NATALIE URQUHART

THE ART OF THE CAYMAN ISLANDS

A JOURNEY THROUGH THE NATIONAL GALLERY COLLECTION

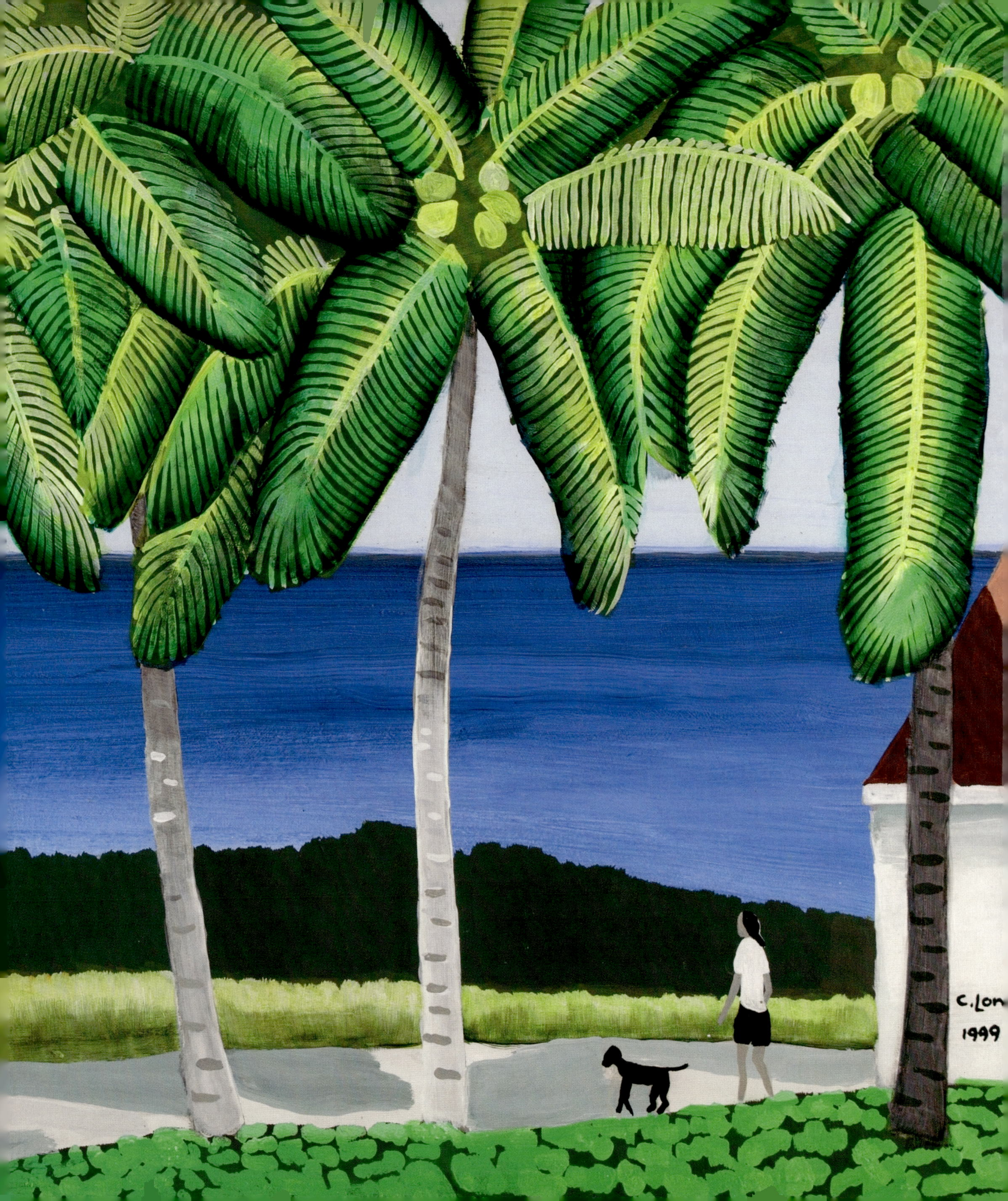
C. Lon
1999

CONTENTS

Figure 1
Charles Long (British-Caymanian, b. 1948)
Pedro's Bluff **(detail), 1999**
Acrylic on masonite; 24 x 36 inches
See also page 92, plates 8–9 and figure 8.

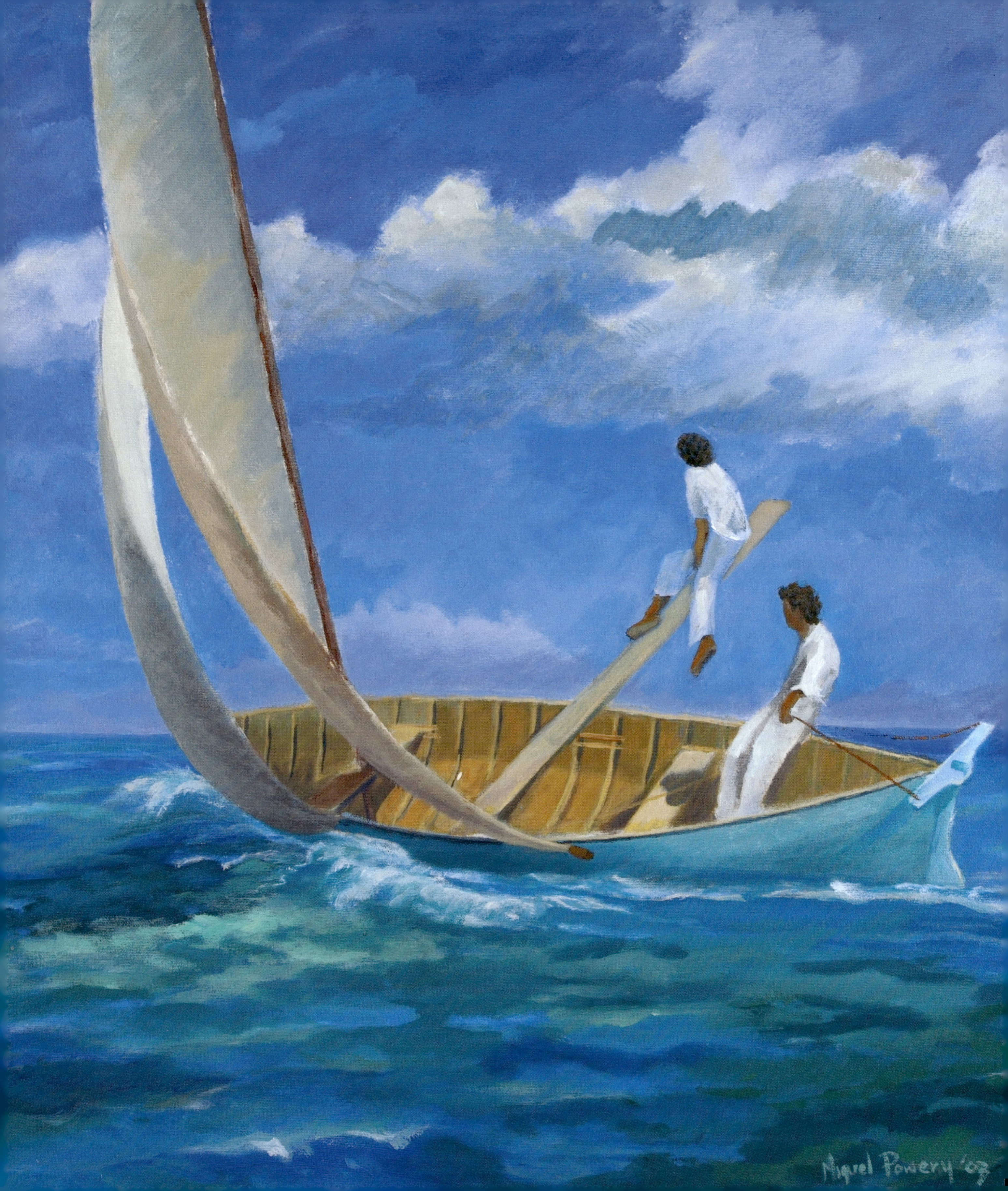

Miguel Powery '07

FOREWORD

It is my pleasure to introduce you to the National Gallery of the Cayman Islands (NGCI) collection guide, which we have created as a general introduction to both the gallery's collection and the wider history of the art of the Cayman Islands. Written in advance of the gallery's twentieth anniversary, it also serves as a celebration of the organisation's own story thus far, highlighting the integral role that it continues to play in the development of art education and fine art for everyone throughout our islands.

Spanning sixty years, the works of art selected for inclusion in this book provide broad insight into the history and creative vision of the Caymanian people, presented through a wide range of media and disciplines: painting, works on paper, collage, mixed-media assemblages, ceramics, sculpture, thatch craft, textiles and photography. These works are but a sample of the cultural treasures in the collection, and many more may be discovered and enjoyed by visiting NGCI. With the great commitment of its curator, Natalie Urquhart, the Collections Committee and supporters, the collection is continually evolving, and yet NGCI remains focused on securing and preserving artworks that represent the unique cultural heritage of these islands, as well as highlighting our flourishing contemporary arts scene.

While this catalogue is by no means a definitive art history of our country, it begins to tell the story of Caymanian visual arts and serves as an important educational resource for the young people of our islands. As a tribute to the people of the Cayman Islands, this guide allows us to share our pride in our culture and gives us an occasion to embrace the gallery and the collection anew.

SUSAN ANNE OLDE, OBE, *Chairperson, NGCI*

Figure 2 (*opposite*)
Miguel Powery (Caymanian, b. 1957)
Riding High, 2007
Acrylic on canvas; 33 x 28 inches
Gift of Truman Bodden
National Gallery of the Cayman Islands Collection
See also page 92 and plates 26 and 40.

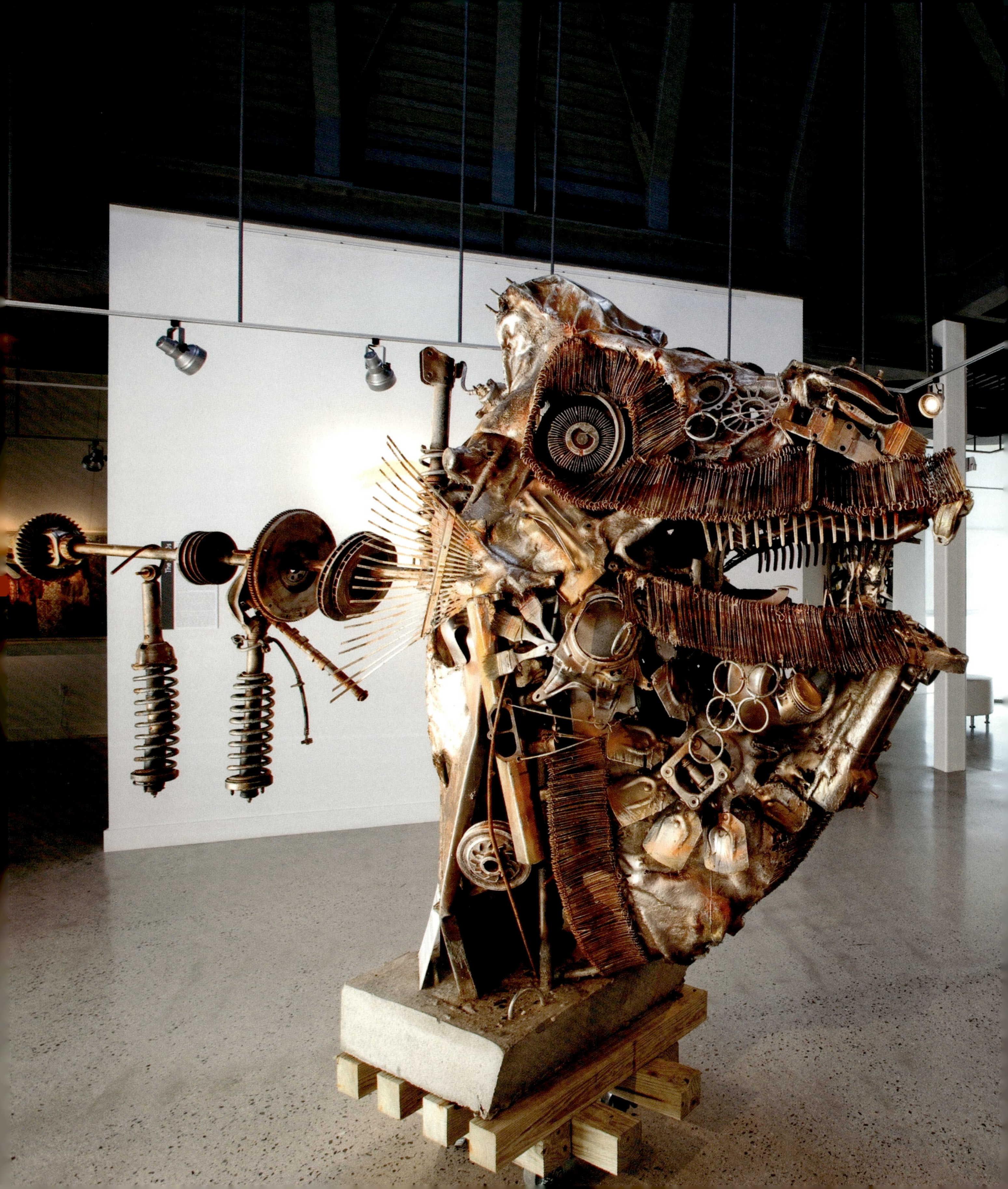

ABOUT THE NATIONAL GALLERY COLLECTION

Founded in 1997, NGCI is the country's leading visual arts museum, charged with preserving, promoting and fostering Caymanian visual culture. Through the permanent collection, changing exhibitions and a dynamic arts education programme, the institution has assumed a central role in the development of fine art while also establishing an invaluable platform for explorations of wider notions of culture and community.

Unlike many national art museums, NGCI was not built on the foundation of a private art collection. In fact, collections development became a priority only in 2010, when construction began on a purpose-built facility with sufficient space to house a suitable collection gallery. For the first fifteen years of its existence, NGCI worked out of a small rented venue and focused purely on temporary exhibitions of local and international work, along with leading art classes and workshops in schools and other loaned facilities. By the mid-2000s, NGCI had grown significantly, offering twenty-five art classes per month and filling a critical gap for art education in both the islands' schools and the wider community. These offerings included on-site weekly programming for youth, adults and seniors; off-site outreach programmes; and six exhibitions and five community festivals each year.

The NGCI Board, founding chairperson Carol Owen, MBE, and founding director Leslie Bigelman, OBE, had envisioned plans for a purpose-built gallery facility as early as 1998, when NGCI patron Helen Harquail, OBE, generously donated four acres of land. It wasn't until late 2010, however, after years of fundraising, that NGCI officially broke ground. The building, which formally opened on 27 January 2012, included expanded temporary exhibition spaces, a library and art studio, an auditorium, a café and gift shop, a sculpture garden, and a new gallery for the permanent collection, the first of its kind in the Cayman Islands.

Figure 3 (*opposite*)
Rasitha Sanjeewa (Sri Lankan, b. 1972)
Fish Skeleton, 2013
Mixed media; 108 x 72 x 45 inches
See also page 93 and plate 56.

The collection, as it stands today, has been assembled slowly over twenty years. It was composed almost entirely of donations in its early years, and the bulk of works acquired during that time were two-dimensional watercolour and acrylic paintings by artists from the Cayman Islands and the wider Caribbean region. Key early acquisitions included four Bendel Hydes works, two Gladwyn K. ('Miss Lassie') Bush paintings, *Mitch Miller and His 'Ting'* (1973) by Charles Long (plate 8), *Poincianas at Government House* (1995) by Carol Owen (plate 25), *Among Friends* (1999) by Al Ebanks (plate 28) and *Pathway* (1998) by Miguel Powery.

By the mid-2000s, under the stewardship of NGCI's second director, Nancy Barnard, the collection had grown to include seventy-seven artworks, with acquisitions continuing to rely solely on gifts. Significant additions from that period included thirteen watercolours from the 2005 *Watermarks* exhibition, each sponsored by a local company; *That Morning* (2004), an assemblage work by Karoly Szücs inspired by Hurricane Ivan (plate 37); and *Rain Gauge* (2007) by David Bridgeman (plate 36).

In 2010, in advance of the building project, collections development began in earnest. NGCI sought out private funding partners to help purchase works by key local artists who were not yet represented in the collection, as well as important works featured in major NGCI exhibitions.

Through donations, artworks such as *3 a Lick, No Taws* (*Ode to Milo* series; 1999) by Wray Banker (plate 30), *Mangrove III* (2005) by Chris Mann (plate 35) and *Blue Meridian: 80° W, Old Isaac's* (2009) by Davin Ebanks (plate 44), along with works by members of the Native

Figure 4
National Gallery of the Cayman Islands
event space, 2012
Photograph by David Wolfe

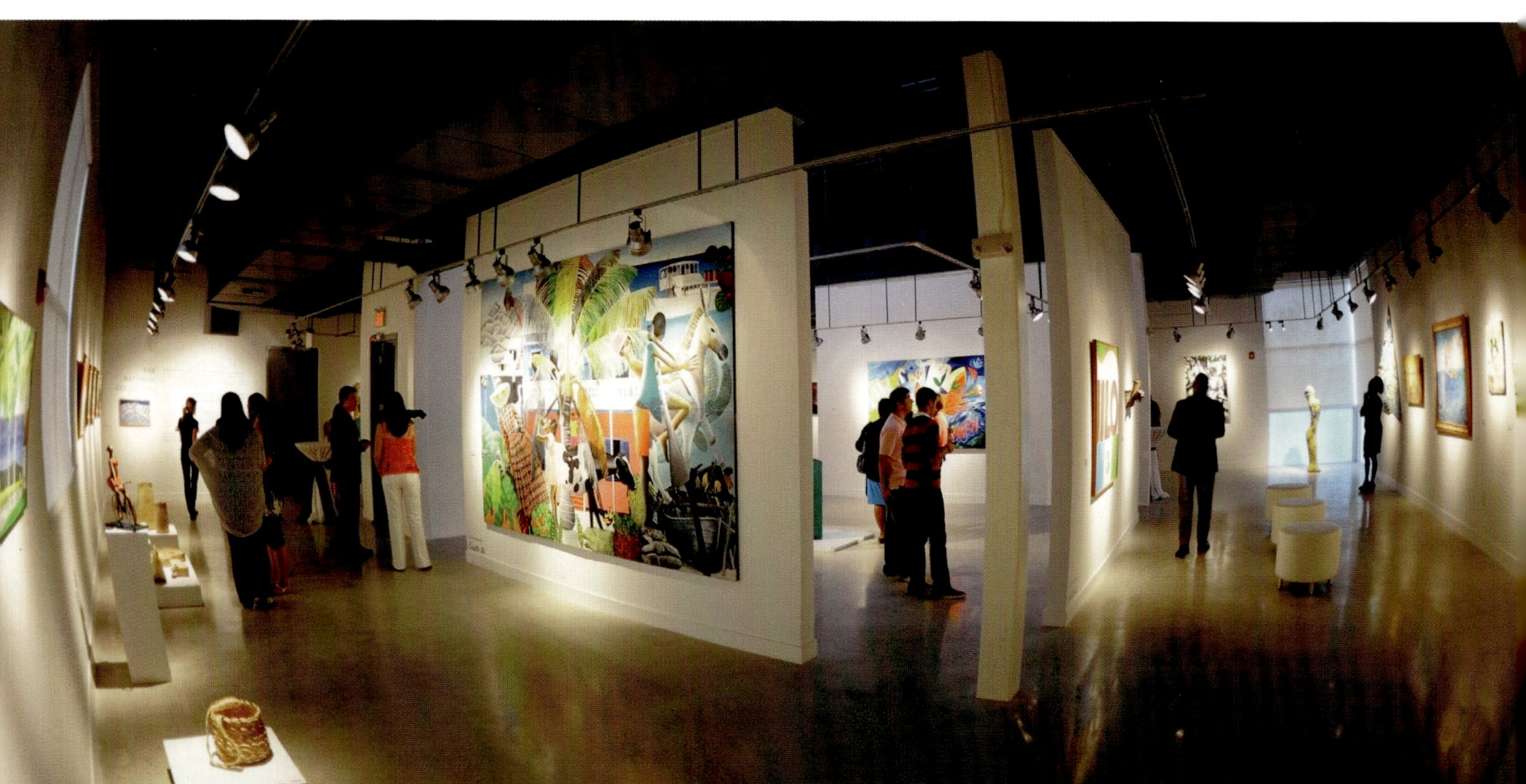

Sons art collective—Randy Chollette, Nasaria Suckoo-Chollette, Gordon Solomon, Nickola McCoy-Snell—and several highly skilled traditional thatchers, were secured. NGCI acquired a further fifty works of historical value in 2014, including a large private donation of *en plein air* watercolours created from the mid-1980s to the 1990s. Recent key additions include four invaluable painted panels by intuitive artist Gladwyn K. ('Miss Lassie') Bush (plates 12a–d), purchased in part via the Susan A. Olde Collection Fund, along with several works of contemporary art that reflect a shift toward a more critically engaged practise within the islands' art community.

Today the collection holds more than two hundred artworks, which together offer an unparalleled record of the Cayman Islands' rich artistic and cultural history and capture the aspirations, character and imagination of its people. Dating primarily from the late 1960s to the present, the works include a wide variety of media, from painting and sculpture to film, photography, new media art, intuitive art and contemporary craft. Approximately 40 per cent of the collection is displayed on rotation in the NGCI Permanent Collection Gallery, and to ensure that the remainder is fully accessible, NGCI's education and collections departments have developed an online collections portal (www.nationalgallery.org.ky/collection-highlights), a collections-focused cross-curricular learning programme for local schools, and scholarship disseminated via publications such as this catalogue.

While NGCI still receives no public funding for acquisitions, we continue our commitment to grow and strengthen the collection by seeking funding partners and donations. These efforts will ensure that works of national significance remain on-island and publicly accessible to both the present and future generations.

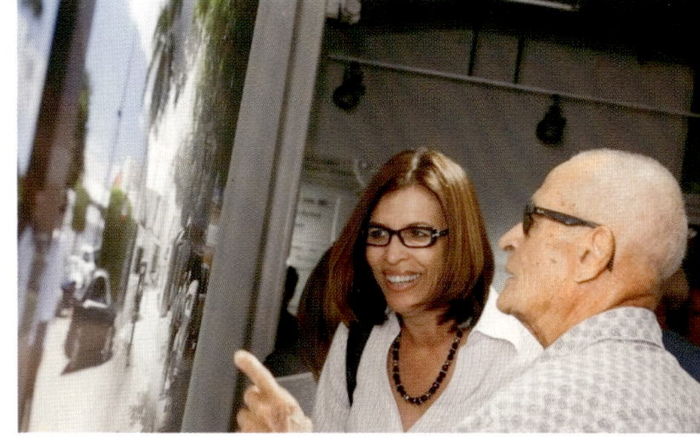

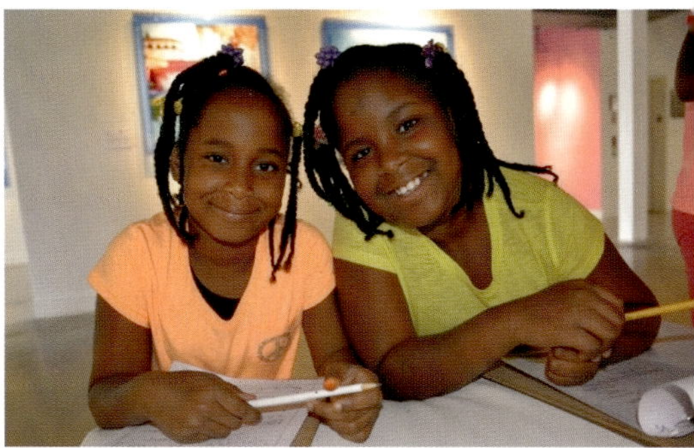

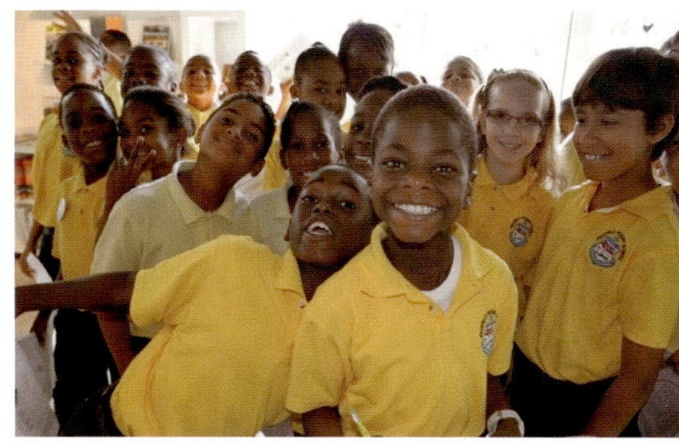

Figure 5
Gallery-goers, *Now and Then* opening,
National Gallery of the Cayman Islands, 2012
Photograph by Veronica Platt

Figure 6
Schoolchildren at the National Gallery
of the Cayman Islands' Family Fun Day, 2015
Photograph by Kaitlyn Elphinstone

Figure 7
Students tour the National Gallery
of the Cayman Islands, 2014
Photograph by Kaitlyn Elphinstone

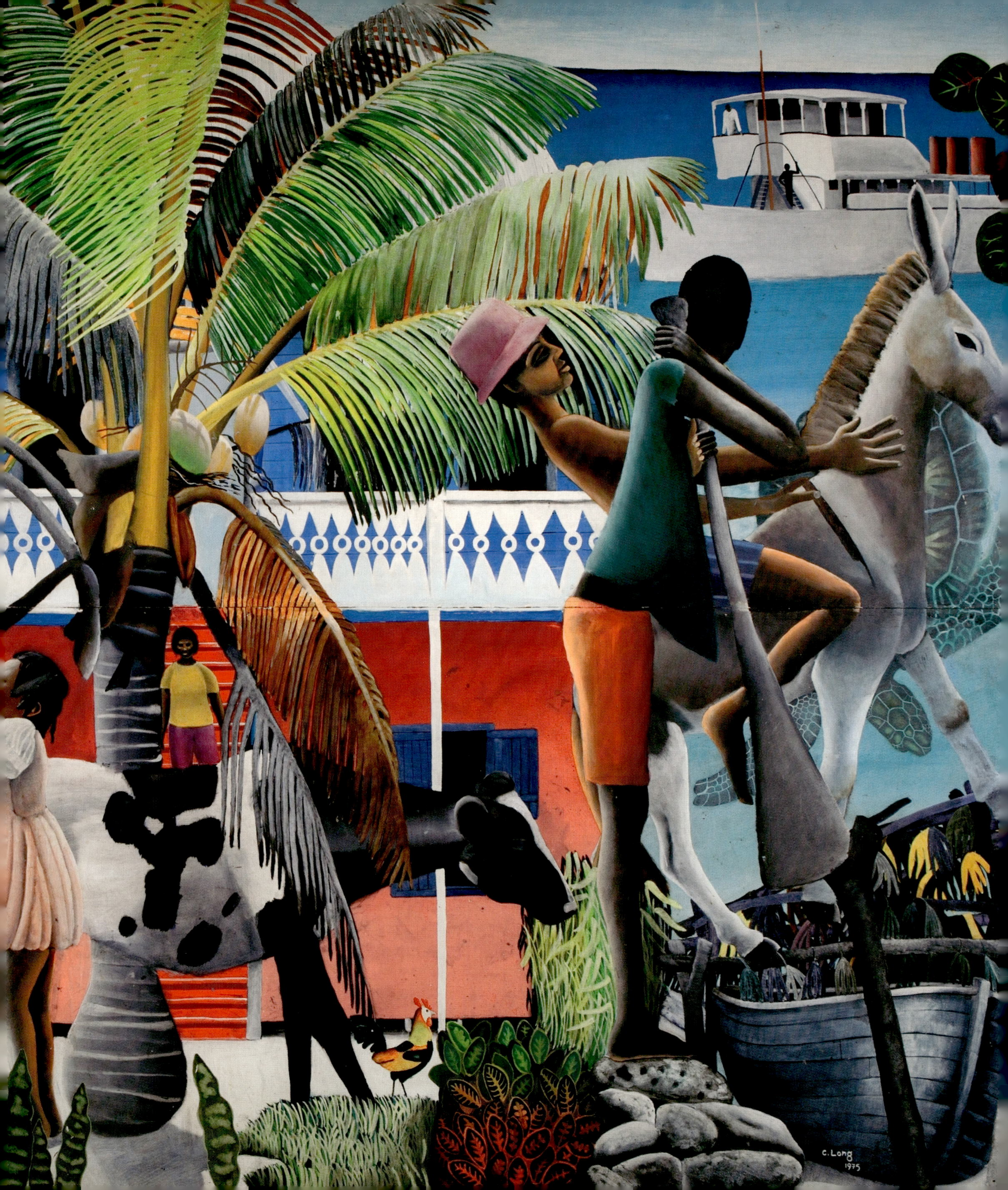

C. Long
1975

A BRIEF HISTORY OF CAYMAN ISLANDS ART

The history of art[1] in the Cayman Islands is relatively short in comparison to our recorded past. Given our isolated geographical location and relatively late permanent settlement, there is no evidence here of the pre-Columbian cultures who so dramatically influenced the development of the fine arts in our neighbouring islands. Instead, early Caymanian identity was created by a series of factors: the primarily European and African cultures of our early settlers,[2] the historical legacy of British colonialism,[3] the small but present plantocracy system,[4] limited natural resources and reliance on the sea for sustenance and industry.

Indeed, the people of these islands were a hardworking, predominantly conservative Christian society, carving out an existence from small landholdings, turtling (figure 9) and seafaring. By the mid-1800s, following the decline in agricultural exports, the economy became almost entirely driven by maritime-related activities.[5] Caymanians soon became known as some of the greatest shipbuilders and mariners in the region. With the male population often away at sea for months on end, women played a central role in both running the home and cultivating the land. To aid themselves in their labours, and using the limited available local resources, women created baskets out of the islands' ubiquitous silver thatch palm (*Coccothrinax proctorii*) for 'backing' (carrying) sand and other heavy goods (see plate 5). Subsequently, functional crafts, such as basket weaving, roofing, embroidery, appliqué, smocking and quilting (figure 10), along with fiddle music, traditional Caymanian songs—primarily narrative ballads and boat-launching songs—quadrille dance, architectural fretwork and shell and wood carving, were the primary forms of cultural expression during this early period, as the tough physical and economic climate rarely afforded residents the luxury of spare time to dedicate to creating art for art's sake.[6] These craft forms, however, were

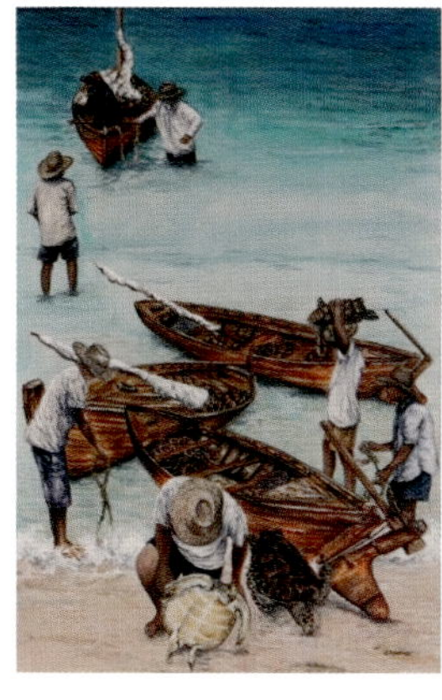

Figure 8 (*opposite*)
Charles Long (British-Caymanian, b. 1948)
Radio Cayman Mural (detail), 1975
Acrylic on Masonite; 22 x 62 inches
Courtesy of Cayman Islands National Museum
See also page 92, plates 8–9 and figure 1.

Figure 9 (*above*)
Sue Widmer (British-Caymanian, ca. 1955–2012)
Turtling, 2007
Acrylic on canvas; 40 x 24 inches
Private collection. Courtesy of the artist's family
See also page 94.

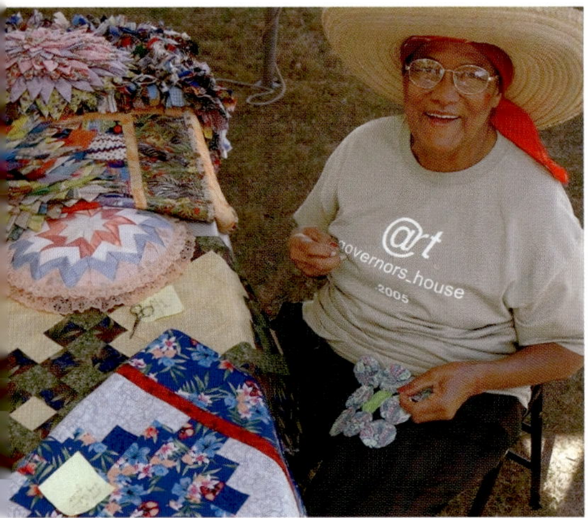

Figure 10
Traditional thatcher Josie Solomon
(Caymanian, b. 1932) at Art@Governors 2005
Photograph by Courtney Platt
See also page 93.

creative, skilful and highly individualised, as is still evident in their present-day counterparts (plates 2–7).[7] A display of Caymanian traditional craft was included in the Jamaica Exhibition in 1891, which speaks to the quality and creativity of the work made in this early period.

With the increasing affluence generated during the Southwell Years,[8] along with growth in the financial services and tourism industries from the 1960s onward, came a transformation in Caymanian society. Substantial investment at this period altered the social, political and cultural profile of the islands, resulting in rapid social development, improved standards of living and increased time for general leisure activities. During this period of globalisation, increased immigration from the United Kingdom, Canada, the United States and Jamaica brought an influx of new residents to the islands, including some with formal fine art training. Many of these new residents made distinct contributions to the development of fine art, including pioneer art teachers Ed and Barbara Oliver and Maureen Andersen Berry and artists such as Janet Walker, Joanne Sibley, Charles Long and Debbie Chase van der Bol.

The late Ed Oliver, or 'Mr Ed,' as he was better known, arrived in the Cayman Islands in the late 1960s after leaving an advertising and industrial-design career in the United States. He worked as a manager for the *Caymanian Weekly* newspaper but soon set up his own design business and later pioneered the postcard industry in the Cayman Islands. It was Mr Ed's love of art and teaching, however, that carved him a place in the Cayman Islands' art history. He started his first art classes in 1969 and taught for thirty-seven years alongside his wife, Barbara. In these classes, hundreds of students received fine art training, including a young artist who would go on to become one of the Cayman Islands' greatest talents: Bendel Hydes.

Still, at the start of the 1970s, Caymanian artists had few opportunities to introduce and sell their work beyond the annual Agricultural Fair and craft days and informally at local hotels. In 1970, the Olivers held the inaugural Art Talent Competition, an annual event that provided one of the first venues specifically intended for local artists to exhibit their work in public. It was here that Hydes first exhibited as a young student before leaving to study at Liverpool College of Art in the United Kingdom. These annual events, along with Mr Ed's store, ARTVentures, were the 'complete face of art in Cayman during the 1960s and early '70s,' remembers Hydes.[9]

The first significant solo exhibition by a Caymanian artist was Hydes's 1974 exhibition at the Royal Palms Hotel. At this same venue, in 1978, Hydes, along with actors and playwrights Geoff Cresswell, Frank McField, Anita Ebanks and others, started the Inn Theatre Company, which would eventually evolve into the National Theatre Company and ultimately the Cayman National Cultural Foundation (CNCF). Recently returned from the United Kingdom, Hydes had been greatly influenced by his experience of living in a post-industrial society, which was a world apart from his unspoiled, idyllic island home. His work in this period was figurative, with echoes of Dadaism and Pop Art and a foreshadowing of the environmental concerns that would become a central theme in his later work.

By the mid-1970s, a group of artists including Margaret Barwick, Eolin Lufthouse and Meg Paterson had begun painting together informally, and in 1976 they mounted an exhibition at the Holiday Inn Hotel that was met with significant critical acclaim and some commercial success. The following year, the group formalised into the islands' first official art organisation, the Visual Arts Society (VAS).[10] Some of the Cayman Islands' most talented resident and visiting artists taught classes for VAS, supporting the organisation's strong education

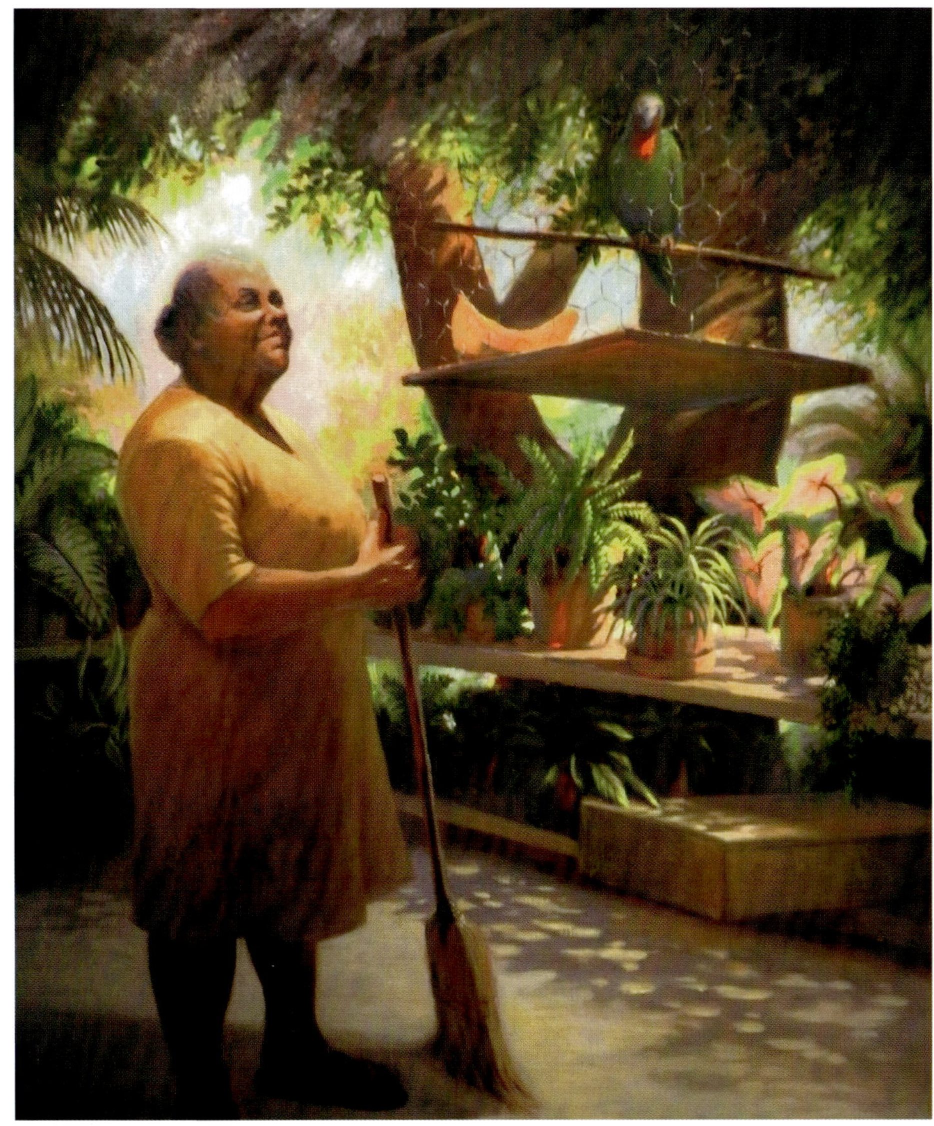

commitment, which continues to this day. VAS held annual art fairs throughout the late 1970s and 1980s, and these became centres of the islands' growing fine art scene.

Stylistically, this period was dominated by Realist painters who sought to capture the picturesque local environment and used oil and watercolour as their primary media. Few artists would experiment with different genres (or subjects) until the 1990s. This choice was driven as much by the strong demand among collectors for representational art[11] as by a genuine desire to capture the remarkable light and colours of the natural landscape.

The 1980s opened with a major event in the development of Caymanian art when the Cayman Islands sent a contingent of artists, led by Margaret Barwick (figure 11), to participate in Carifesta IV (the Caribbean Festival of the Arts) in Barbados in 1981. Carifesta IV offered the first real chance for artists to promote their work regionally and exposed them to new techniques and ideas, which they brought back home.

Support for the arts community also gained momentum during this period with the emergence of the first government-funded arts institutions, national festivals[12] and commercial galleries—including Pure Art, which was opened by artist Debbie Chase van der Bol, and the short-lived McField Square Gallery, which was opened by Frank McField and Bendel Hydes on Mary Street, George Town. The National Children's Festival of the Arts began in 1982 to showcase young talent, and in 1984, CNCF was established: the first national organisation specifically tasked with stimulating, facilitating and preserving cultural and artistic expression. In addition to providing visual arts workshops led by local and visiting Caribbean artists, the Young at Art youth initiative and other cultural programmes, CNCF's Cayfest (the Cayman Islands Festival of the Arts, established in 1995) offered a chance for artists to exhibit at a national level. The festival emphasised an eclectic mix of local arts and culture, including visual arts, music, theatre, dance, fashion design and cultural discussions, and showcased the finest local talent.

One of CNCF's most important contributions to the history of Caymanian visual art was artistic director Henry Muttoo's early recognition and support of Gladwyn K. ('Miss Lassie') Bush, who began painting at the age of sixty-two after an epiphany that she described as a 'visionary experience.' Miss Lassie's 'markings' became legendary, and in the years before her death in 2003, she created a prolific body of work on the walls, windows and furnishings of her home and later on canvas. Strong Christian themes run throughout her paintings, which she executed in her unique self-taught style. Due to CNCF's promotion of her work, Miss Lassie is now considered to be a serious intuitive artist within the Caribbean region, ranked alongside artists such as Guyana's Philip Moore and Jamaica's Kapo, and her home was recognised on the 2012 World Heritage Watch List. Rebecca Hoffberger, founder and director of the American Visionary Arts Museum, describes it as 'an oasis for folk and visionary art lovers worldwide.'[13] This recognition has paved the way for the emergence of other intuitive artists in the Cayman Islands, including Harvey Ebanks, Edrid Banks Jr. (figure 12) and Luelan Bodden.

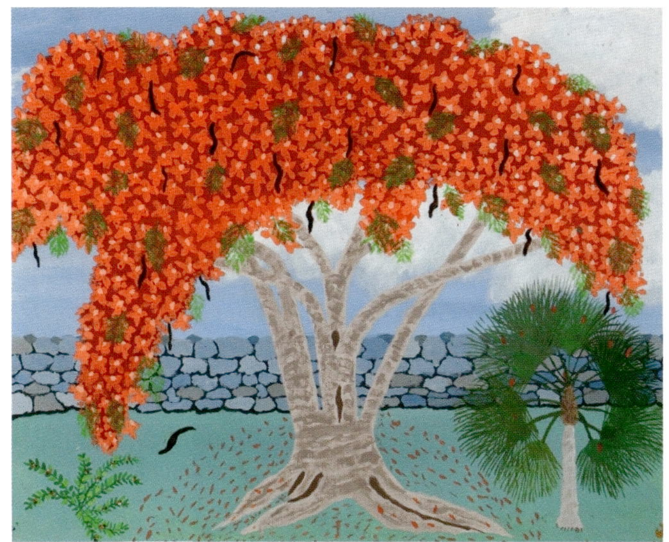 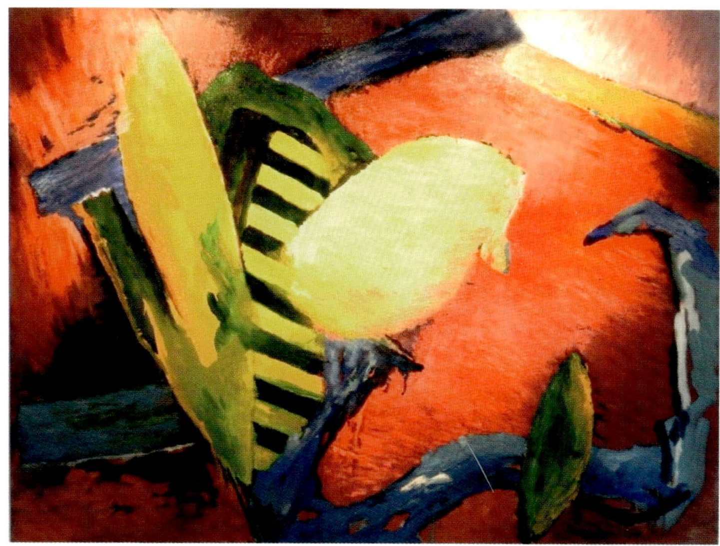

Aside from Miss Lassie's intuitive markings, Bendel Hydes's style was the exception to the representational work still practised by the majority of artists in the early 1980s (figure 13). He had begun to move away from figurative work and toward abstraction, and in 1981, his solo exhibition, *Elements in a Free Space*, at the Government Assembly Building displayed a series of abstract paintings that constituted his stylistic breakthrough. Yet it was not a commercial success, and, disenchanted, he left Cayman for New York a year later. This move would prove to be of critical importance to Hydes's career, as soon afterward he participated in two international exhibitions—*New Painting*s at the Commonwealth Institute, London, and *Caribbean Art/African Currents* at the Museum of Contemporary Hispanic Art, New York— which were the first of several major exhibitions for him over the coming decade.

The 1990s saw an unprecedented number of new initiatives and opportunities for local artists. At the start of the decade, the Cayman Islands National Museum (CINM)[14] was formed to collect historical, natural and scientific objects of interest. Importantly, CINM also became the first organisation to actively collect fine art. Each year, the museum's founding director, Anita Ebanks, in keeping with its mission, secured the strongest works from VAS exhibitions, along with other artworks that depicted scenes of Caymanian history and society.

The Cayman Islands' participation in *Carib Art: Contemporary Art of the Caribbean*—a UNESCO-funded Caribbean-wide travelling exhibition—in 1993–94 played a significant role in raising the profile of Caymanian art overseas.[15] Bendel Hydes, John Broad (who provided the catalogue cover illustration), David Bridgeman, Joanne Sibley, Teresa Grimes and Gladwyn K. ('Miss Lassie') Bush were among the 137 Caribbean artists whose work travelled to North America, Europe and the Caribbean, including the Cayman Islands, over an

Figure 12 (*above left*)
Edrid Banks Jr. (Caymanian, 1923–91)
Poinciana, 1971
Acrylic on canvas; 18 x 24 inches
National Gallery of the Cayman Islands Collection
See also page 88.

Figure 13 (*above right*)
Bendel Hydes (Caymanian, b. 1952)
Yellow Leaves, 1988
Oil on canvas; 40 x 60 inches
From the collection of the Cayman Islands National Museum
See also page 91, figure 18 and plates 14 and 45.

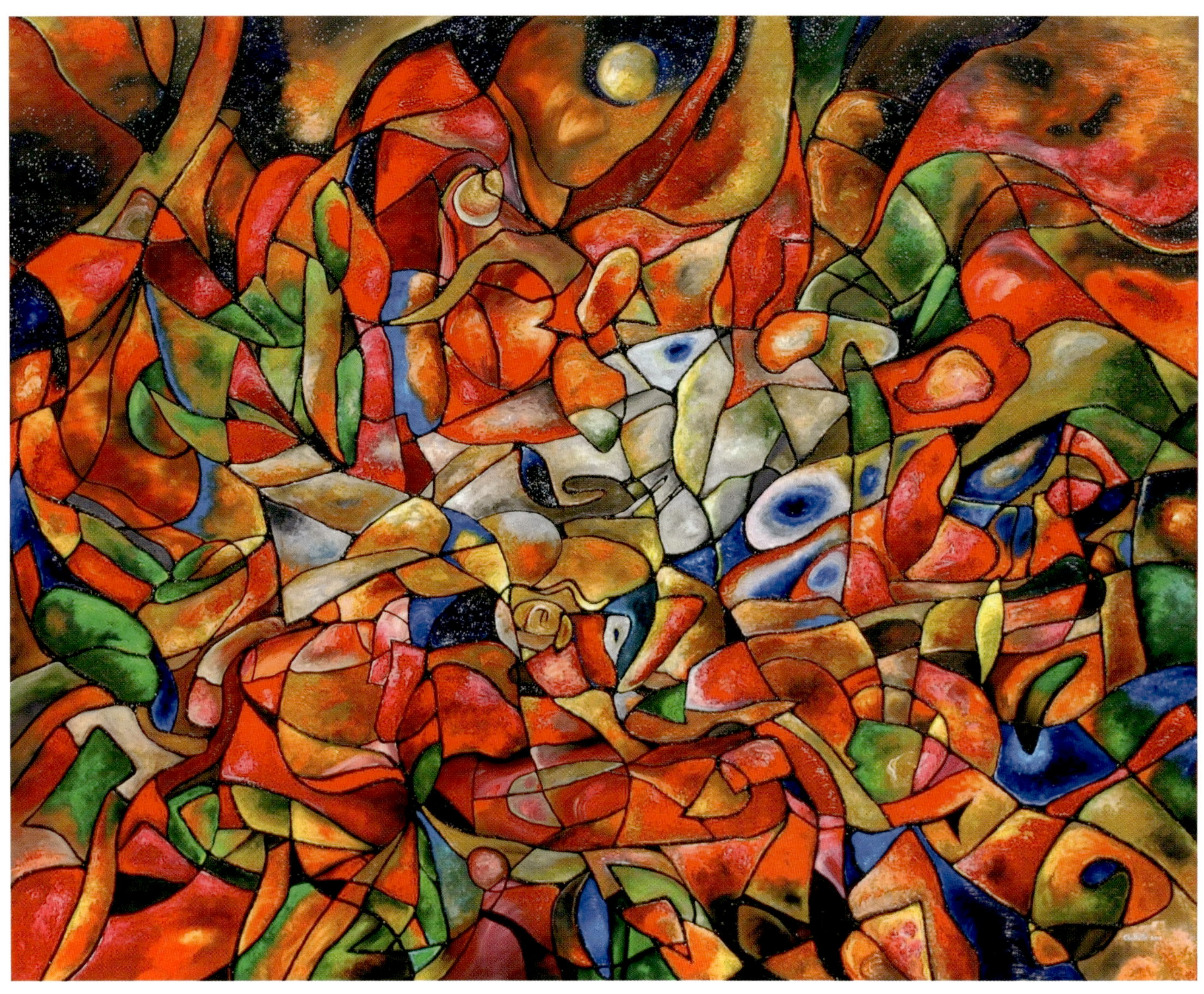

eighteen-month period. CNCF hosted *Carib Art* at the Harquail Theatre, showcasing Caymanian art alongside works from thirty-two countries. At the same juncture, Bendel Hydes was featured in several high-profile international Caribbean exhibitions, including *500 Years After: Caribbean and Central American Painting* at the Art Museum of the Americas, Washington, DC; *Caribbean Visions: Contemporary Painting and Sculpture*, a North American travelling exhibition; and the International Biennial de São Paulo,

Brazil. The increased regional visibility of Caymanian art led to a newly acquired confidence
at home.

Meanwhile, during the early 1990s, a new generation of artists came to the forefront.
Young Caymanians such as Wray Banker, Paul Jordison and Nasaria Suckoo-Chollette were
returning home from the United States with degrees in graphic design, fine art and the
dramatic arts while an increasing number of self-taught artists were gaining popularity, such
as Al Ebanks, Miguel Powery and Horacio Esteban. There was a mobilisation toward a new,
home-grown discourse that challenged the persistent dominance of landscape painting and
which resulted in the creation of the Native Sons collective in 1996.[16]

While stylistically individual, the Native Sons were united by the principle of promoting
a uniquely Caymanian aesthetic inspired by their heritage and sociocultural experiences,
including their African heritage, which had been relatively removed from artistic content until
this period. Initially most drew heavily on archival images of bygone Cayman found at the
Cayman Islands National Archives (CINA) and in family collections. Some did so directly,
as in the work of Miguel Powery, Gordon Solomon and Chris Christian, while others, including
Al Ebanks and Nickola McCoy-Snell, explored these histories through a purely abstract
language. Later the group diversified into more personal themes. Today Wray Banker uses
installation and often humorous Pop Art–inspired graphic sketches to comment on erosion of
traditional Caymanian heritage; race and feminism are recurring themes in Nasaria Suckoo-
Chollette's work, which combines traditional Caymanian crafts techniques with contemporary
fine art materials. Randy Chollette's large-scale, vibrantly coloured 'stained glass paintings'
are heavily informed by his Rastafarian faith (figure 14).

Several new commercial galleries were established in this period, and new display
opportunities arose in traditional retail establishments. In addition to the long-running Pure
Art gallery, which was opened by artist Debbie Chase van der Bol in the 1980s, the island now
boasted Kennedy Gallery; Frames, Trains & Things; and Island Art and Framing, all of which
greatly increased exhibition and sales opportunities for local artists.

With the establishment of NGCI in 1997, the visual arts were formally recognised as a
critical component of Caymanian cultural expression. It was the first national institution
devoted entirely to the promotion, appreciation and practise of the visual arts, and it heralded
a growing professionalism in visual arts administration and curatorial practise.

Even before a temporary facility was found for the fledging organisation, chairperson
Carol Owen and founding director Leslie Bigelman launched NGCI via an island-wide
education initiative to raise awareness of the visual arts within the school system. This
wide-reaching programme was soon followed by a series of exhibitions designed to highlight
the diverse genres of art that were practised within the Cayman Islands and internationally,
and to challenge traditional notions of what art could be. Works on display included
everything from traditional crafts, painting, photography, ceramics and assemblage to
the first installation and video-art pieces to be exhibited in the Cayman Islands. NGCI also

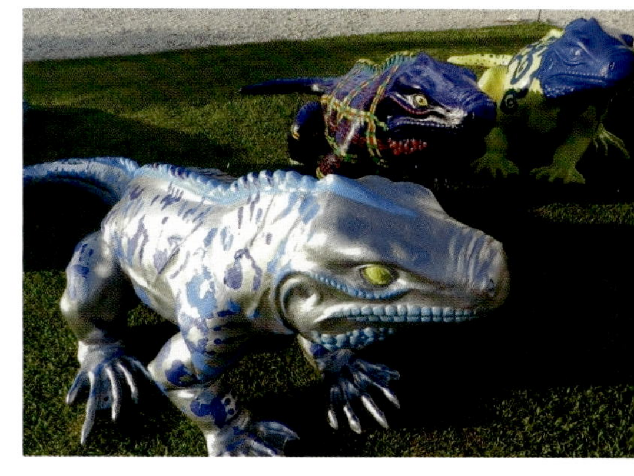

Figure 15
The Blue Dragon Project, 2004
Courtesy of the National Gallery
of the Cayman Islands
See also page 89.

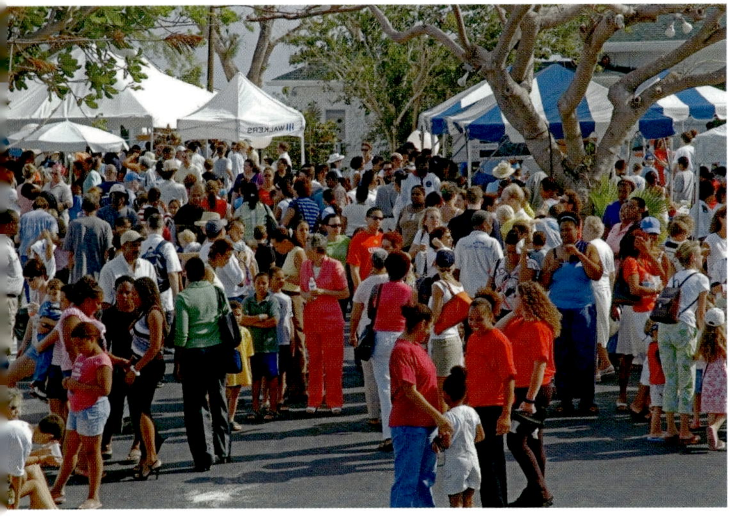

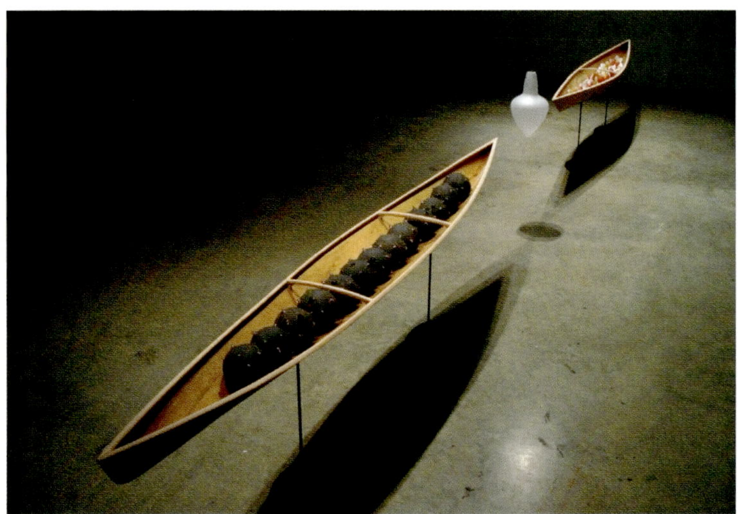

worked to bring art outside the gallery space and into the wider environment via island-wide public art projects, including giant carved Styrofoam sculptures in various districts, Gordon Solomon's travelling 'art car,' and *The Blue Dragon Project* (figure 15), undertaken with the National Trust for the Cayman Islands.

With the start of the new millennium came a new wave of opportunities for the art community that helped the scene to further flourish. NGCI's Art@Governors opened in 2000 with more than seventy[17] featured artists and craftspeople demonstrating their work (figure 16). Visitors had a chance to view the diverse visual art forms being produced in the Cayman Islands, and the family-friendly festival atmosphere helped to widen the audience for fine art by attracting three thousand visitors annually. The following year saw the launch of The McCoy Prize and exhibition, co-administered by CINM and NGCI, funded by the McCoy family of North Side, and designed to encourage and reward excellence in Caymanian contemporary arts. The inaugural exhibition, featuring twenty-five artists, opened in 2002.

The year 2001 also witnessed the opening of Kensington-Lott Fine Art (KLFA), a contemporary gallery founded and run by artist Paul Jordison. Jordison represented many of the Cayman Islands' emerging contemporary artists, and the gallery became known for hosting fresh, innovative exhibitions and events. It was at KLFA that Randy Chollette first received recognition. While the gallery was short-lived, it made a long-lasting contribution to the art scene, most importantly by encouraging several large private firms to begin collecting original, contemporary Caymanian art rather than featuring prints in their corporate offices. This in turn increased sales opportunities for local artists and helped to instigate the development of several large corporate art collections.

Figure 16 (*above left*)
Art@Governors, 2005
Photograph by Courtney Platt

Figure 17 (*above right*)
Davin Ebanks (Caymanian, b. 1975)
Waterline: Eastern and Western Passages, 2003
Featured in the 2011 *Persistence of Memory* exhibition
Blown, hot-worked, metalised glass, wood, steel;
16 x 198 x 13 inches
Courtesy of the artist
See also page 91 and plates 44, 46 and 55.

By the mid-2000s, commercial opportunities for local artists had increased dramatically, fuelled by the growing demand from collectors. Several new commercial art galleries opened, including The Morgan Gallery, Arteccentrix, Bodden Town Art Gallery and Sandon Feat Gallery, while hotels and cafés incorporated mini-galleries into their premises.

2003 marked a half-millennium since Christopher Columbus's sighting of the Cayman Islands, and a year-long cultural programme ensued under the direction of the Quincentennial Celebrations Committee. The visual arts community played a significant part in the events through a series of important exhibitions, including Bendel Hydes's retrospective *Soundings* and the *Visual Arts Society 25 Year Retrospective*,[18] as well as community art festivals and district heritage displays. Several important commemorative public sculptures were created to mark the anniversary, such as *The Wall of History* by John Broad in Heroes Square, which was a joint project of the Quincentennial Committee and NGCI.

This period also saw more exhibition opportunities for local artists overseas via NGCI initiatives, including a Caymanian contingent at the Dominican Republic Biennale (2002),

Figure 18
Bendel Hydes (Caymanian, b. 1952)
***Circumnavigating the Globe*, 2012**
This exhibition (curated by the author) opened the new National Gallery of the Cayman Islands facility in February 2012
Courtesy of the National Gallery of the Cayman Islands
See also page 91, plates 14 and 45 and figure 13.

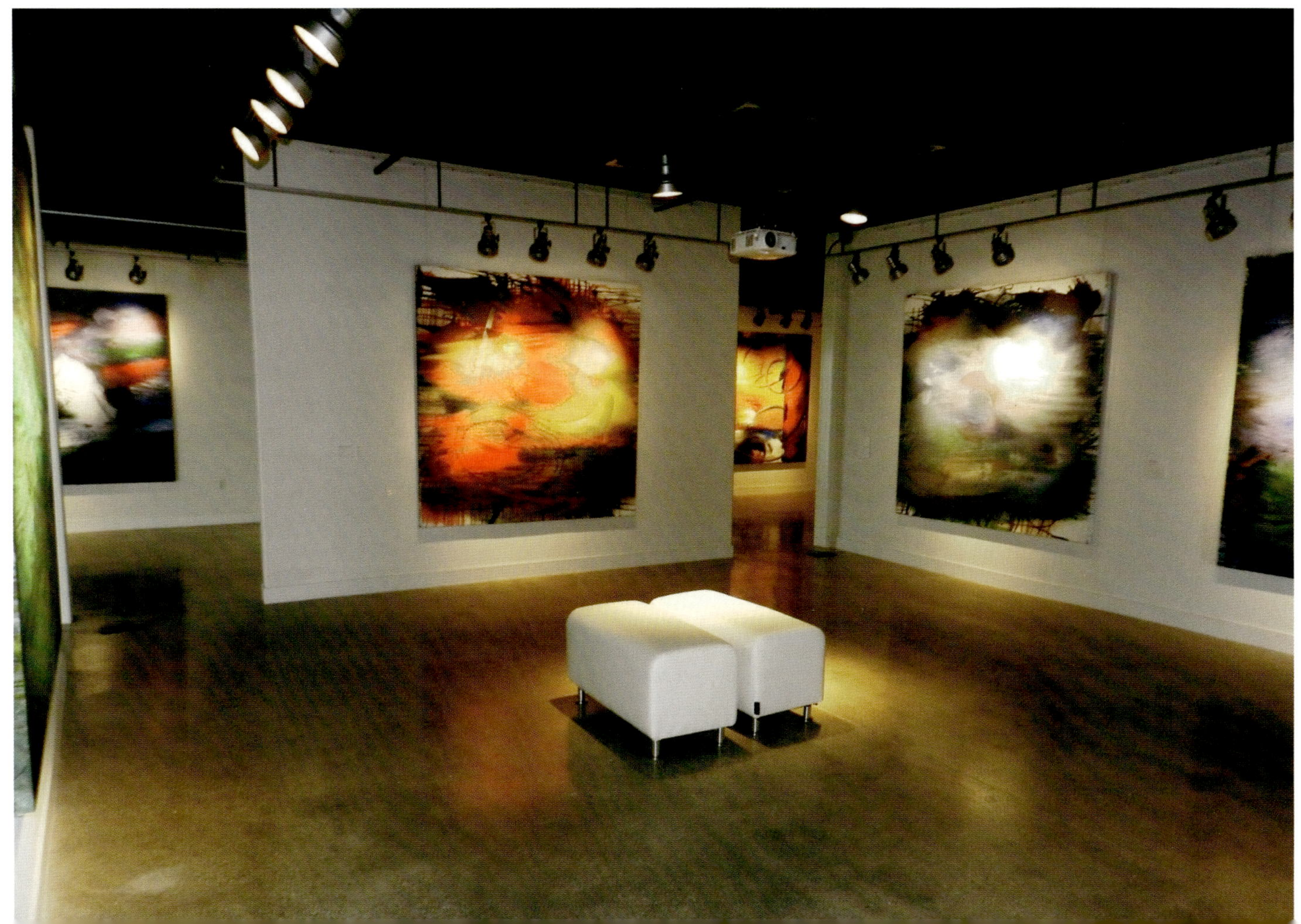

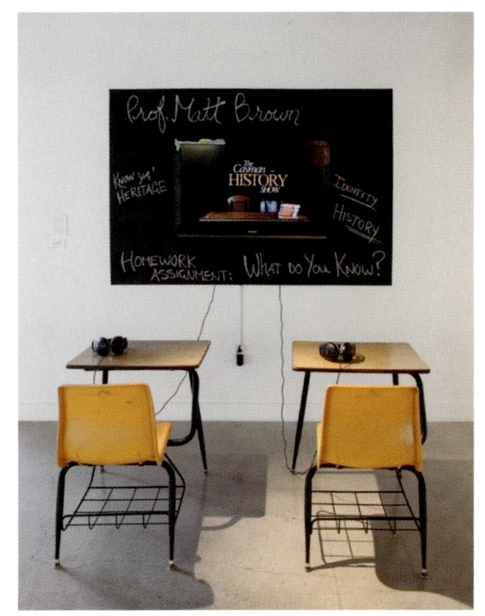

Figure 19
**Ben Hudson (Belizean, b. 1976)
and Matt Brown (Caymanian, b. 1985)
The Cayman History Show, 2014**
Featured in the 2015 National Gallery of the
Cayman Islands exhibition *tIDal Shift: Explorations
of Identity in Contemporary Caymanian Art*
(curated by the author)
Digital video, acrylic, plastic, metal, wood, chalk;
71½ x 64 x 72 inches
See also pages 89 and 91 and plate 61.

NGCI's *Dos Visiones* exhibition[19] in Cuba and London (2003) and group exhibitions in the United Kingdom and United States (2005). As the decade drew to a close, NGCI partnered with CNCF to send the largest contingent of Caymanian art ever to travel abroad to Carifesta X in Guyana.

While much was happening locally, artists also took opportunities to train and to promote their work abroad, many through grants provided by CNCF's Grants for the Arts and NGCI's Artists Away programme.[20] In addition, the Cayman Islands government began to award fine art scholarships to Caymanian students. Several opted to further their studies not only in fine art, but also in arts administration, museum management and curating, which increased professionalism within the arts sector.

The role of the curator as a contextualising force in the development of art became increasingly prominent during this decade,[21] as NGCI exhibitions developed around central critical premises rather than as surveys, retrospectives or 'open-call' group shows. Exhibitions such as *Arreckly* (2007) and *Persistence of Memory* (2011; figure 17)[22] provided challenging platforms for artists' experimentation and creation of work that directly addressed socio-political issues.

The global financial crisis that marked 2008 affected the Cayman Islands' economy and in turn its arts community. Art sales—to both the corporate sector and private collectors— suffered significantly. Several commercial galleries closed, while budget cuts forced partially government-funded organisations to downsize or dissolve grant programmes. Still, artists showed remarkable resilience to these challenges, finding new venues in which to display their work and new ways to connect directly with potential collectors. At the same time, arts organisations streamlined programming and sought to create new public/private partnerships to support the continuation of art education, programmes and exhibitions.

Despite such setbacks, 2012 was a very important year in Cayman's art history: the purpose-built NGCI facility was completed (figure 18), and it included the first permanent gallery for the National Art Collection, temporary exhibition areas and a multipurpose education centre, all funded primarily through corporate and private-sector donations. Meanwhile, CNCF's advocacy efforts to gain international recognition for Miss Lassie succeeded when her cottage was placed on the World Heritage Watch List that year. Both achievements evidenced a growing maturity in the development of Caymanian art as well as increasing interest from local and overseas audiences. Approximately twenty thousand people visited NGCI in 2012–13, a 100 per cent increase from previous years, and footfall has remained consistent in the years since.

This growing interest in the visual arts parallels the increasing number of artists currently practising, which exceeds that of any time in the country's past. While many artists still choose to create primarily representational work, often for commercial ends, others are seeking to articulate a uniquely Caymanian experience and striving to express their location within twenty-first-century Caymanian society. Contemporary art forms such as installation, photography and assemblage have become as common as more traditional media such as painting and sculpture and are being executed with increased clarity and confidence (figure 19). Wray Banker (figure 20), for example, appropriates popular commercial graphics and humour to draw attention to more serious concerns such as the erosion of his cultural heritage. London-based British-Caymanian artist Pippa Ridley uses mythology and symbolism to explore her position as a first-generation Caymanian. Aston Ebanks is a mixed-media artist whose work addresses urban development. Kaitlyn Elphinstone addresses environmental concerns by meticulously 'wrapping' seedpods and other found natural objects. David Bridgeman uses collage and mixed media to create works that explore themes of cultural identity, nationality and transformation in an increasingly globalised environment. Greg Lipton's recent installations reflect the social isolation that can be driven by technology. Davin Ebanks's glass sculptures comment on his maritime heritage in a wholly contemporary format. These are but a few examples of the vibrant output currently produced both within the Cayman Islands and by Caymanian diaspora artists living abroad.

At the time of writing, the arts in the Cayman Islands are thriving, and yet much still needs to be addressed if they are to continue to grow and prosper. Most pressing, perhaps, is the acknowledgment that Caymanian art and culture, while firmly rooted in our maritime heritage and traditions, are in fact in a state of on-going transition and that the islands' present-day multicultural outlook must be considered an additive rather than a diluting factor in this development. The establishment of a National Cultural and Heritage Policy (currently under development) should help to create safeguards for the preservation of traditional Caymanian heritage while providing a healthy climate in which contemporary Caymanian creativity can flourish.

Consideration must be given to increasing arts education in primary and secondary schools and to the establishment of tertiary/associate-level arts education, as is found in the neighbouring islands of Jamaica, the Bahamas and Cuba, whose artists are now celebrated in the global arena. The growth of the fine art sector and the wider creative industries[23] in Cayman could play a critical role in future economic diversification, but only if young people are provided the education and skills needed to succeed in these areas. Simultaneously, Caymanian artists and curators must seek to create a more critical environment through which to view art at home if they are to begin seriously engaging in regional and international artistic discourse. These challenges are not unique to the Cayman Islands, but they need urgent attention and support by both the public and private sectors in order to ensure a vibrant future for the arts in Cayman.

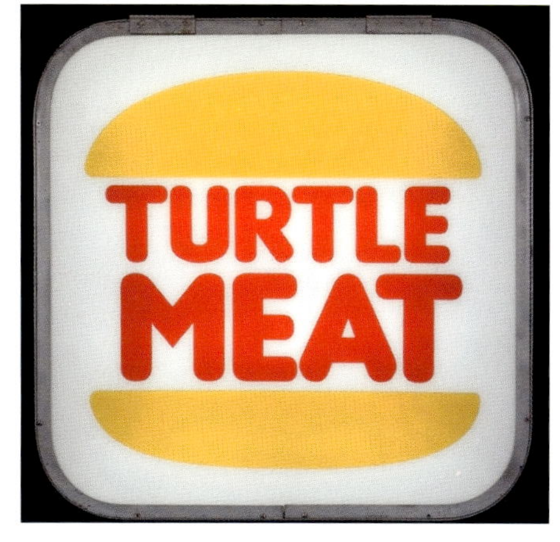

Figure 20
Wray Banker (Caymanian, b. 1968)
Our Way 1994–99, **2015**
Commercial signage, metal, electrical fixtures;
48 x 48 inches
Courtesy of the artist
See also page 88 and plate 30.

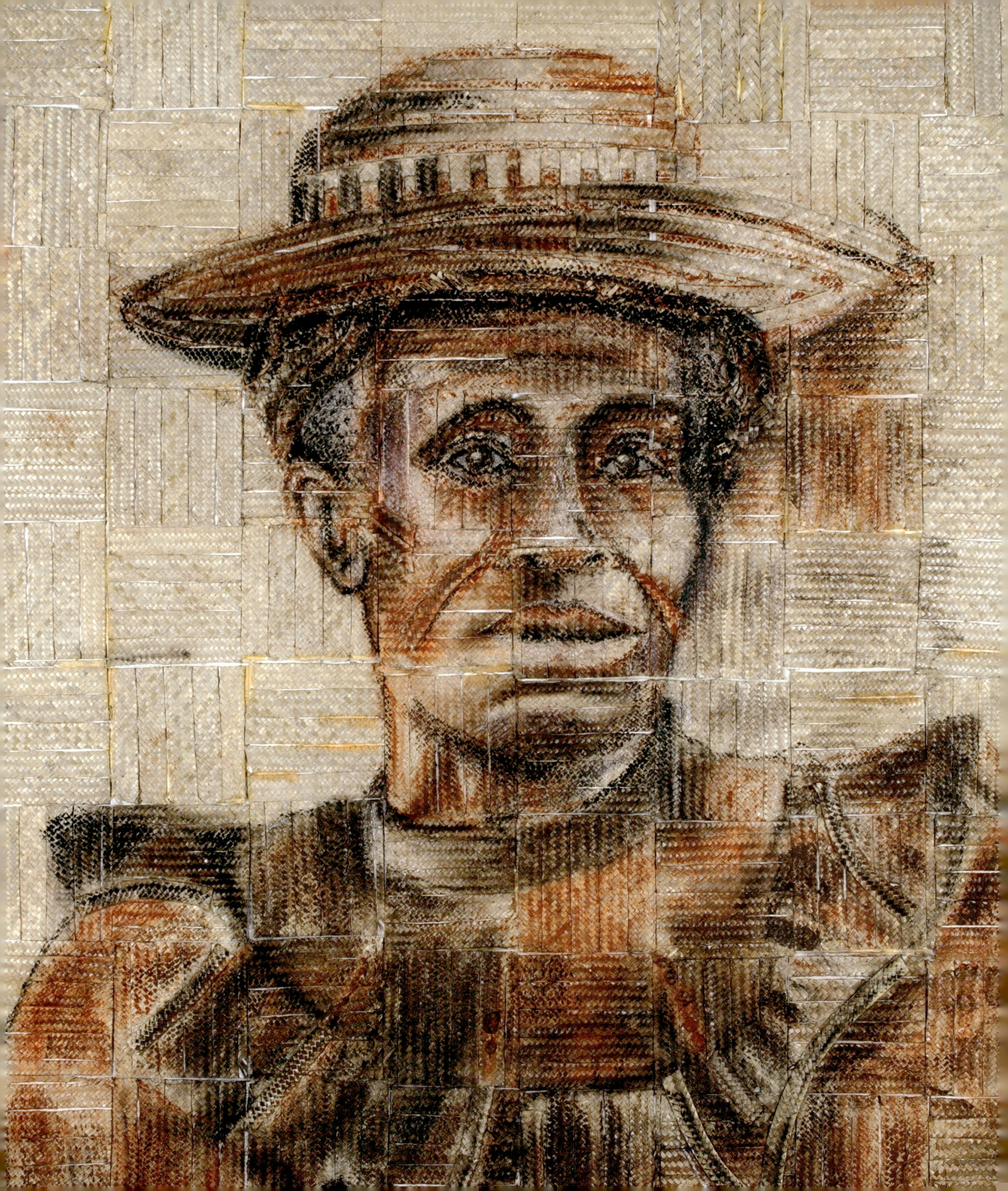

PLATES

John Broad (British-Caymanian, b. 1947)
and Rose May Ebanks (Caymanian, b. 1951)
Portrait of Susanna Connolly of
East End. Born 1838 **(detail), 2010**
Chalk, silver thatch palm; 48 x 36 inches
See page 89 and plate 42 for
information on Broad, and page 91
for information on Ebanks.

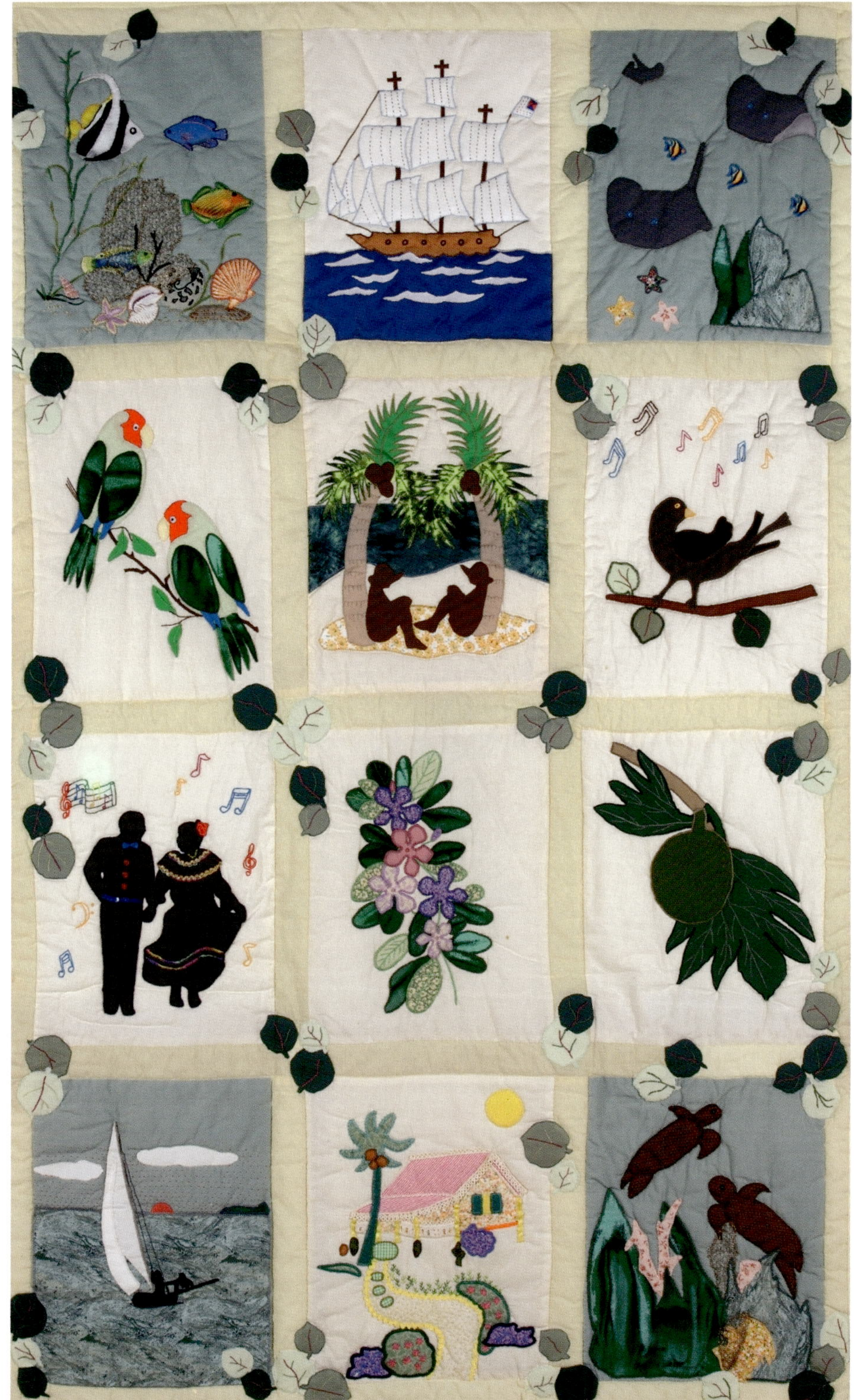

PLATE 2
Cayman Quilters (est. 1993)
Love Quilt, 2001
Fabric, thread; 68 x 43½ inches
See also page 90.

Love Quilt was created for NGCI's 2012 *Love* exhibition and was donated to the collection by the quilting group. It celebrates the islands' unique flora and fauna, maritime heritage and cultural pastimes.

The Cayman Quilters are a group of local craftspeople who work collectively to continue the long tradition of quilting in the Cayman Islands and to raise funds for charitable organisations. The group was started in 1993 and has met weekly in one another's homes since that time.

TRADITIONAL CRAFTS

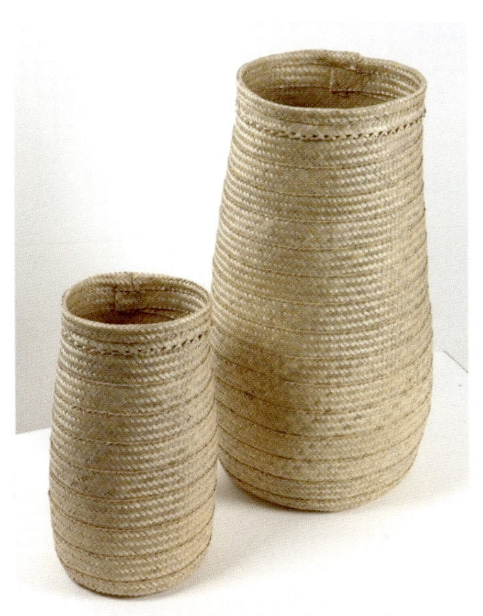

While the history of the formal visual arts in the Cayman Islands stretches back only to the mid-twentieth century, the islands have enjoyed a rich heritage of silver thatch craft for generations. Our collection begins with these traditional craft objects in an effort to put more recent artistic developments into context. The beautiful craft items featured here were commissioned by NGCI and are subsequently more contemporary and experimental in style than their historical counterparts.

The silver thatch palm (*Coccothrinax proctorii*) is a sturdy, salt-tolerant palm that is endemic to the islands and used primarily for rope making, roofing and basketry. Traditionally the thatch fronds, also known as 'tops,' would be harvested under a full moon, when the silvery undersides of the leaves were particularly prominent. These fronds would then be dried and cut into strips for weaving baskets or rope making. As evidenced in these images, basketry was creative, skilful and highly individualised, with weaving patterns varying from district to district. Caymanian thatch rope was also highly prized both locally and in Cuba and Jamaica for use in the shipping, fishing and sugar industries. It played an important role in the Caymanian economy until it was replaced in the 1950s with synthetic rope.

Elizabeth ('Lizzie') Powell (Caymanian, b. 1937)
Vases, **2010**
Silver thatch palm; 13 x 6½ x 7 inches (*left*)
and 20½ x 8½ x 11 inches (*right*)
See also page 92.

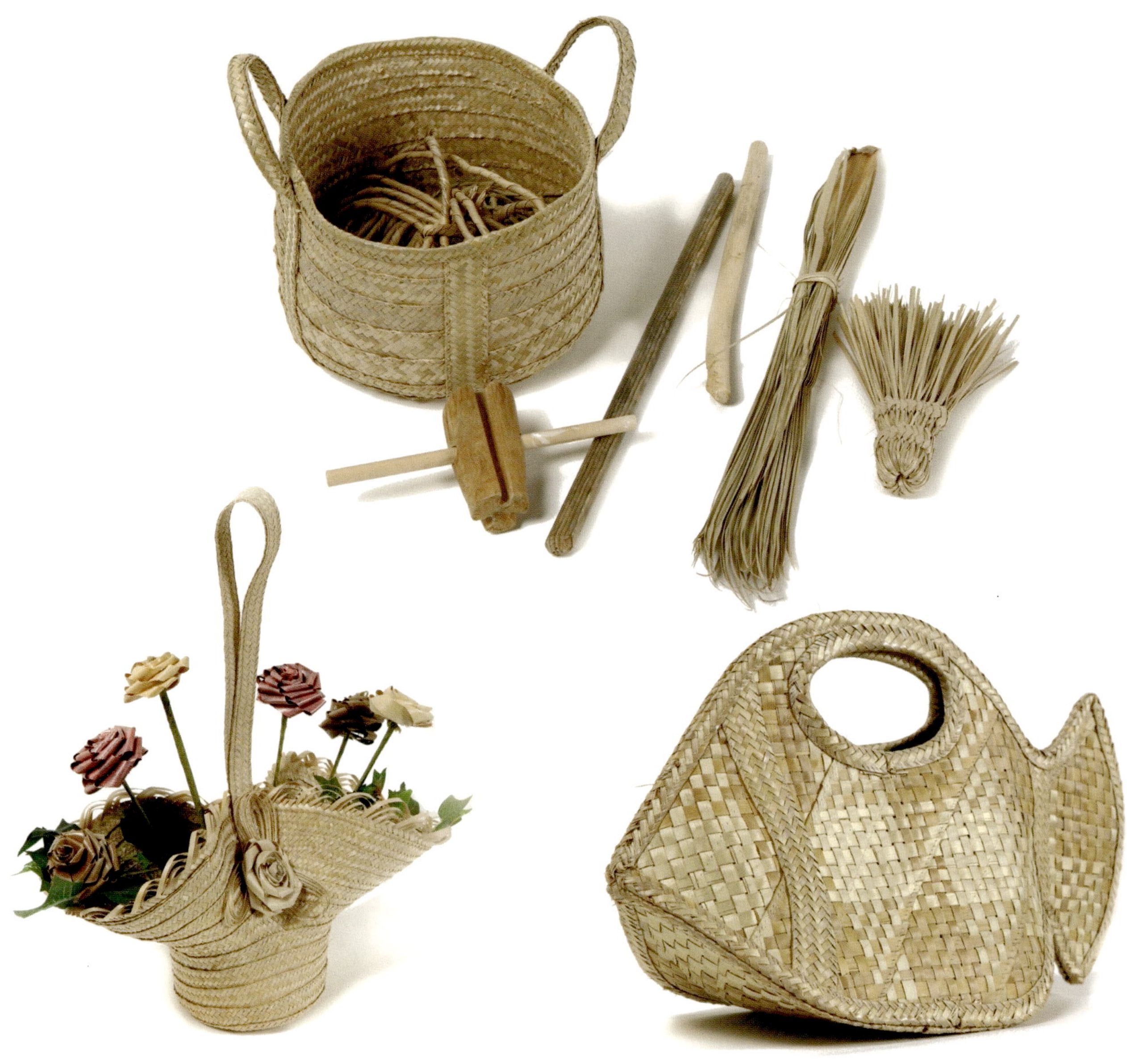

PLATE 4 (*lower left*)
Carmen Connolly (Caymanian, b. 1936)
Basket of Flowers, 2012
Silver thatch palm, natural dye, raffia;
18 x 14 x 7 inches
See also page 90.

PLATE 5 (*top*)
Marlena Anglin (Caymanian, b. 1933)
Basket with Utensils, 2013
Silver thatch palm; 26½ x 10 x 10 inches
See also page 88.

PLATE 6 (*lower right*)
Annalee Ebanks (Caymanian, b. 1933)
Thatch Fish Hand Basket, 2007
Silver thatch palm; 11 x 19 x 6½ inches
See also page 90.

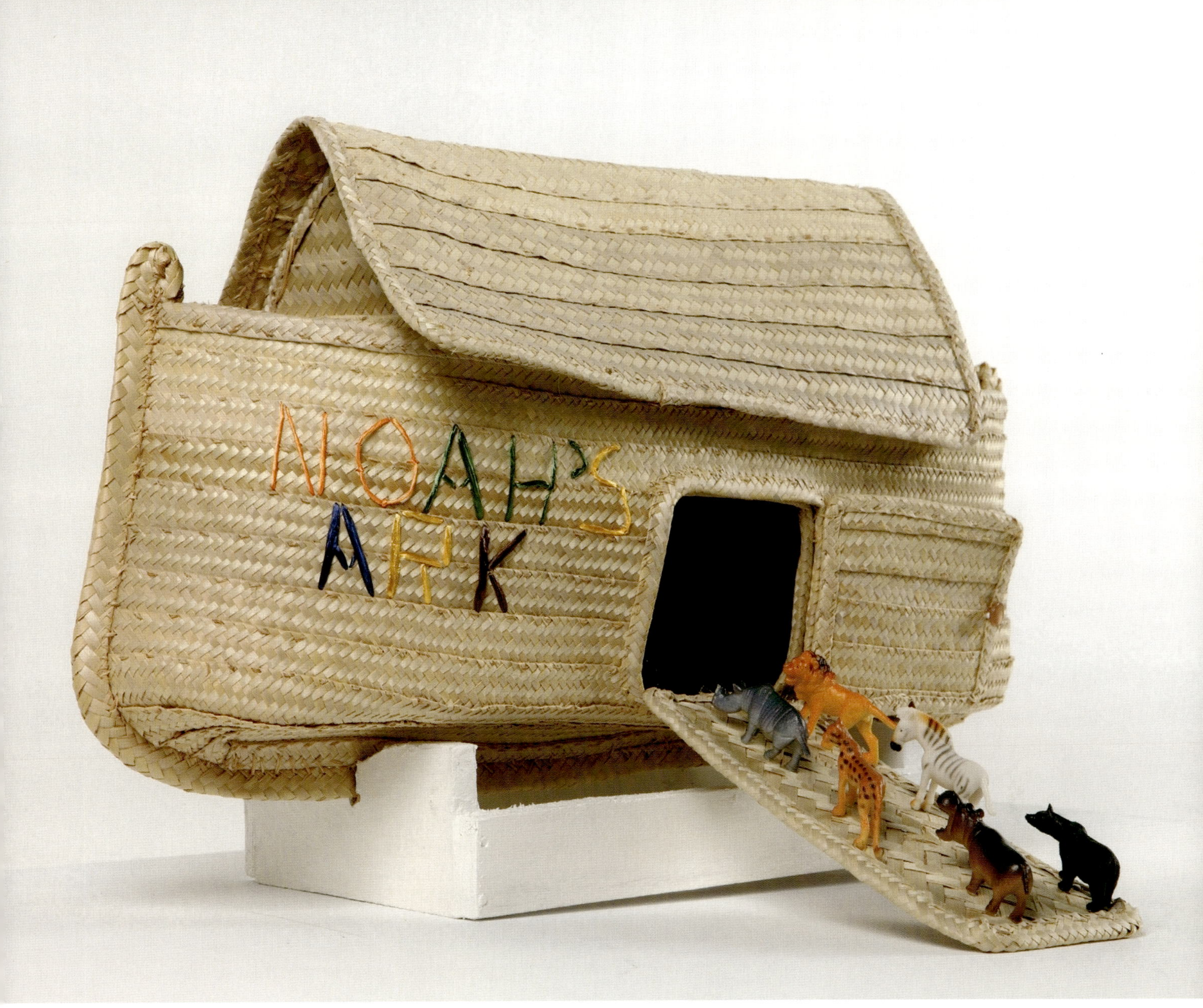

PLATE 7
Annie Joy ('Mrs Annie') Ebanks (Caymanian, b. 1950)
Noah's Ark, 2012
Silver thatch palm, raffia, plastic figurines;
16½ x 20 x 16 inches
See also page 90.

Charles Long (British-Caymanian, b. 1948)
Mitch Miller and His 'Ting,' 1973
Acrylic on Masonite; 22 x 62 inches
Gift of Mitch Miller
See also page 92, plate 9 and figures 1 and 8.

The famed American musician Mitch Miller, who vacationed on the island regularly from 1964 onward, is depicted here driving his yellow Volkswagen, known locally as a 'Ting.' The backdrop is a typical Caymanian street of the early 1970s, when reliance on the maritime industry (symbolised by the vessel in the background) was dwindling and the financial and tourism sectors were on the rise, bringing with them a rapid influx of foreign nationals and cultural influences. The flat, decorative style is typical of the artist's work.

Long began documenting scenes of daily life in the Cayman Islands soon after arriving in Grand Cayman from West Africa in 1968. He has been dubbed a chronicler of our times for his whimsical depictions of local flora and fauna, seascapes, street life and everyday activities.

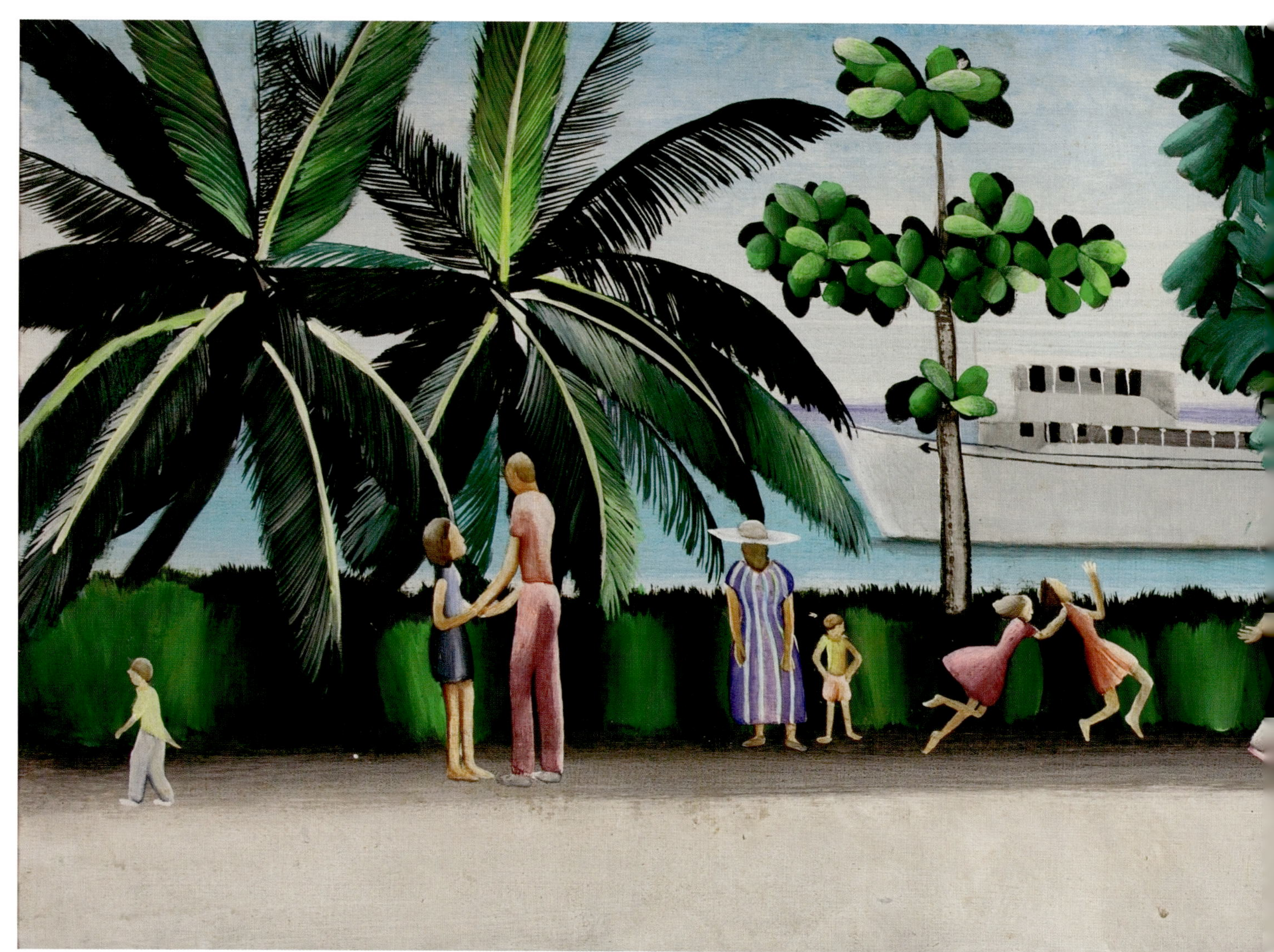

PLATE 9
Charles Long (British-Caymanian, b. 1948)
Girls at the Vanity Table (detail), 1975
Acrylic on Surinamese wood; 24 x 24 inches
Gift of George and Nita Wheaton-Tully
See also page 92, plate 8 and figures 1 and 8.

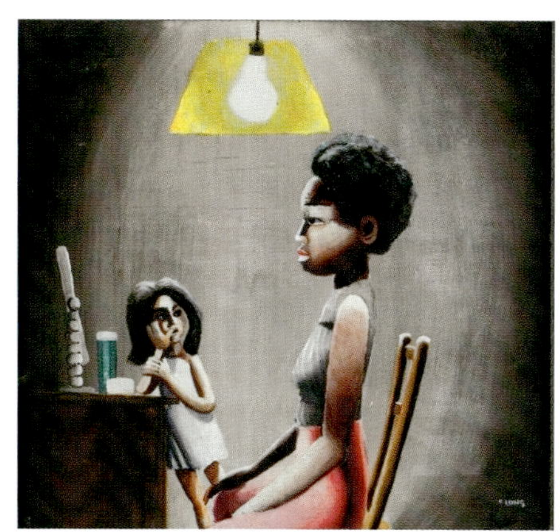

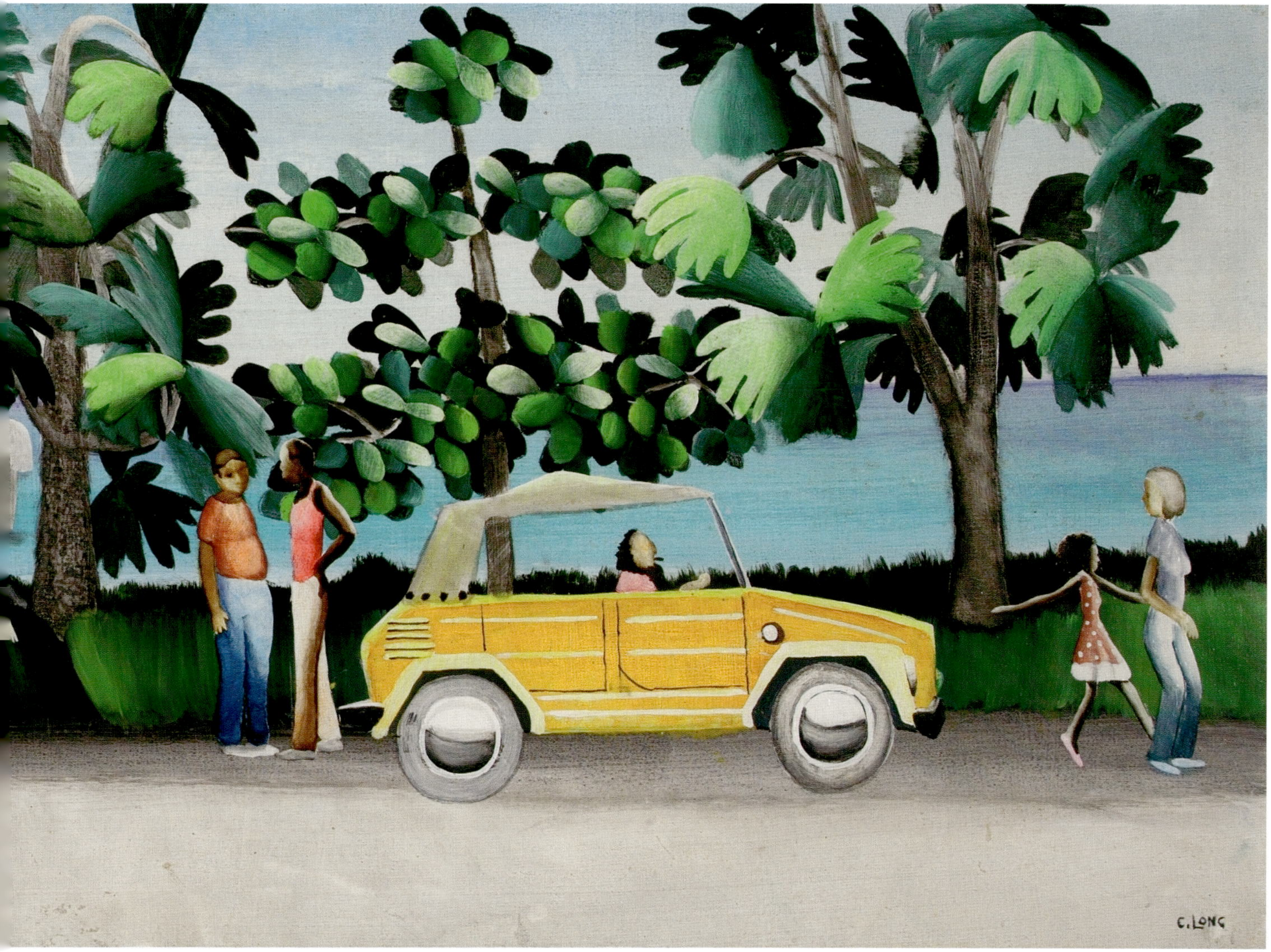

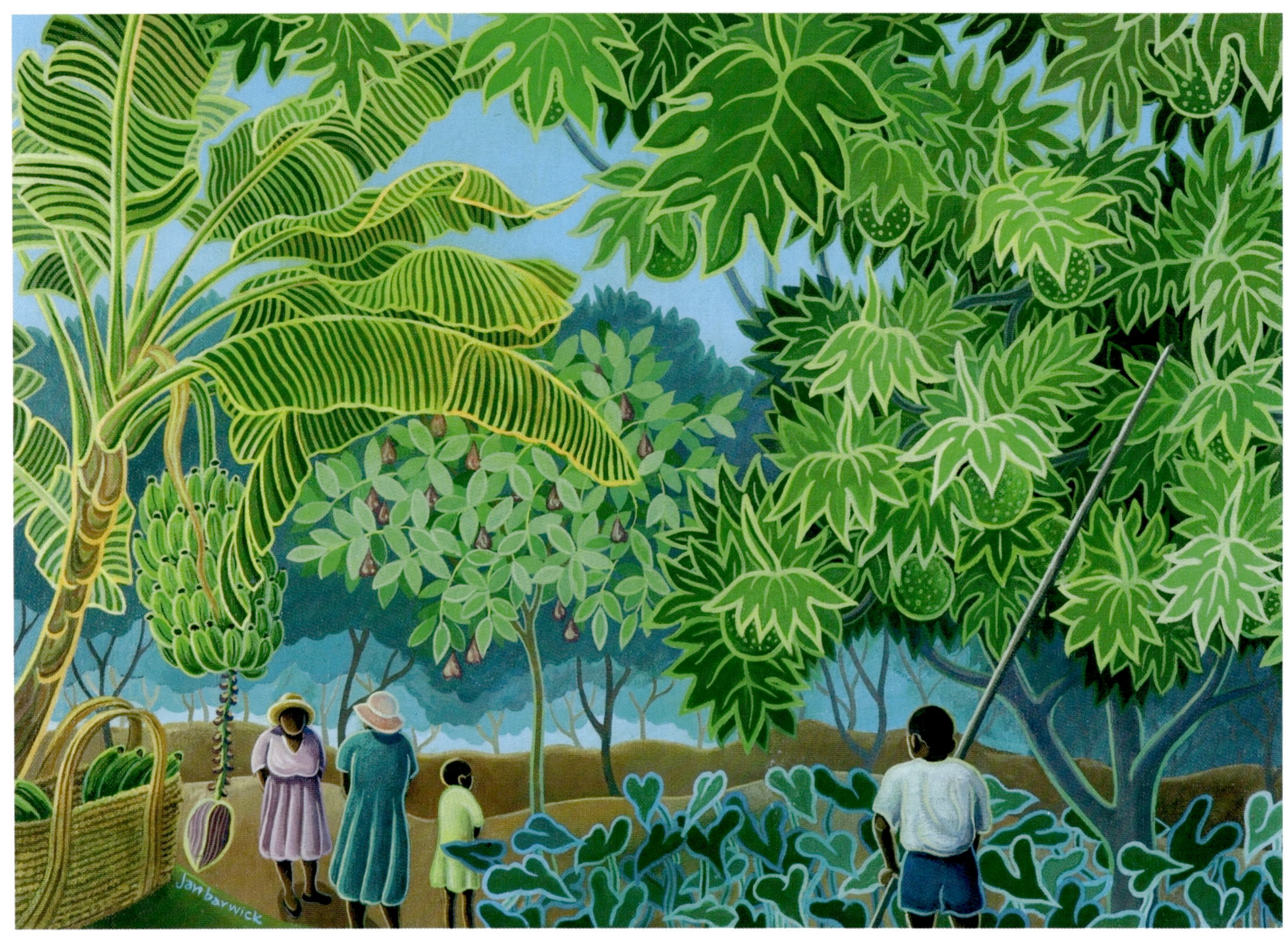

PLATE 10
Jan Barwick (New Zealander–British, b. 1953)
Picking Breadfruit, ca. 1988
Acrylic on canvas; 11 x 14 inches
Gift of Leslie Bigelman
See also page 88 and plate 13.

Breadfruit has been a mainstay of the Caymanian diet for centuries. In this image, inspired by a photograph from the Cayman Islands National Archives, Barwick captures a typical Caymanian family, imagined circa 1930, gathering breadfruit for sustenance and using the ubiquitous silver thatch basket for 'backing' (carrying) produce home. The tropical palette and flat, decorative style are typical of her work of this period.

Born in New Zealand, Barwick spent her childhood in the Solomon Islands, Kiribati and Malawi before moving to the Cayman Islands with her family. She was highly prolific through the late 1980s and early 1990s before relocating to France. Travel, a keen interest in ecology and wildlife, and an exceptional colour sense combine to make her a painter of unique vision.

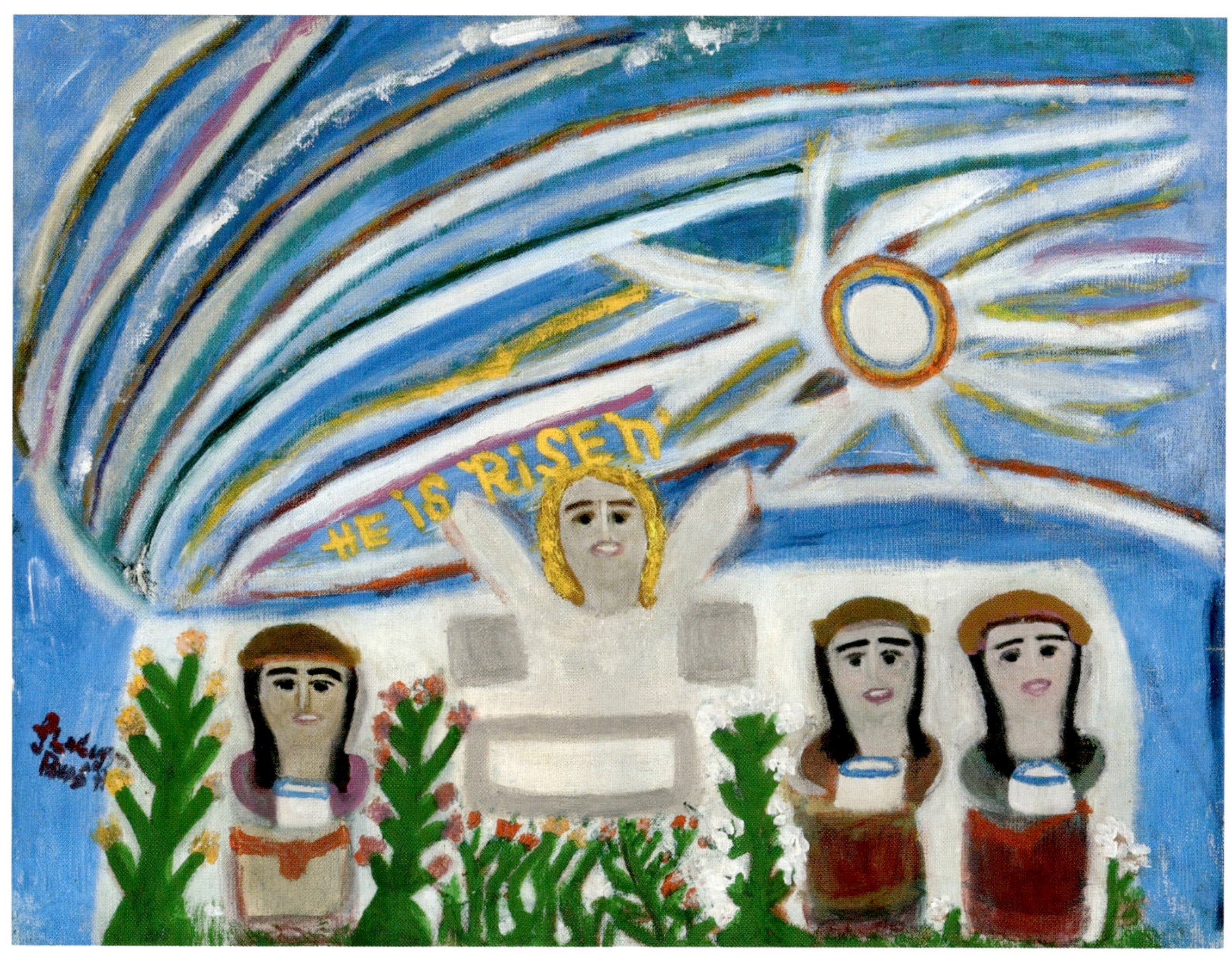

PLATE 11

Gladwyn K. ('Miss Lassie') Bush
(Caymanian, 1914–2003)
He Is Risen, ca. 1983
Acrylic on canvas; 16 x 20 inches
Gift of Michael and Monica Gore
Image reproduced with permission of
the Cayman National Cultural Foundation
See also page 89 and plates 12a–d.

A fourth-generation Caymanian, the late Gladwyn K. ('Miss Lassie') Bush began to paint only at the age of sixty-two, following what she described as a 'visionary experience.' Her 'markings,' as she referred to her work, are executed in a naïve style reflecting her status as an intuitive, self-taught artist. As evidenced in this reference to Christ's resurrection, strong Christian themes run through her art, which she initially painted on the walls, windows and furnishings of her home and later created on canvas.

Miss Lassie was considered a serious intuitive artist in the Caribbean region, alongside the likes of Guyana's Philip Moore and Jamaica's Kapo. Her cottage was recognised on the World Heritage Watch List in 2012 and has become a destination for folk and visionary art lovers worldwide.

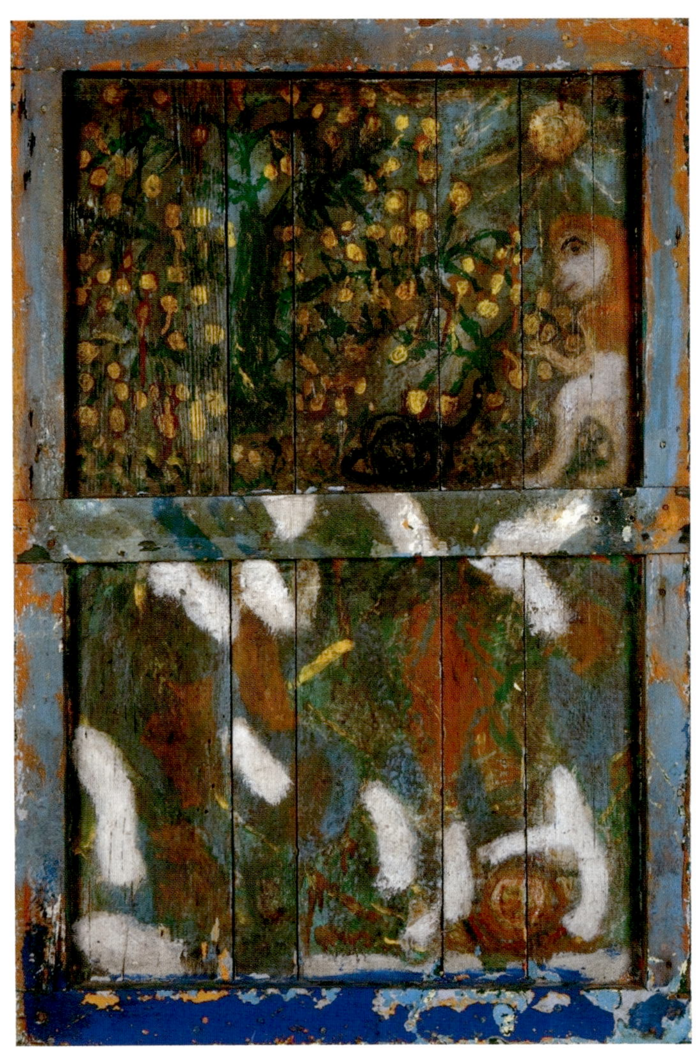 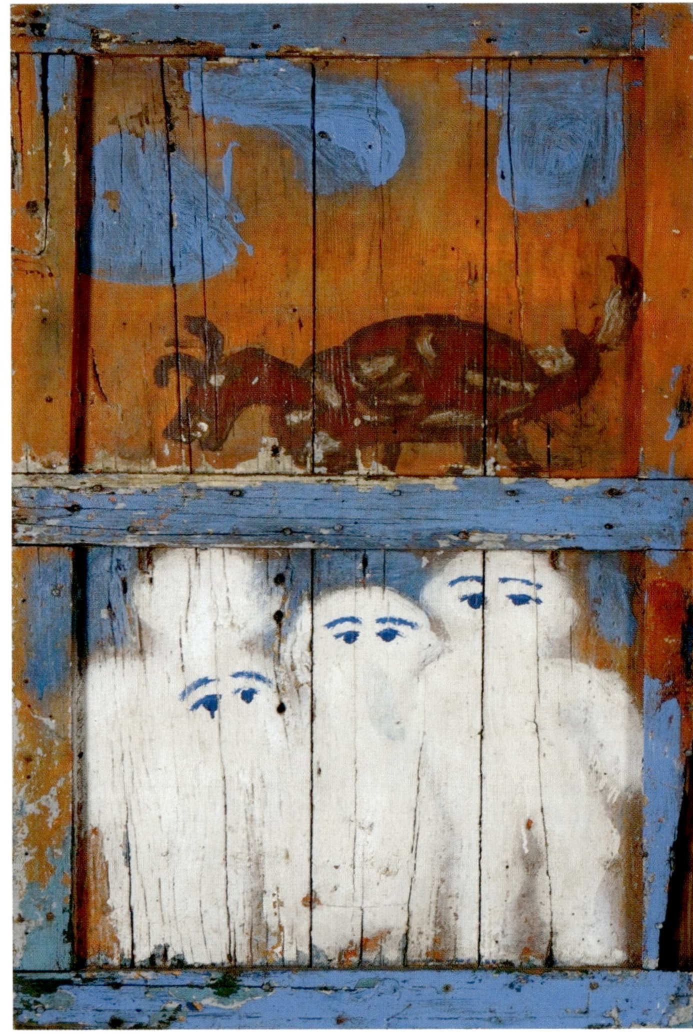

PLATES 12A–D

Gladwyn K. ('Miss Lassie') Bush
(Caymanian, 1914–2003)
Kitchen Window I–IV, ca. 1980
Acrylic on wood; 43 x 29½ x 2 inches,
43½ x 28 x 2 inches, 43 x 29½ x 2 inches,
and 44 x 30 x 1½ inches
Part gift of Michael and Alejandro Joseph
Purchased in part via the Susan A. Olde Collection Fund
Images reproduced with permission of the
Cayman National Cultural Foundation
See also page 89 and plate 11.

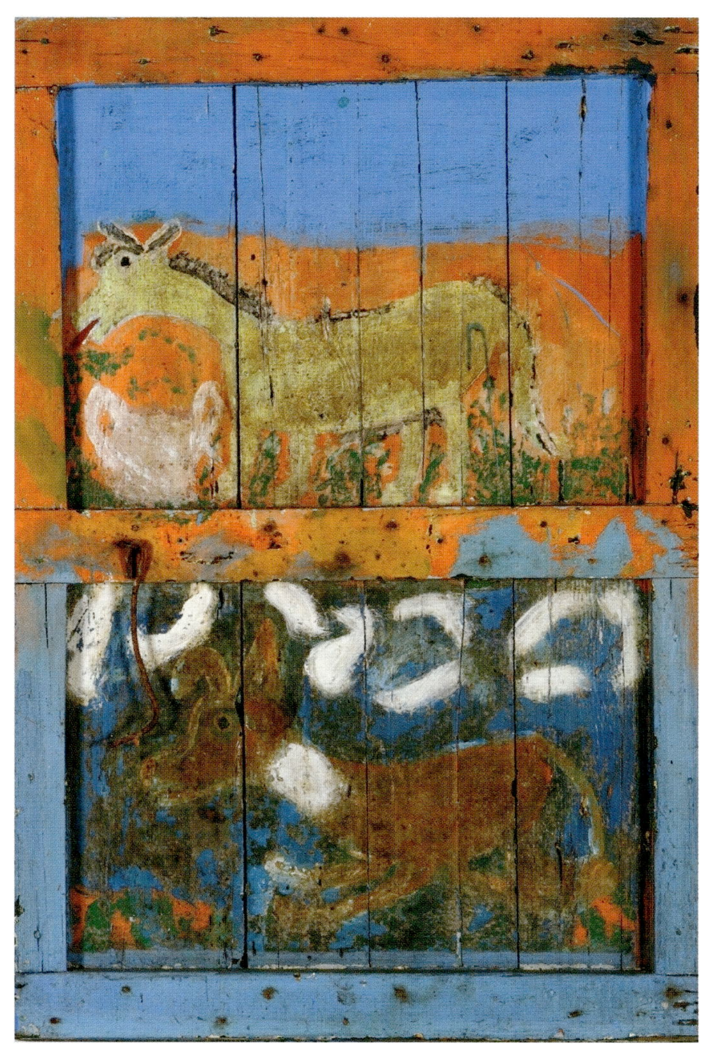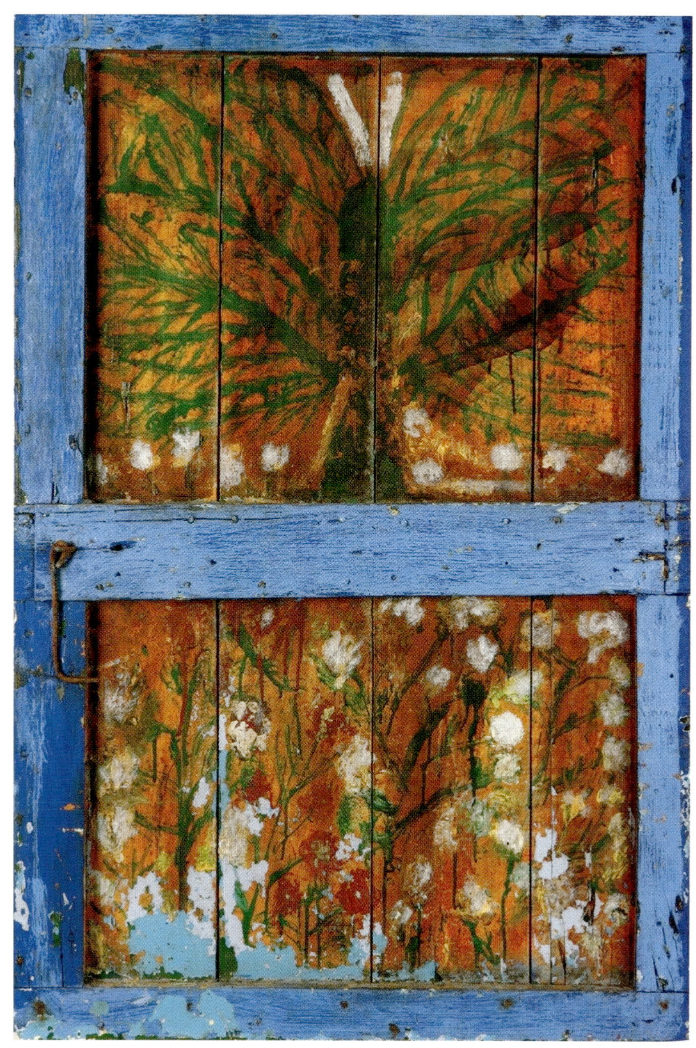

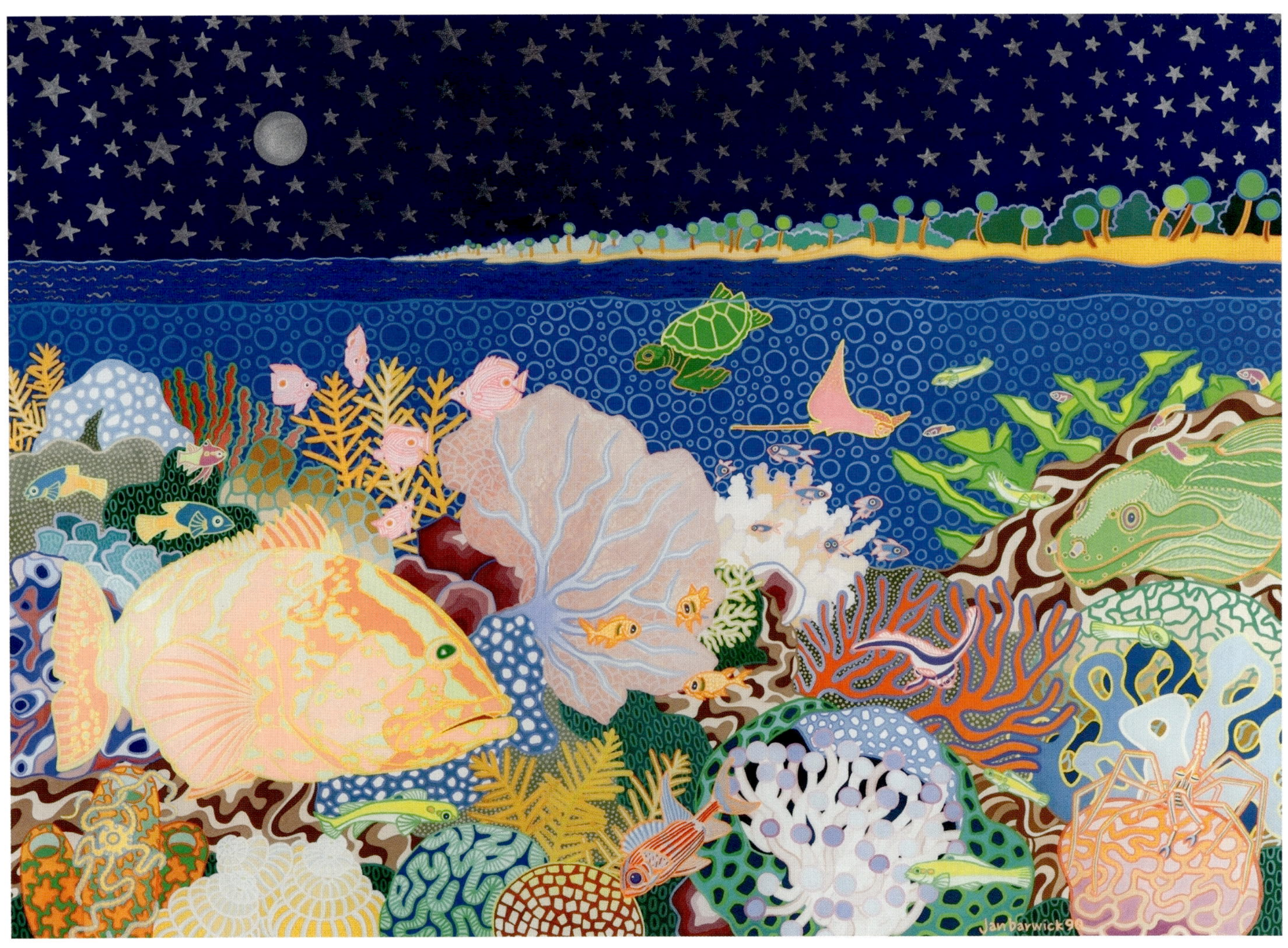

PLATE 13
Jan Barwick (New Zealander–British, b. 1953)
Coral Reef by Night, 1990
Gouache on paper; 30 x 40 inches
Gift of King and Lisa Flowers and
Ralph and Jennifer Woodford
See also page 88 and plate 10.

As illustrated in *Picking Breadfruit* (plate 10), Barwick's keen interest in ecology and wildlife and her remarkable sense of colour create a unique vision of the Cayman Islands' underwater environment. In a period dominated by Realist painters, her highly decorative style became iconic when it was reproduced in poster format and in merchandising across the islands. The series included several variations, depicting the reef in both sunlight and moonlight, but *Coral Reef by Night* is perhaps the most recognisable.

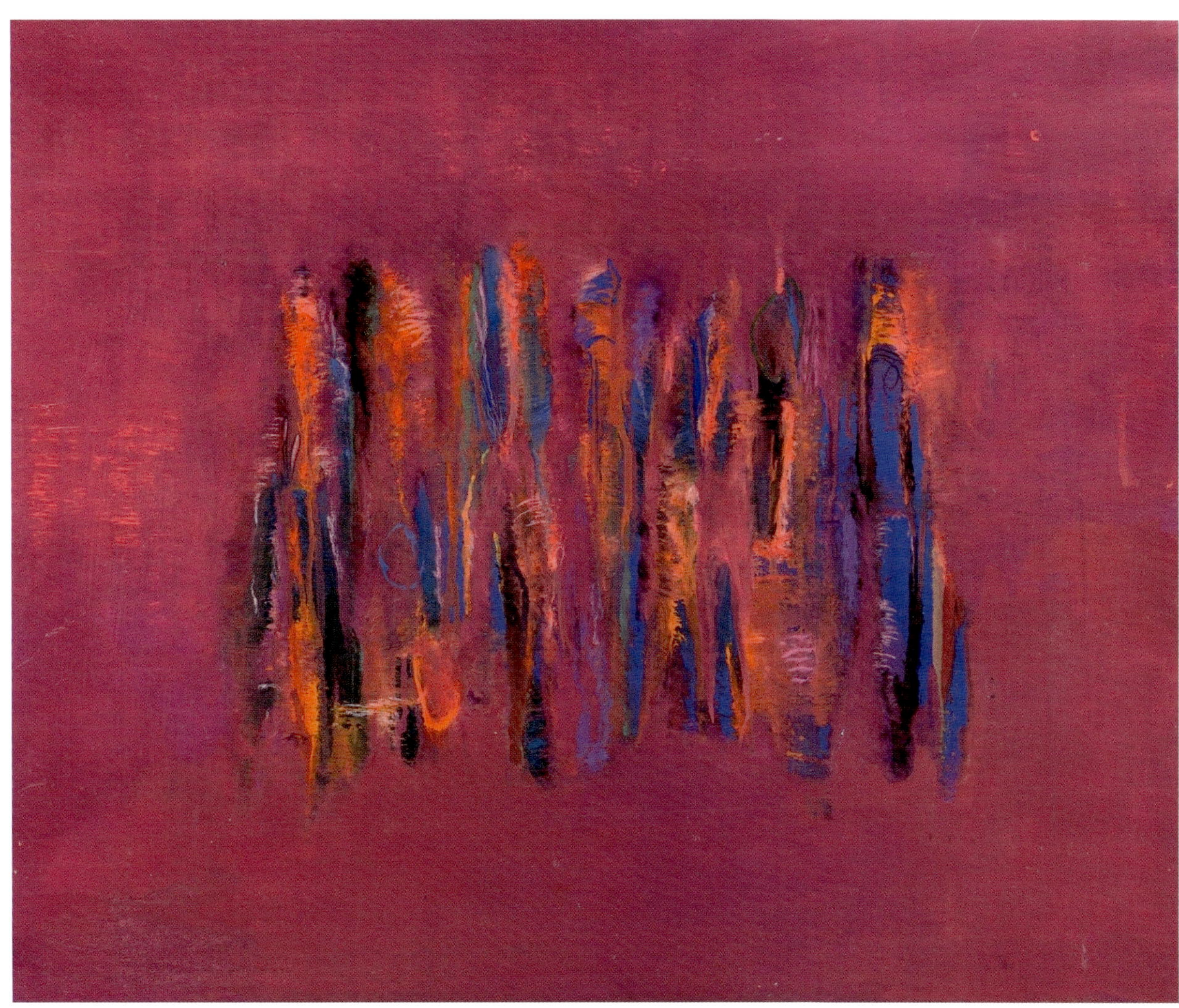

Bendel Hydes (Caymanian, b. 1952)
Ovid's Conch III, 1983
Acrylic on canvas; 16 x 20 inches
Gift of Beverly Banks
See also page 91, plate 45 and figures 13 and 18.

Initially a proponent of Realism and Pop Art, Hydes began to experiment in the early 1980s with the abstract visual language for which he is known today. *Ovid's Conch III* shows a composition that exists with a measure of independence from its subject. However, the title's allusion to poetry announces the artist's preference to deal with ideas rather than the mere formal qualities of his style, which he refers to as 'luminescent abstraction.' Hydes was the first Caymanian to study fine art abroad, and he is considered a forefather of Cayman Islands art. He moved to New York in the 1980s, and the dichotomy between his locations, in addition to his maritime heritage, continues to play a central role in his work.

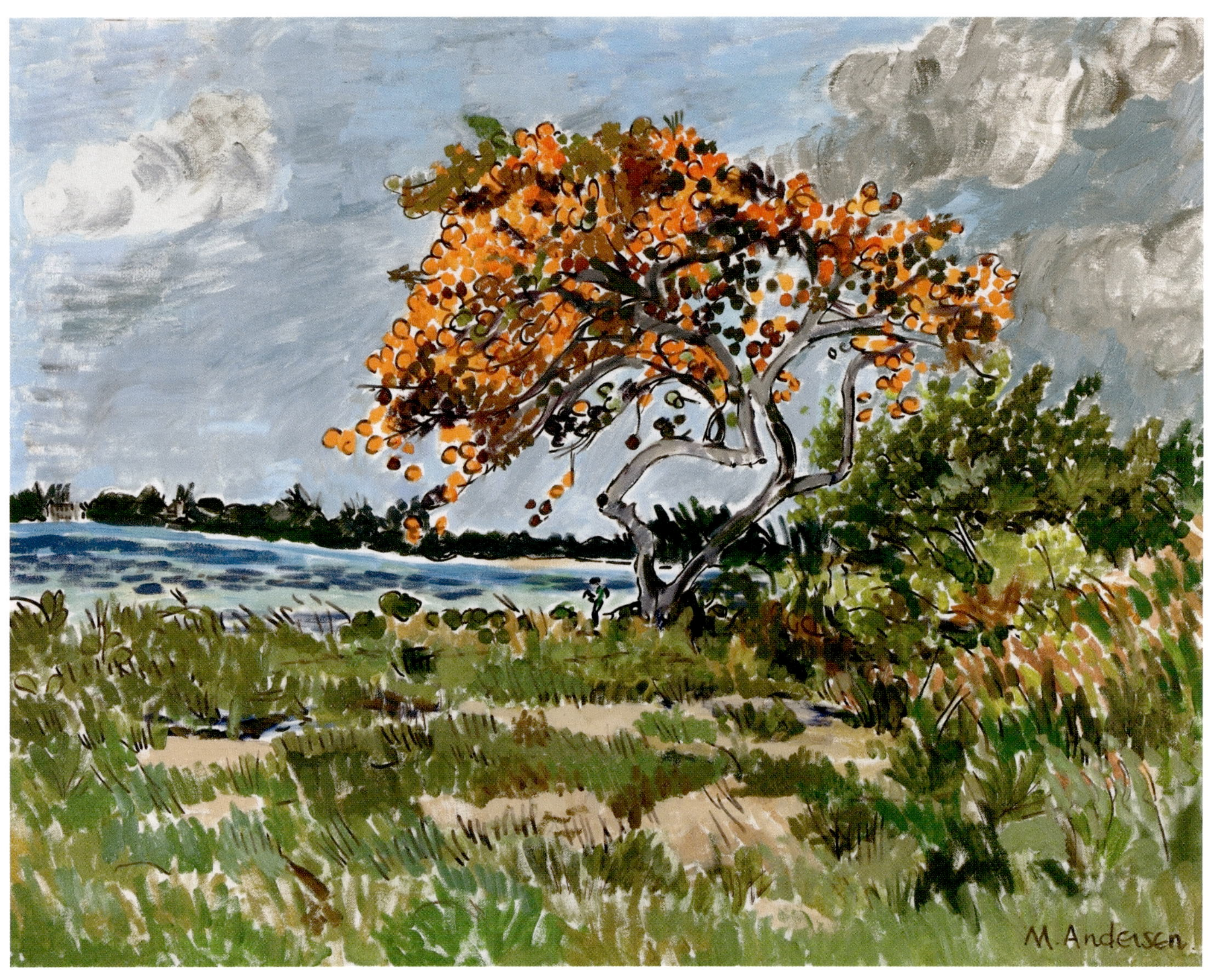

Maureen Andersen Berry (British-Caymanian, b. 1927)
Sea Grape Tree, 1985

Ink, acrylic on canvas; 24 x 30 inches
See also page 88.

Native to the West Indies, the sea grape (*Coccoloba uvifera*) is conspicuous for its large, circular leaves with red veins and its edible purple grapes. It is these features, along with the gnarled shape of the trunk, which has been sculpted by the wind and salt spray, that the artist beautifully renders using a combination of ink and acrylic.

Andersen Berry was born in Derby, United Kingdom, and she studied at the Slade School of Fine Art, London, before moving to the Cayman Islands to teach in 1976. Her work is heavily influenced by Post-Impressionism and is predominantly concerned with the vibrant flora and vistas of the three Cayman Islands.

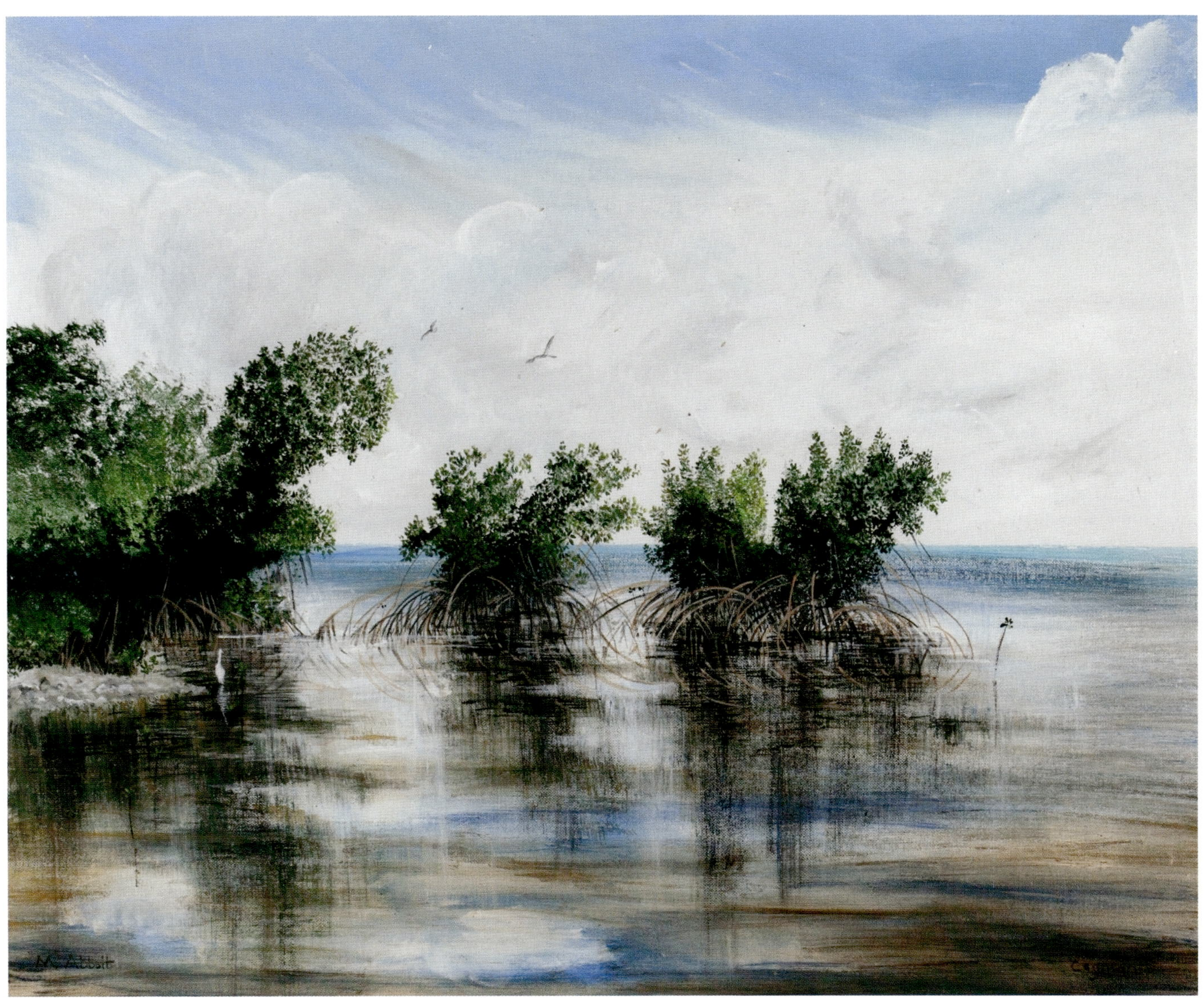

PLATE 16
Moira Abbott (British-Caymanian, b. 1945)
Mangroves, ca. 1980
Acrylic on canvas; 28 x 34 inches
See also page 88.

Landscape was a typical subject for artists working in the 1980s, a period that was dominated by Realist painters who sought to capture the picturesque local environment. Here the artist has created a highly rendered image with a drag-and-scrape technique. The interesting contrast of texture creates a rich dialogue between the opposing elements of land and sea, moderated by the mangroves themselves.

Abbott studied textile design at Manchester College of Art and worked as a conservation officer at the Victoria and Albert Museum, London, before moving to Jamaica in the 1970s to teach art. She arrived in the Cayman Islands in 1983 to work at Cayman Prep and High School and became an active member of the Visual Arts Society and the country's growing art scene.

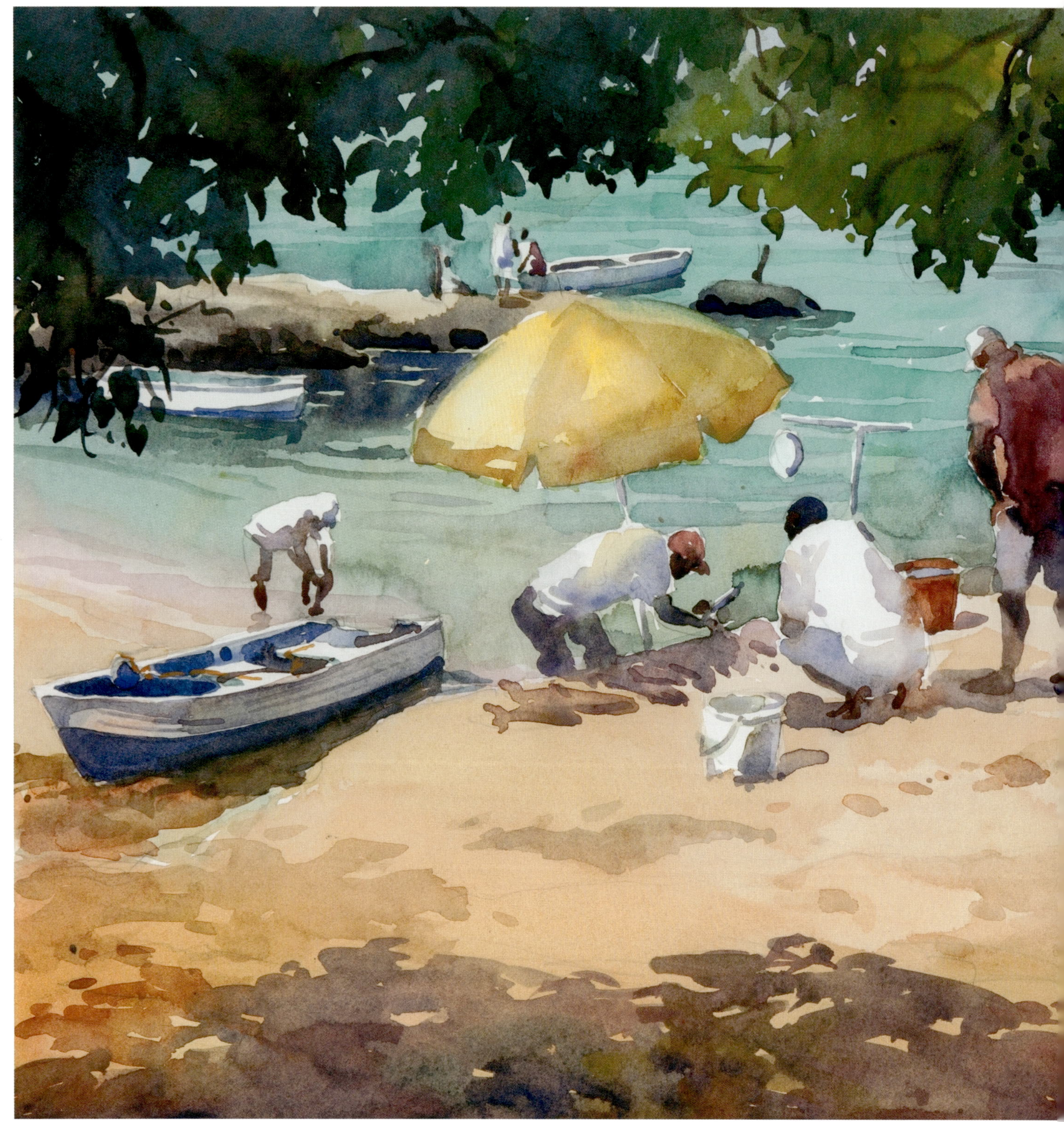

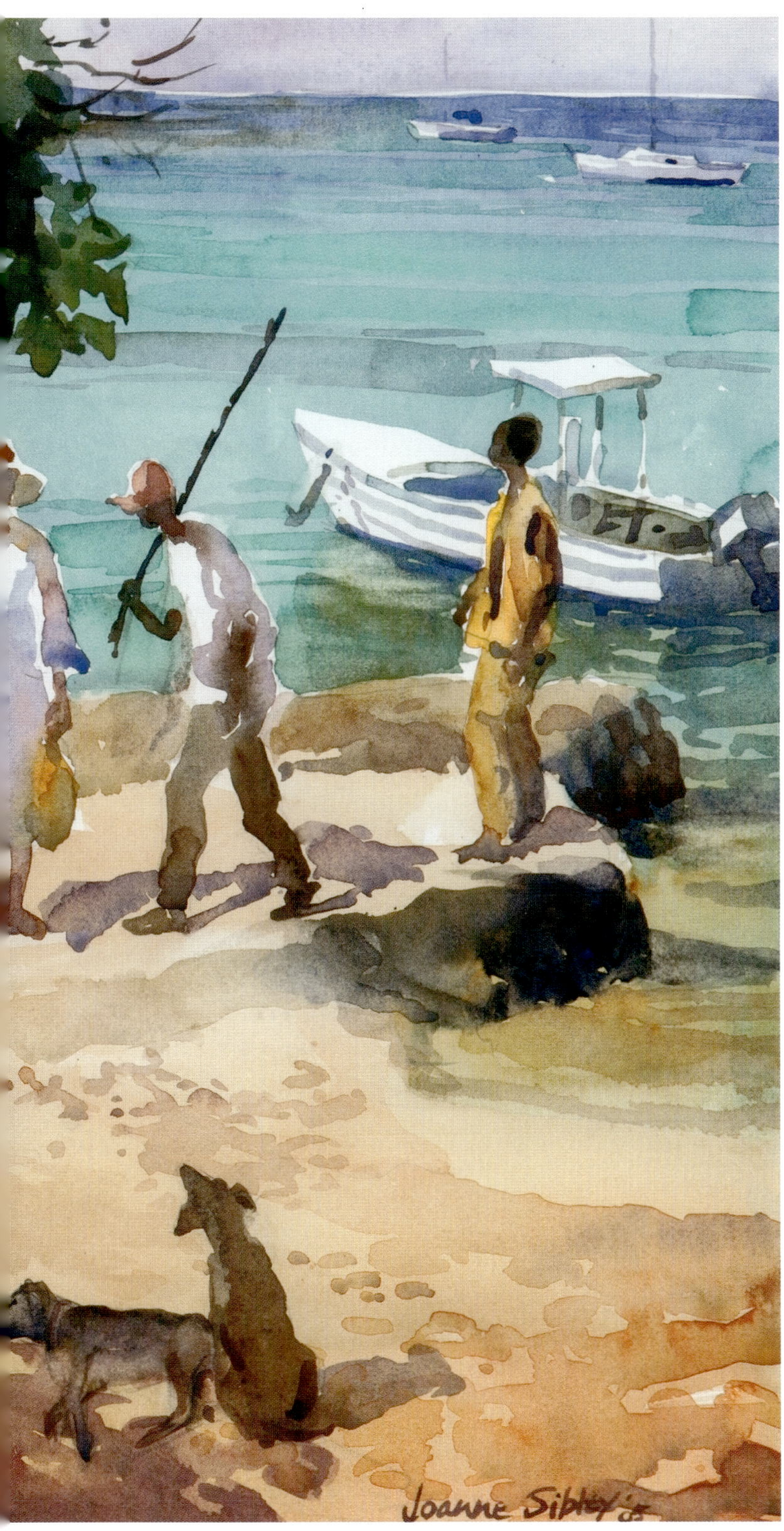

PLATE 17

Joanne Sibley (Canadian-Caymanian, b. 1930)
Fishermen, 2005
Watercolour on paper; 20 x 26 inches
Gift of Bank Austria Cayman Islands Ltd
See also page 93 and plates 18–20.

This image depicts Hog Sty Bay in central George Town, once the centre of the turtling industry and now the location of an informal daily fish market. The richly pigmented and highly textured medium of watercolour is skilfully wielded by the artist to capture a crisp scene of daily maritime life with meticulous detail.

Sibley arrived in the Cayman Islands from Canada in 1980 via Jamaica, where she had already established herself as a successful artist. An interior designer by trade, Sibley has a signature style highly influenced by her formal training in architectural rendering. She has become one of the islands' most prolific and recognisable artists.

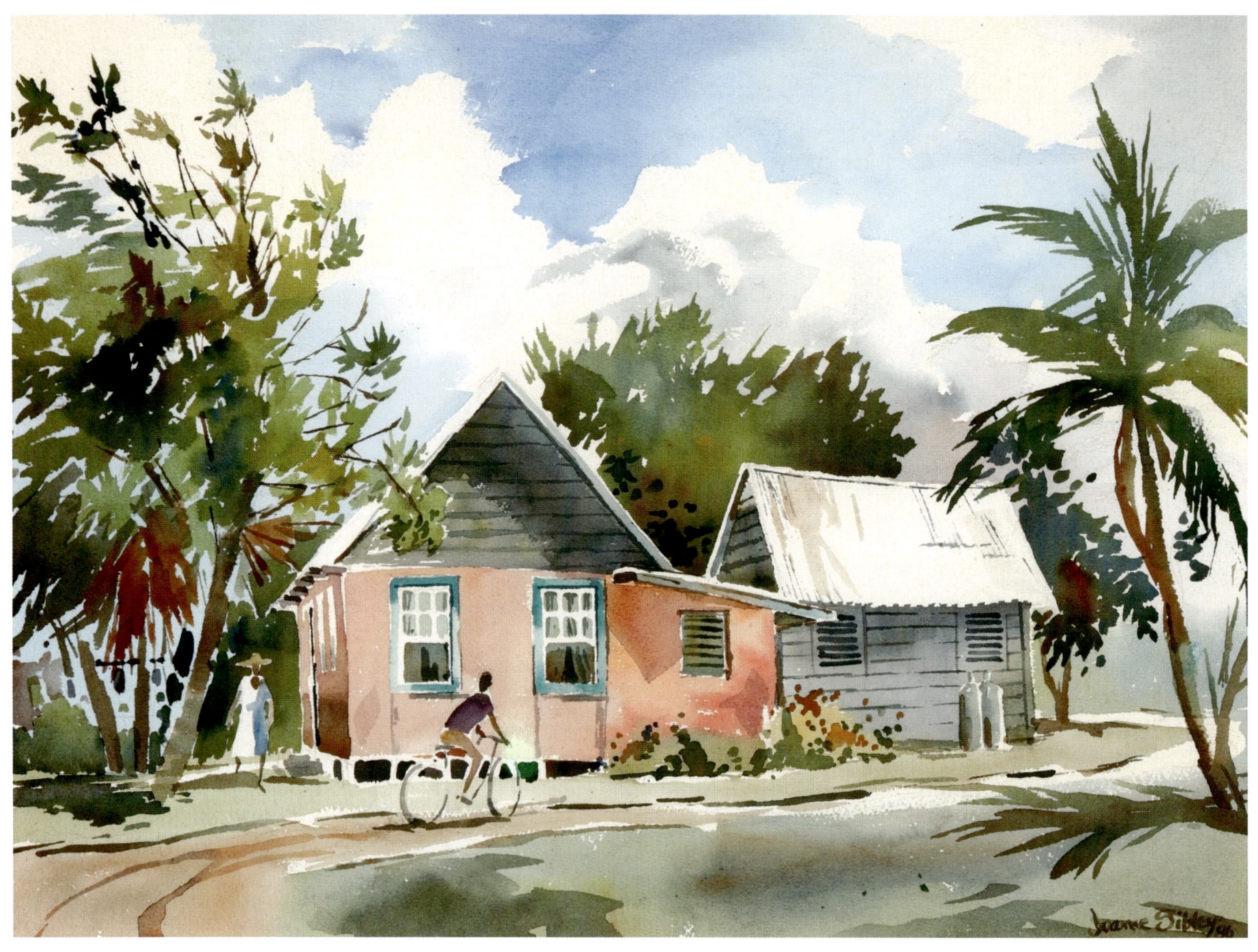

PLATE 18
Joanne Sibley (Canadian-Caymanian, b. 1930)
Pink Cottage, 1986
Watercolour on paper; 27 x 32 inches
See also page 93 and plates 17 and 19–20.

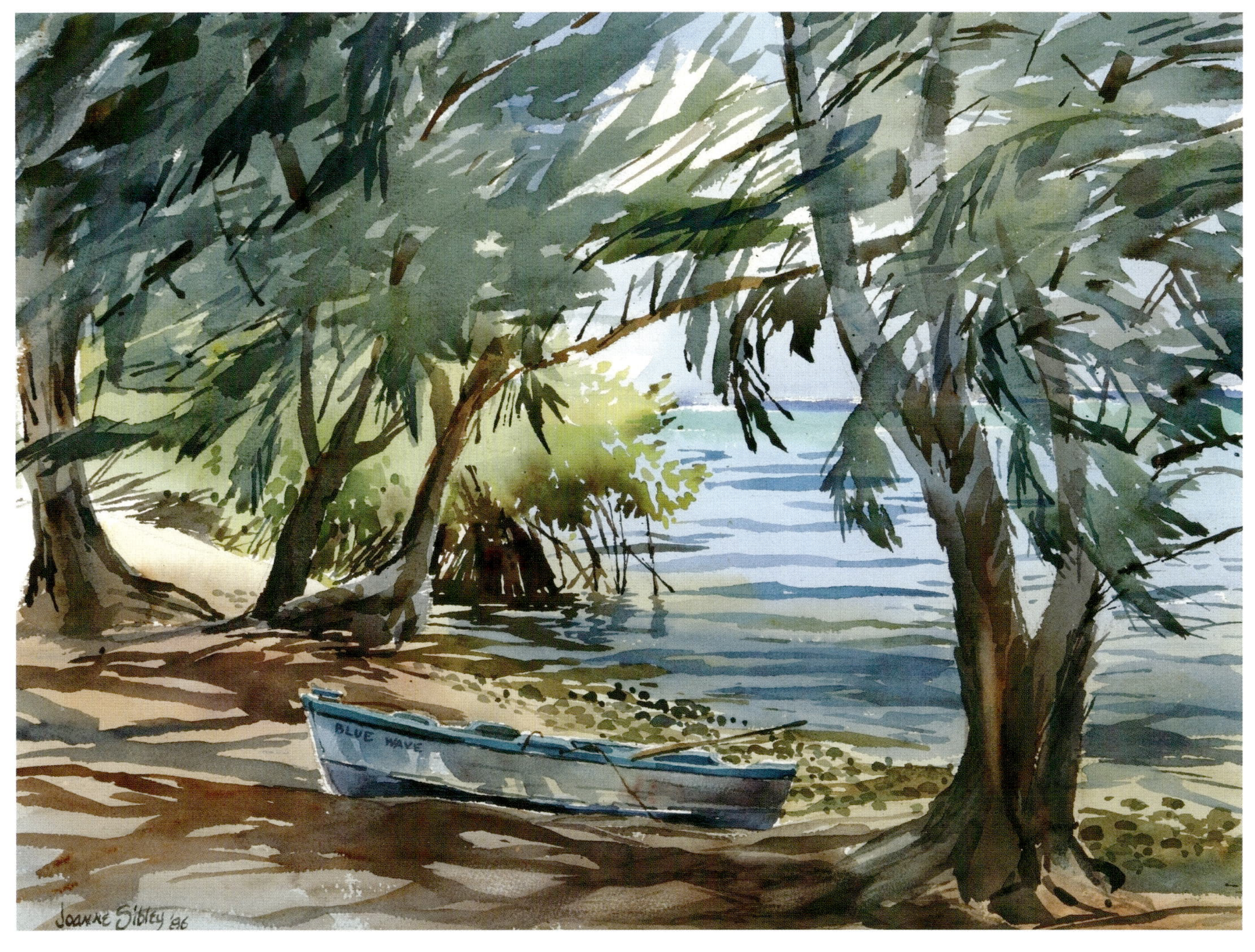

PLATE 19
Joanne Sibley (Canadian-Caymanian, b. 1930)
South Sound, 1986
Watercolour on paper; 17 x 23 inches
See also page 93 and plates 17–18 and 20.

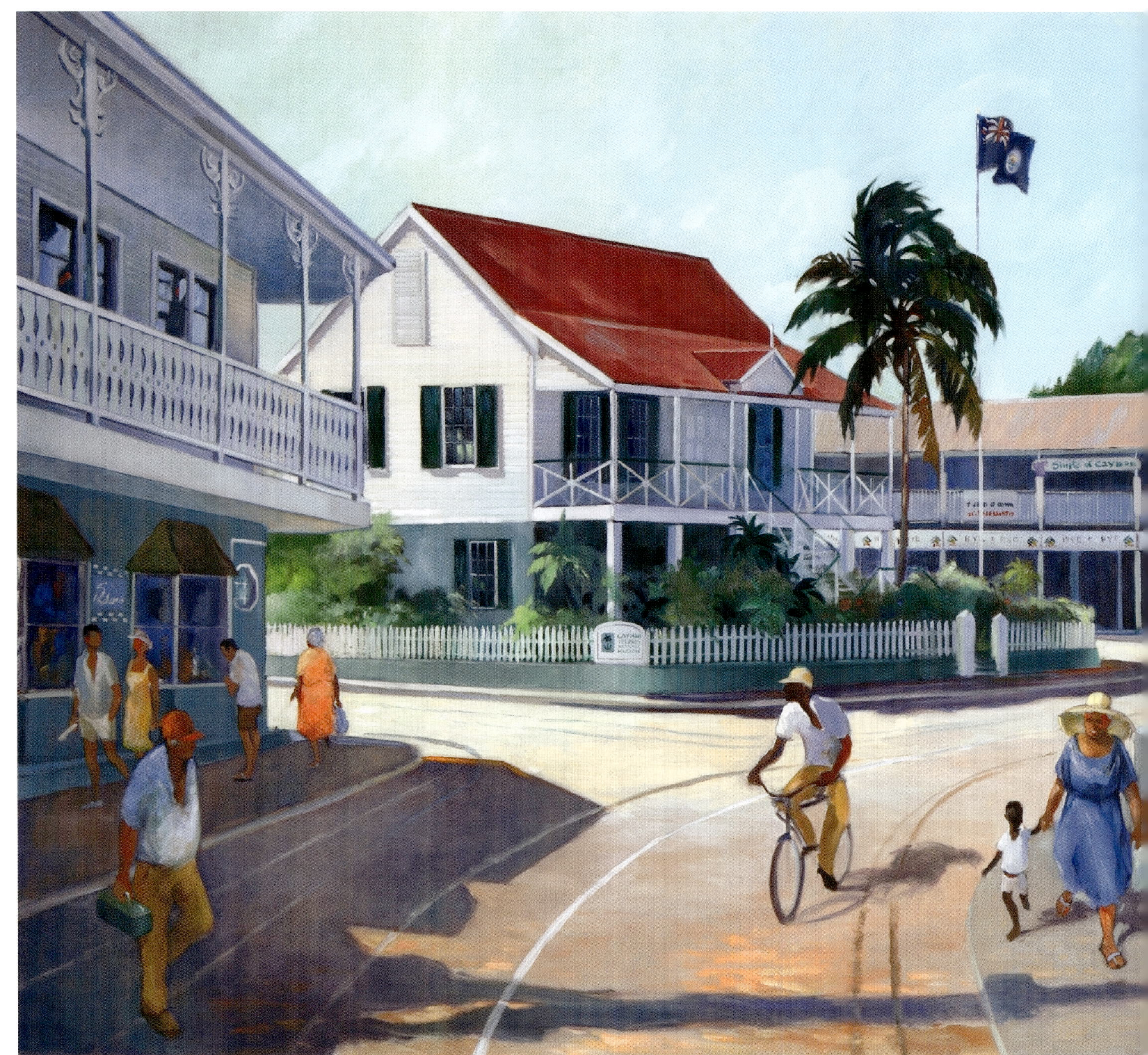

PLATE 20

Joanne Sibley (Canadian-Caymanian, b. 1930)
Harbour Drive, **1995**

Oil on canvas; 50 x 104 inches
Gift of Coutts (Cayman) Ltd
See also page 93 and plates 17–19.

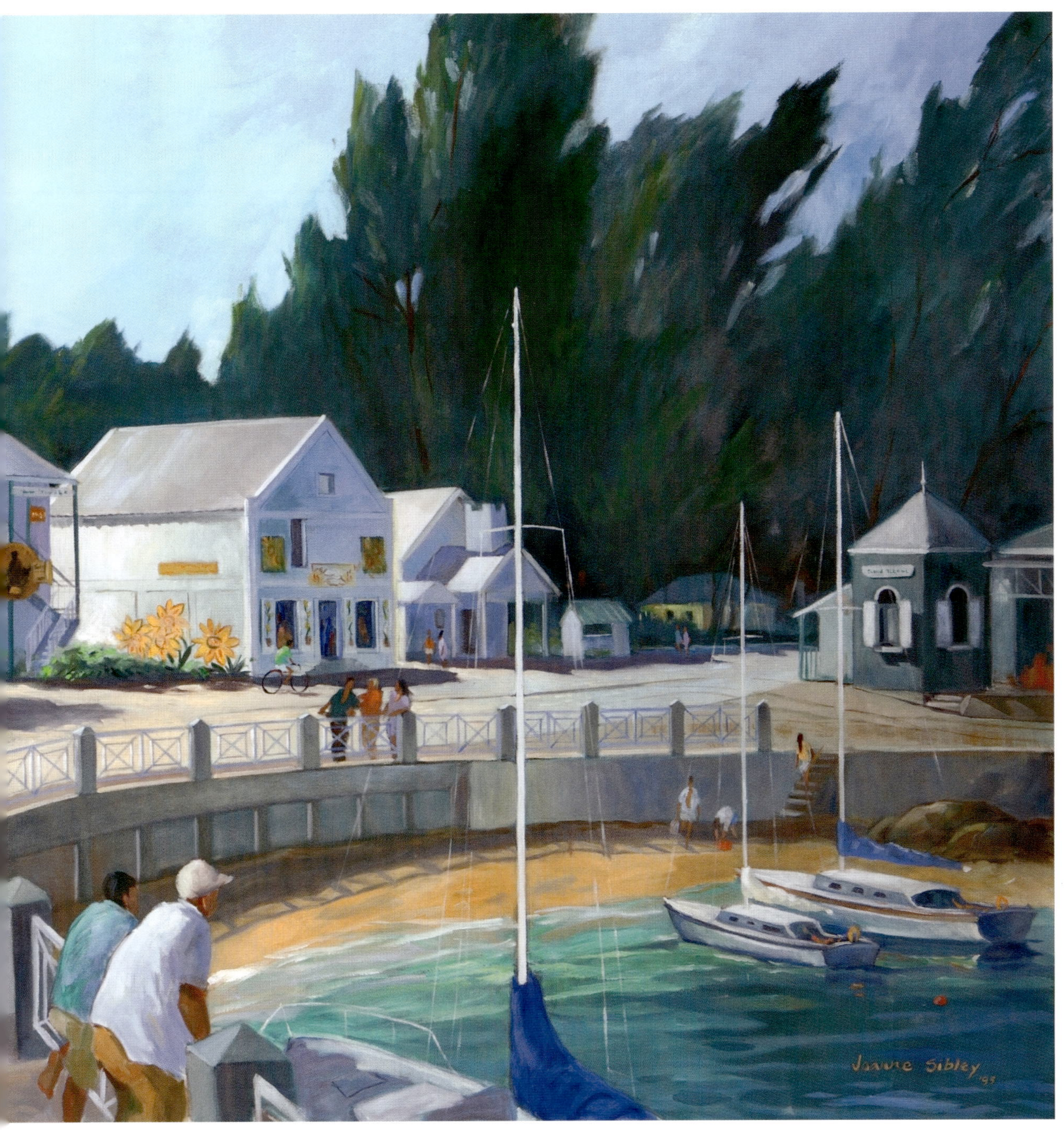

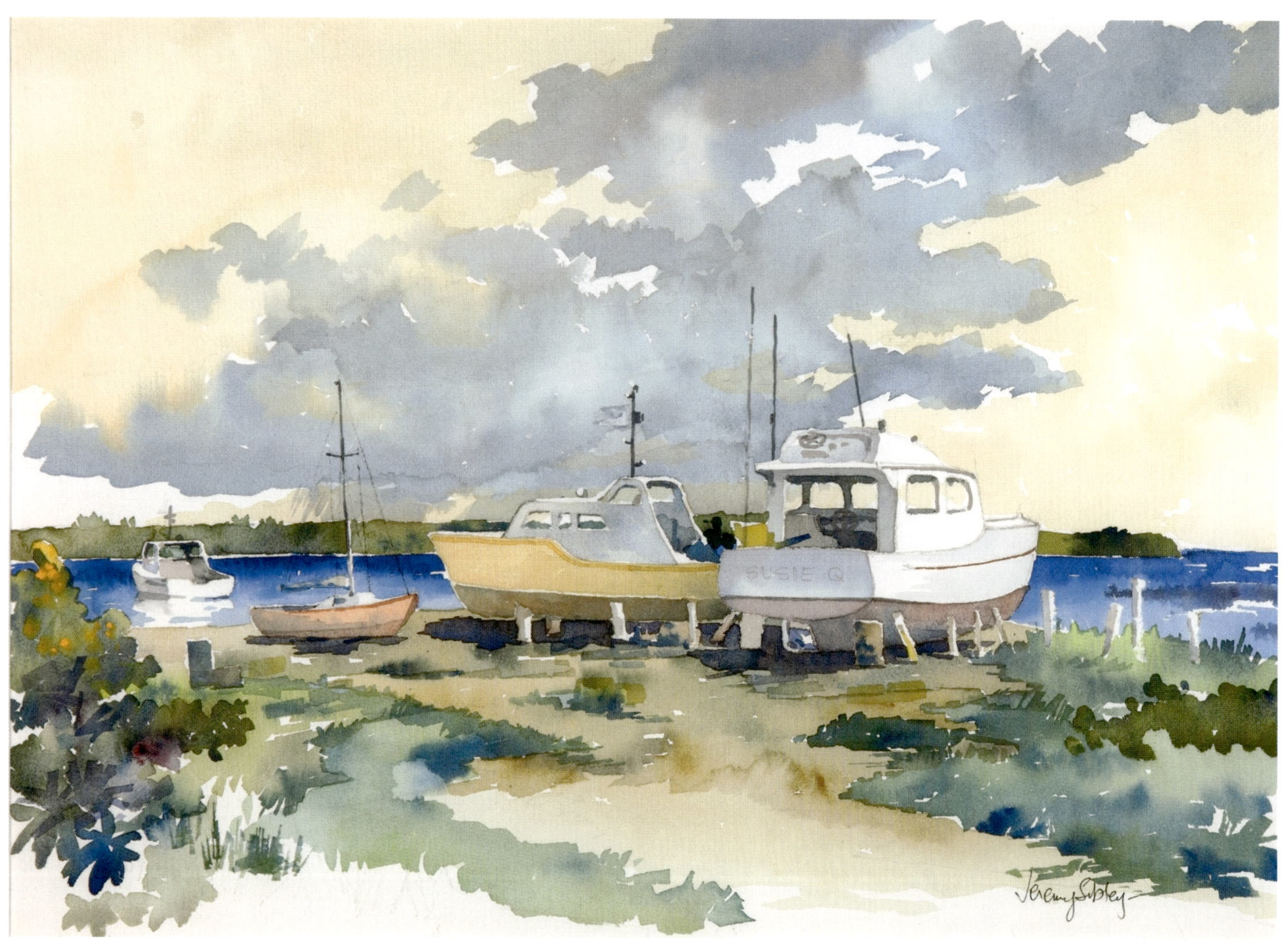

PLATE 21
Jeremy Sibley (Jamaican-Caymanian, b. 1929)
A Quiet Beach with Boats, 2004
Watercolour on paper; 21 x 27 inches
Gift of Appleby
See also page 93.

This watercolour is both a beautifully executed study of light and colour and a carefully rendered illustration of maritime industry. Sibley skirts away from idealised Caribbean representations by using realistically earthy sepia colours, to the effect that his painting is both atmospheric and expressive.

A watercolourist, sketcher and drawer, Sibley was born in Jamaica, where he practised as an architect before retiring to the Cayman Islands with his artist wife, Joanne (see plates 17–20). His work has been exhibited by the Visual Arts Society and in galleries in Salt Spring, British Columbia.

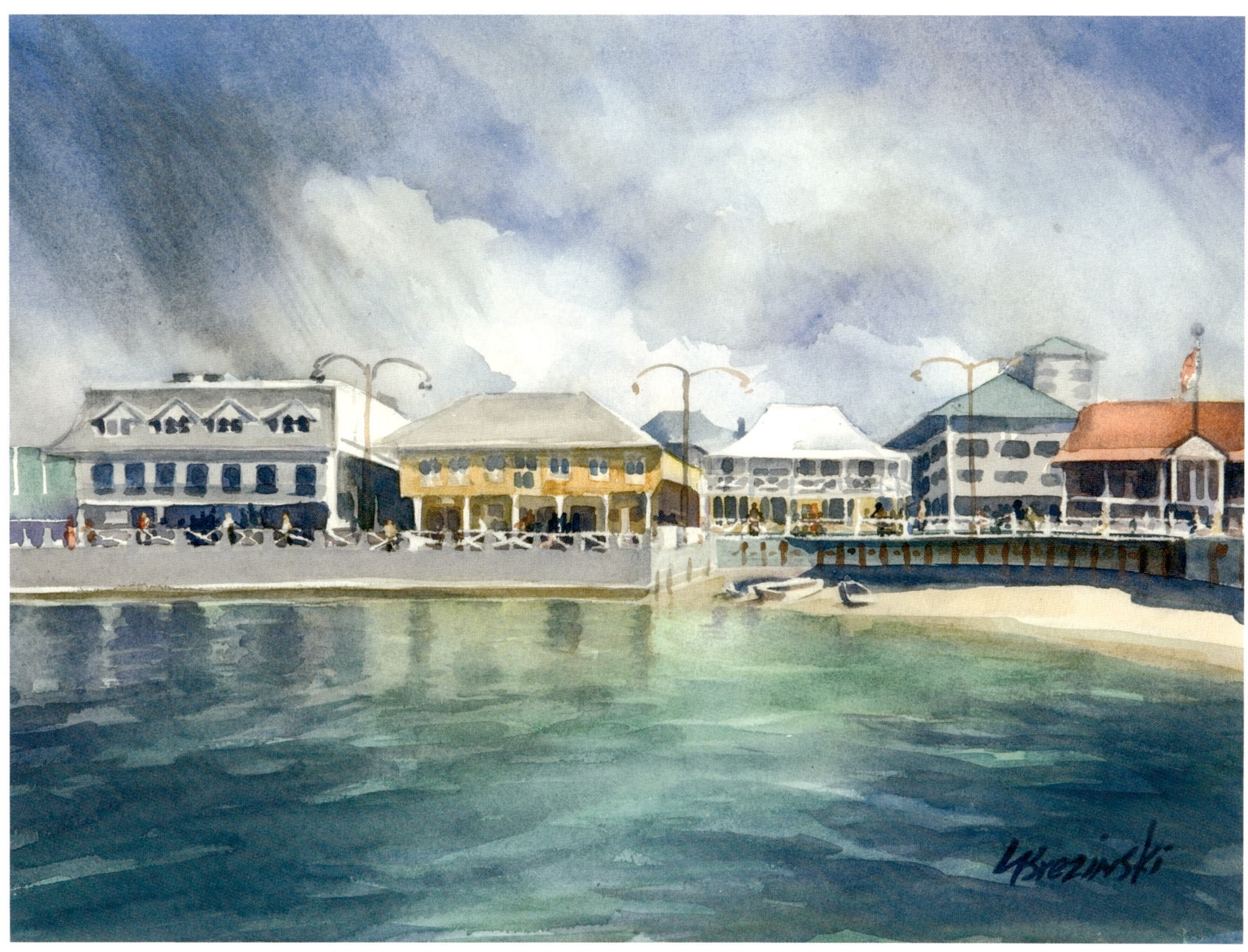

PLATE 22
Lois Brezinski (American, b. 1952)
George Town Harbour, 2004
Watercolour on paper; 20 x 25 inches
Gift of LOM Securities Ltd
See also page 89.

Brezinski has exploited the harbour's varied architecture, geography and Caribbean climate in this distinctive maritime watercolour. The landscape is composed entirely of overlapping small glazes of pure colour, while the artist has successfully deployed the 'wet on wet' technique in the sea and sky to strikingly painterly effect. A painter, textile designer, printmaker and gallerist, Brezinski lived in the Cayman Islands in the 1990s before relocating to Florida. She was an active member of the Visual Arts Society, exhibiting widely and helping to reinvigorate the *en plein air* tradition of painting in the islands.

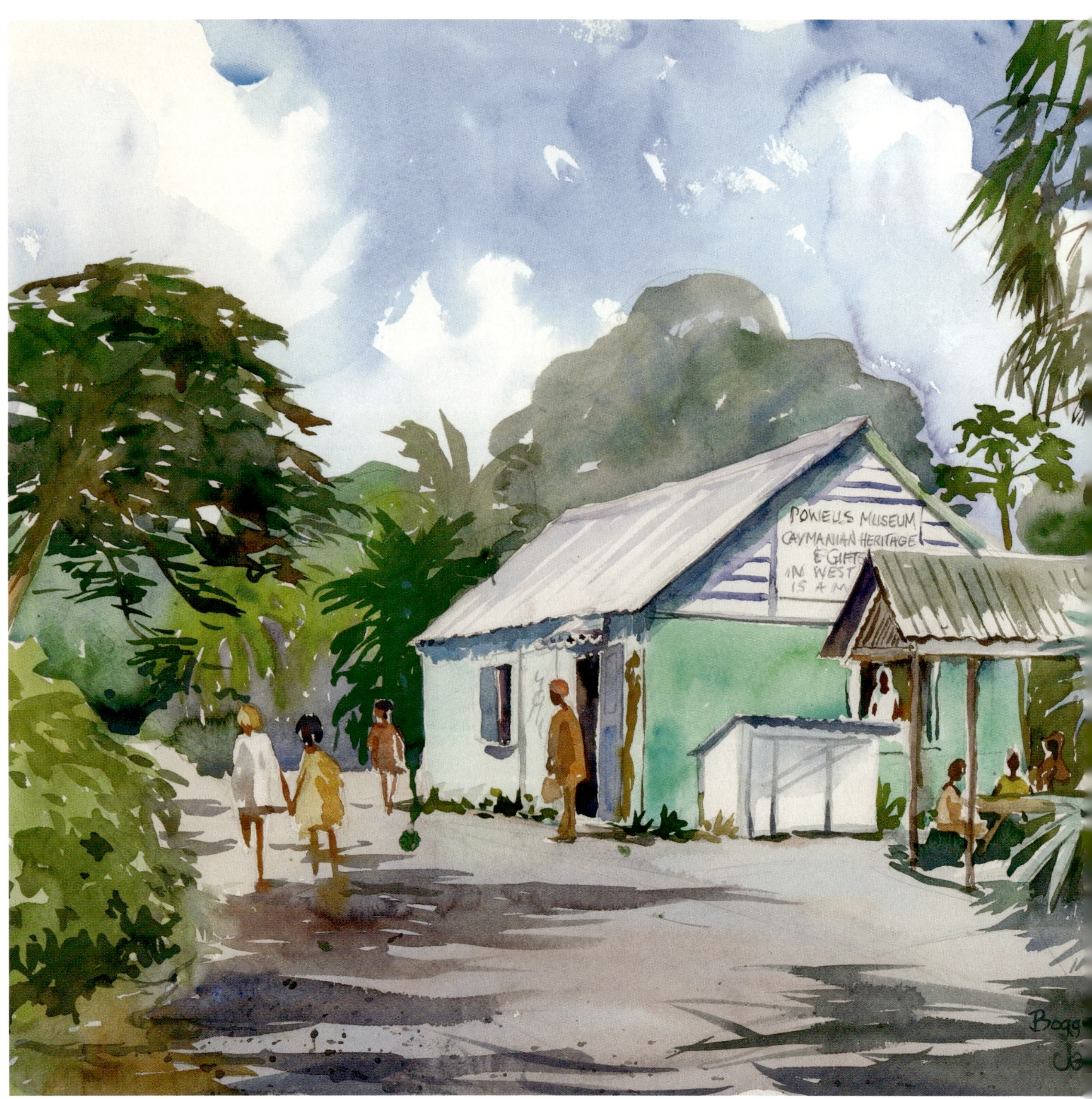
POWELLS MUSEUM
CAYMANIAN HERITAGE
& GIFTS
IN WEST
IS A M
Boggs

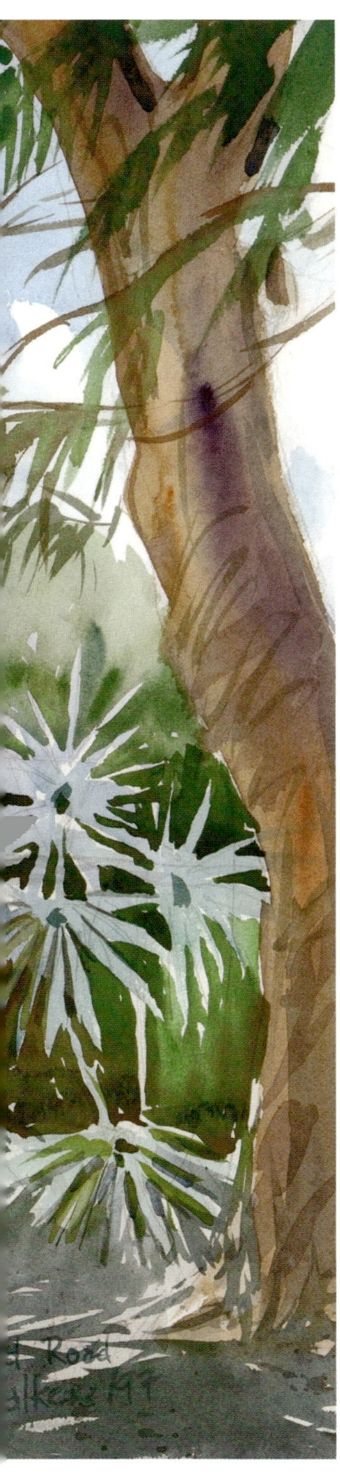

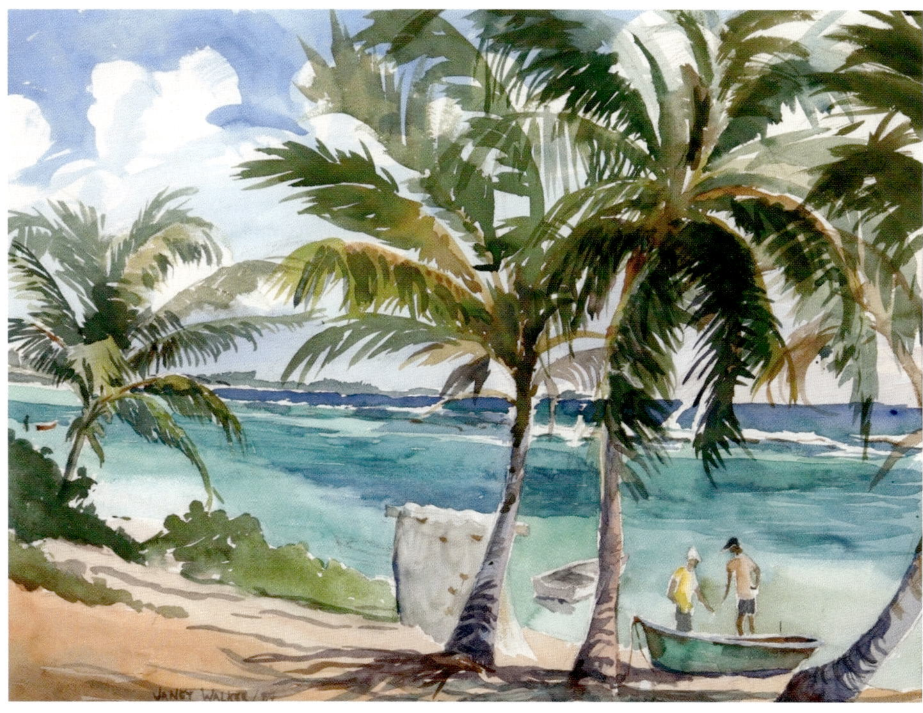

PLATE 23 (*opposite*)
Janet Walker (Canadian-Caymanian, b. 1938)
Boggy Sand Road, 1997
Watercolour on paper; 26 x 30 inches
Gift of Appleby
See also page 94 and plate 24.

PLATE 24 (*above*)
Janet Walker (Canadian-Caymanian, b. 1938)
Mending Nets, 1987
Watercolour on paper; 25½ x 31 inches
See also page 94 and plate 23.

This watercolour has all the hallmarks of the difficult medium, from its layered transparency of pigment to its successful 'reserves' (areas of the paper left unpainted). The dynamic vibrancy of the colours enhances the strong sense of movement, both the light bouncing off the traditional tin roofs and the daily human activity occurring along the charming West Bay street.

A longstanding member of the Cayman Islands arts community, Walker trained at the Ontario College of Art before moving to the Cayman Islands in 1963 with her husband, the late William Walker. She soon traded oil paint for watercolours and began working outdoors to authentically capture Cayman's rapidly changing light. She has exhibited widely in subsequent years and had a retrospective at the National Gallery of the Cayman Islands in 2009.

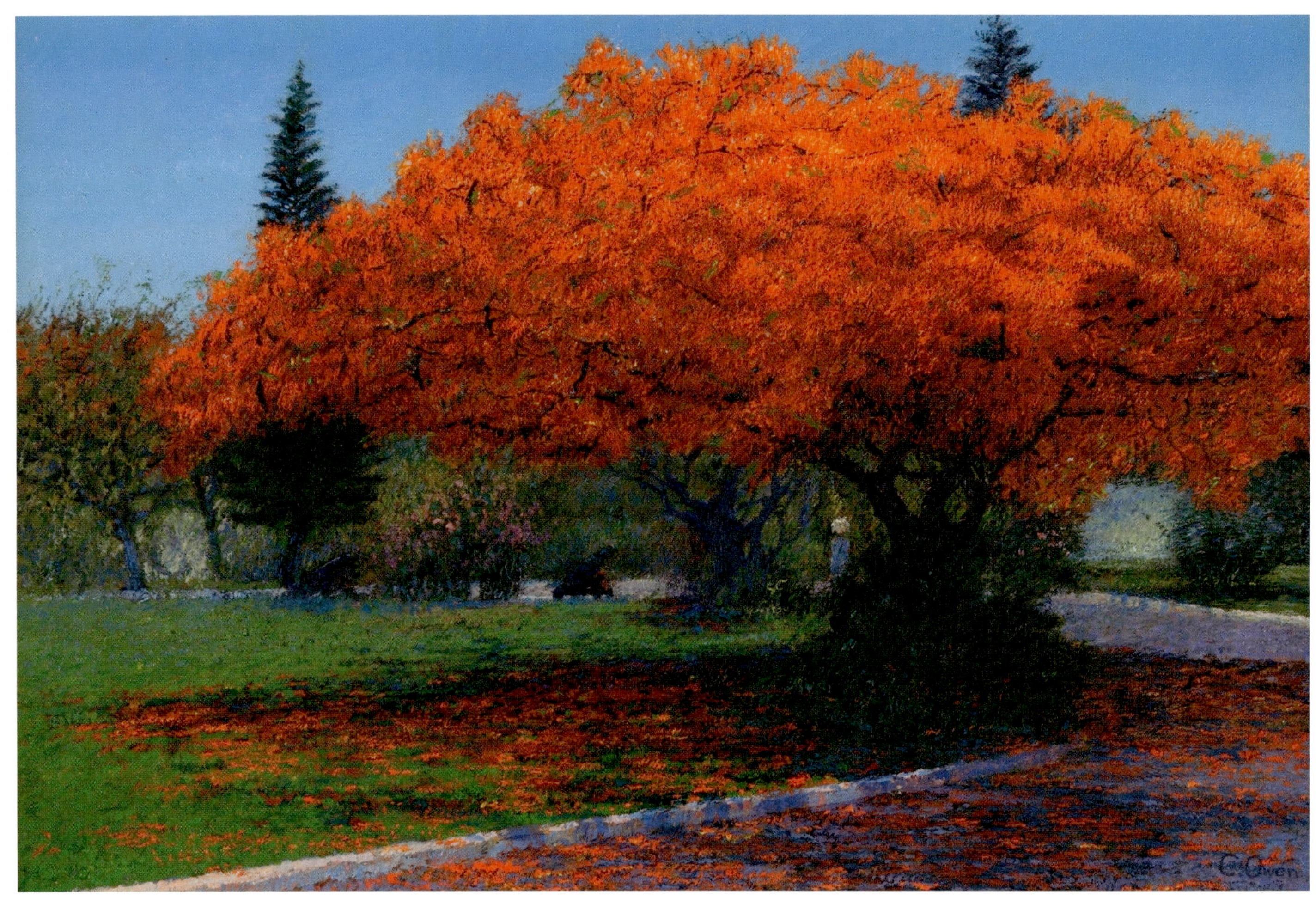

PLATE 25
Carol Owen, MBE (British, b. 1948)
***Poincianas at Government House,* 1995**
Oil on canvas; 23½ x 33 inches
See also page 92.

The artist captured this striking poinciana tree at Government House, where she resided with her husband, Governor John Wynne Owen, CBE, from 1995 to 1999. Her meticulous attention to detail and thick pigment overlays portray the well-loved tree in all its vibrant beauty.

Founding chairwoman of the National Gallery of the Cayman Islands, Owen has worked in various media, including plaster and welded steel. However, it is her portraiture for which she is best known and which led to an invitation by Buckingham Palace to paint Anne, HRH The Princess Royal.

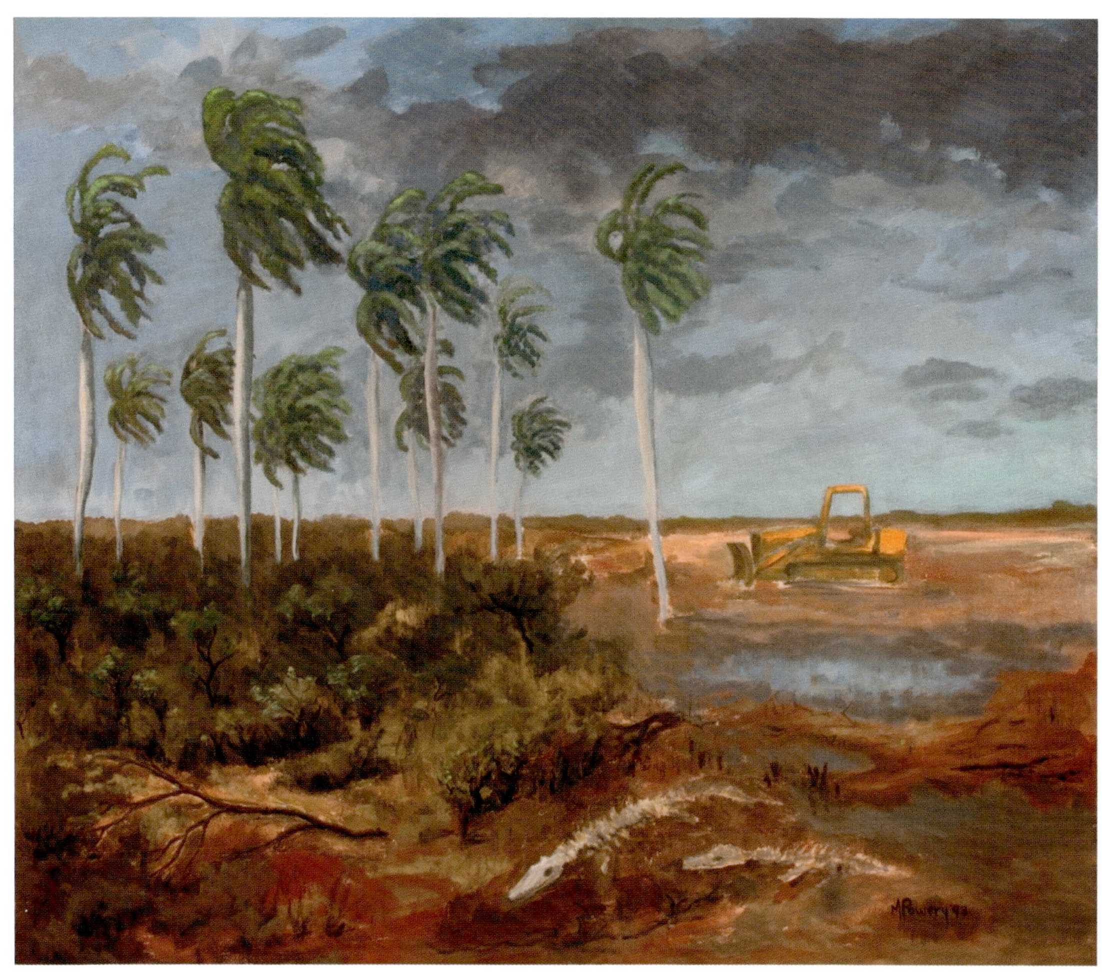

PLATE 26
Miguel Powery (Caymanian, b. 1957)
Paradise Found, Paradise Lost, **1998**
Acrylic on canvas; 43½ x 37½ inches
Gift of the family of Charles Adam, OBE, JP
See also page 92, plate 40 and figure 2.

The darkening sky and stripped landscape set an ominous tone in this scene. As the title implies, the painting refers to the slow destruction of the islands' natural environment by wide-scale urban development in the 1990s. The silver thatch palms—the country's national tree—appear isolated and fragile, while the skeletal remains of two 'caymanes' (caimans), symbolising Caymanian heritage, lie exposed. The narrative is highly poignant and a marked departure for the artist, who is best known for his maritime-inspired paintings.

A painter, sculptor and jewellery maker, Powery is a founding member of the Native Sons collective. Inspired by the Cayman Islands' maritime heritage, he studies boats and the sea, with focus on movement and colour.

PLATE 27 (*this page*)
Debbie Chase van der Bol
(American-Caymanian, b. 1956)
Driftwood, 1986
Pastel on paper; 26 x 19½ inches
See also page 94.

While best known as a watercolourist, Chase van der
Bol here wields the medium of pastel to record and
reproduce the soft yet intense hues of the Caribbean,
which she strives to convey as faithfully as possible.
The realistic treatment, however, is offset by the
geometric and almost abstract composition, an
aesthetic that can be found in nature itself.

A painter, graphic designer and printmaker, Chase
van der Bol moved to the islands in the early 1980s
and soon opened the art store and gallery Pure Art,
which today is the oldest commercial gallery in the
Cayman Islands. She is a prolific member of the arts
community and a longstanding board member of
the Visual Arts Society.

PLATE 28 (*opposite*)
Al Ebanks (Caymanian, b. 1963)
Among Friends, 1999
Acrylic on canvas; 40 x 30 inches
Gift of Richard and Elaine Christiansen
See also page 90.

Although best known for his large abstract works,
Ebanks was still painting in his semi-figurative style
in the mid to late 1990s. *Among Friends* depicts
the Carnival group Mudders, of which Ebanks and his
friends were members. Batabano and Carnival are
recurring themes in his work, and he has completed
several series of paintings inspired by the music,
dance and flowing colours of various Carnival troupes.

Ebanks is a founding member of the Native Sons
art collective and has exhibited individually and
collaboratively since its inauguration. Known for his
large-format acrylics, he is also an accomplished
sculptor of stone and ceramics.

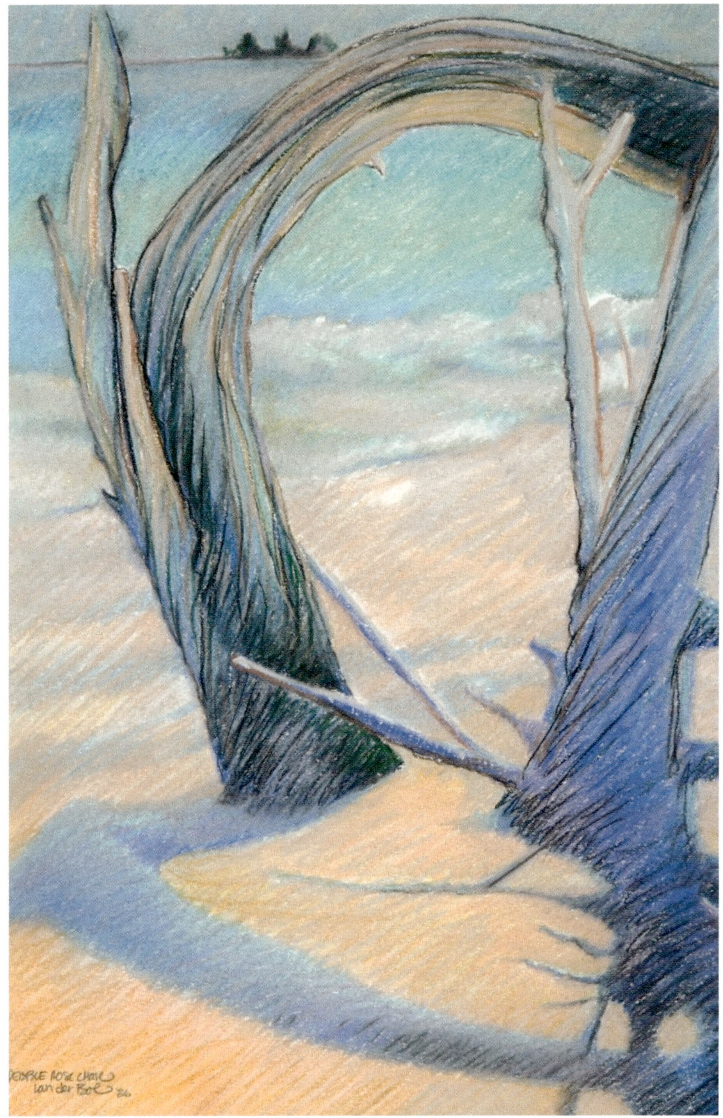

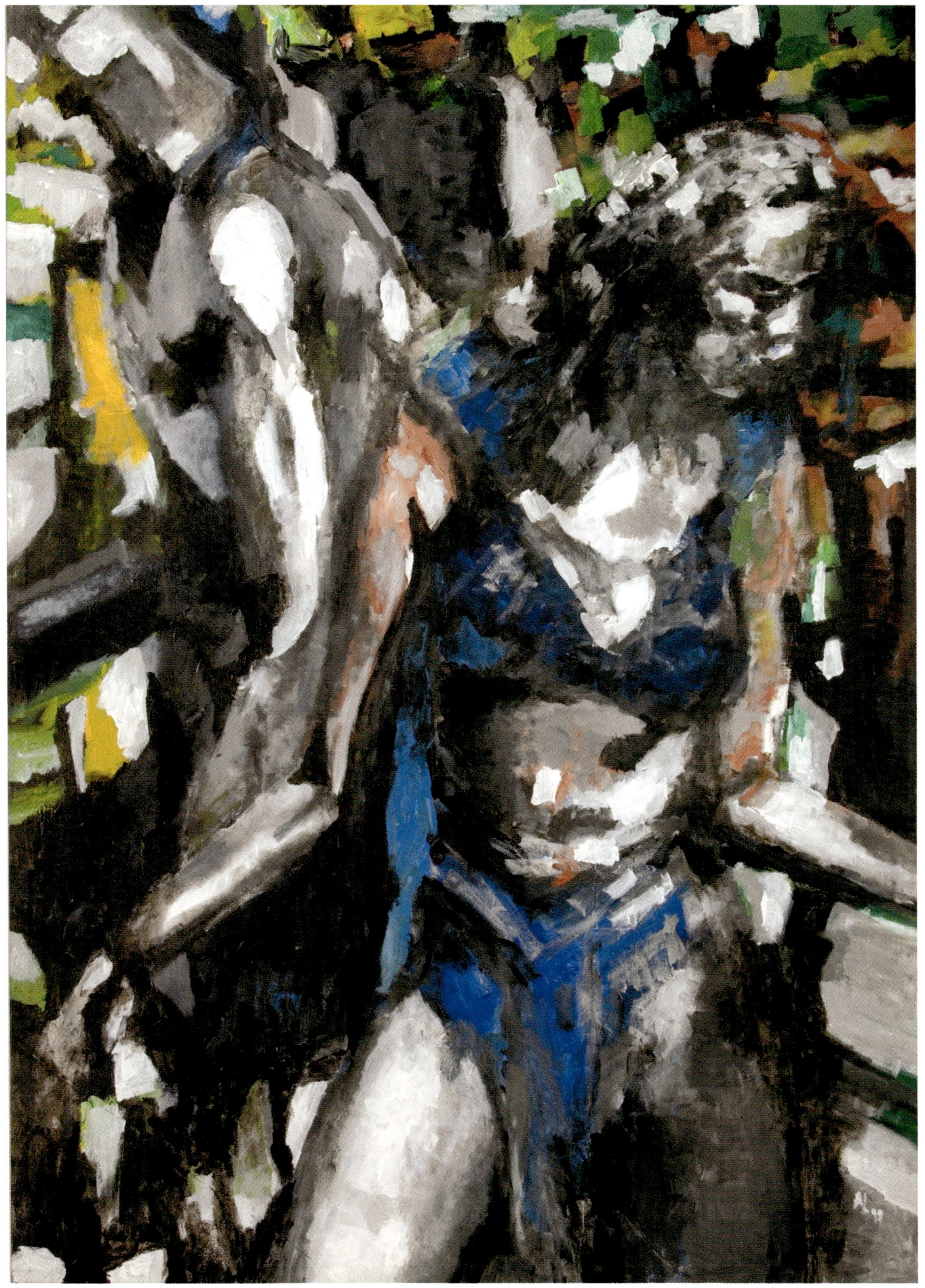

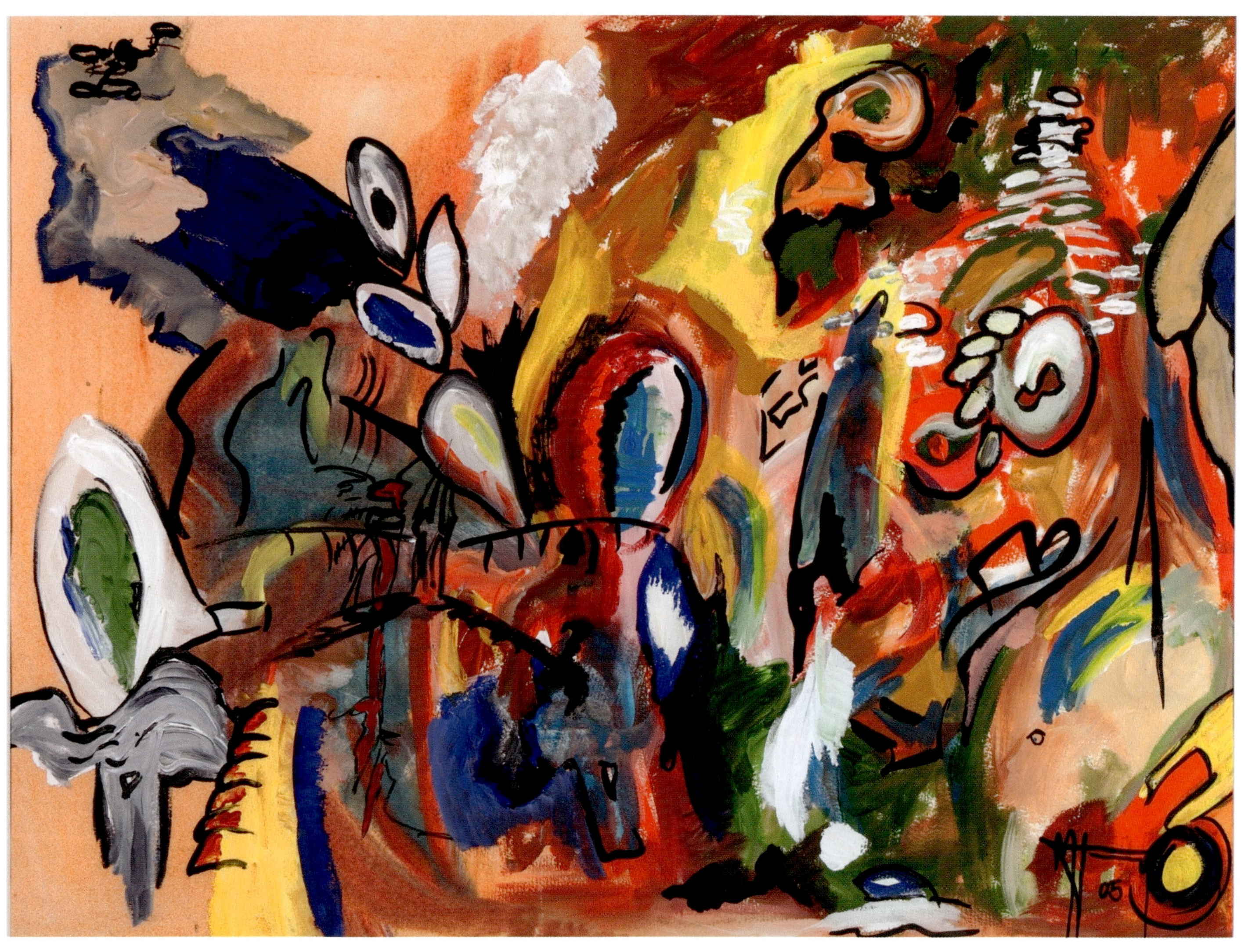

Nickola McCoy-Snell (Caymanian, b. 1974)
Meneage Street (*Black Hat* series), 2005
Acrylic on paper; 36½ x 44 inches
See also page 92.

Meneage Street is one of several paintings that the artist created as part of her *Black Hat* series, inspired by her husband and their developing relationship. Rather than depict him literally—the only recognisable figurative element is her husband's black-outlined Stetson hat at lower right—she uses an abstract language to convey her inner feelings. The expressive, boldly coloured shapes escape the limits of form and line and overlap freely to create an image of extraordinary force.

McCoy-Snell has dealt with an array of moral, political and social themes. Her paintings often evoke the imagery and iconography of street art—running paint, epigrams and bolts that evoke vandalism, graffiti and urban public spaces—to denounce our dependence on authority, tradition and dogma. She is the recipient of several awards, including the inaugural McCoy Prize for Excellence in Caymanian Art (2002).

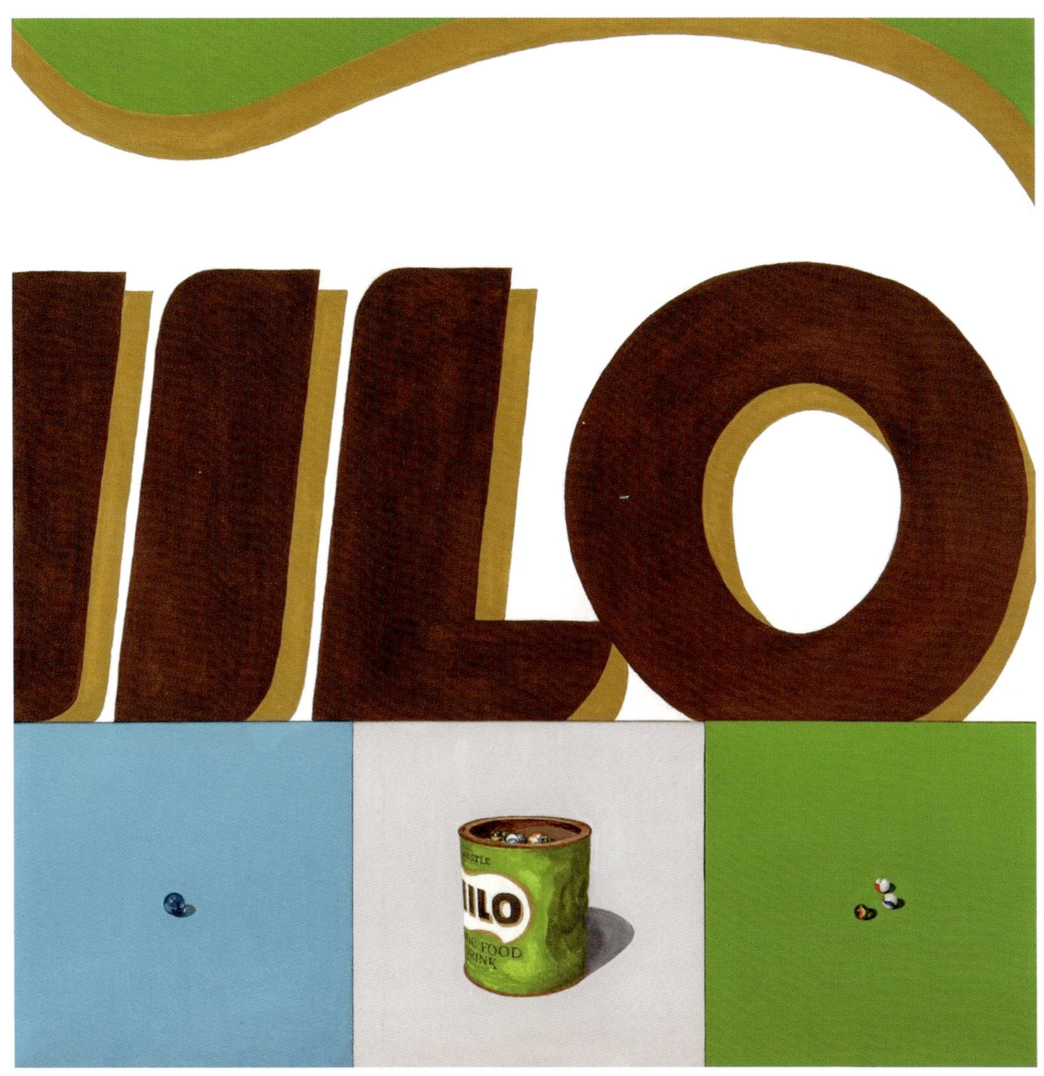

PLATE 30

Wray Banker (Caymanian, b. 1968)
3 a Lick, No Taws (Ode to Milo series), 1999
Acrylic on canvas; 49 x 49½ inches
See also page 88 and figure 20.

The *Ode to Milo* series remains artist Banker's most iconic body of work to date. He uses the much-loved Milo powdered chocolate drink as a symbol of his experience as a child in the Cayman Islands, a touch point shared by many West Indians. For Banker, it is in such seemingly mundane objects (à la Warhol's soup cans) that his culture dwells. Using bold graphics and humour in his work, he also draws attention to more serious concerns, such as the erosion of Caymanian cultural heritage.

Banker is a founding member of the influential Native Sons art collective and has gone on to become one of the Cayman Islands' most recognisable artists. A graphic designer by training, he works in a wide variety of media, including formal painting, photography, assemblage and film. In 2001, he was the youngest artist to be invited for a solo exhibition at the National Gallery of the Cayman Islands, with *Serious bout Makin' Fun.*

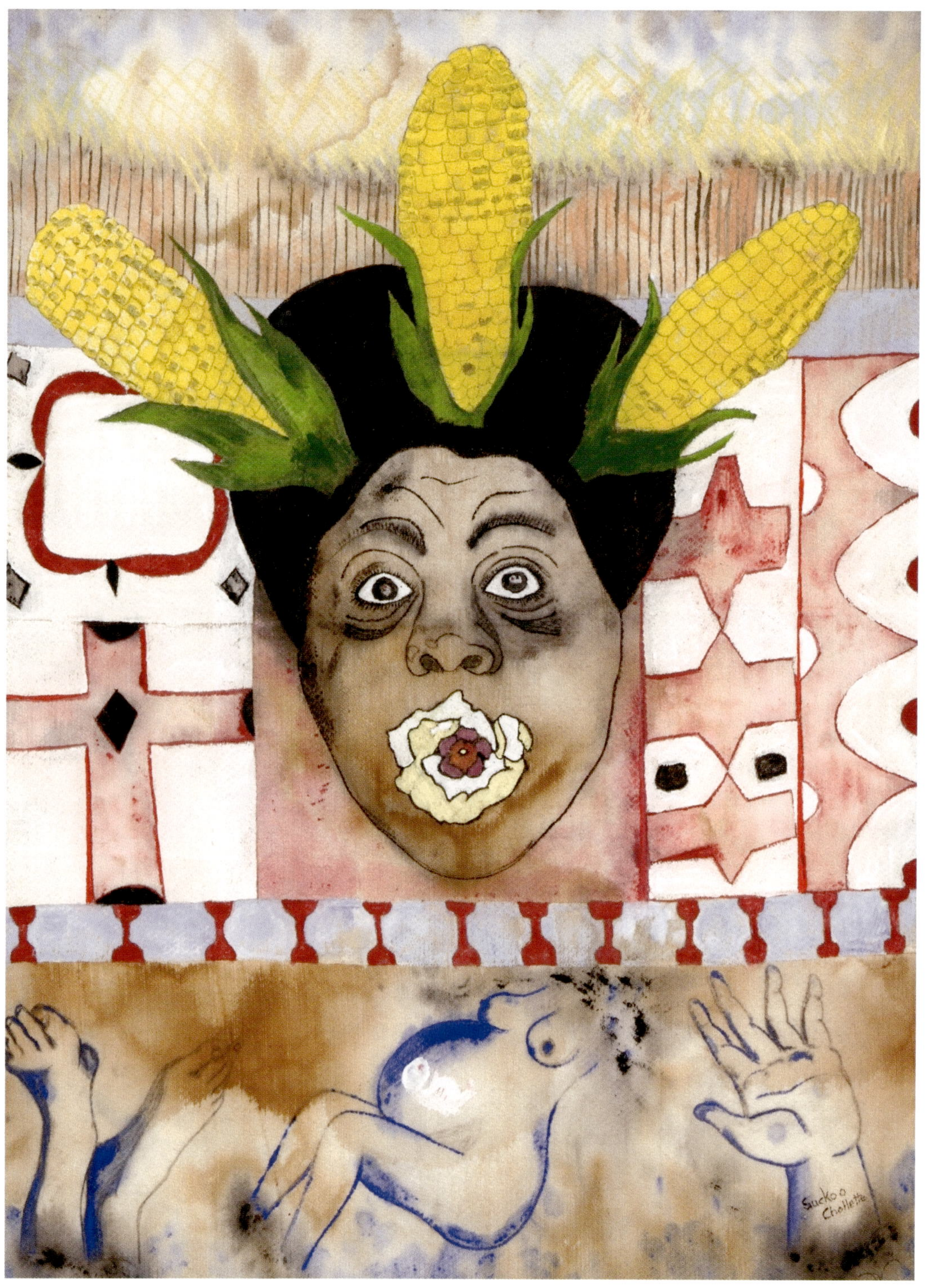

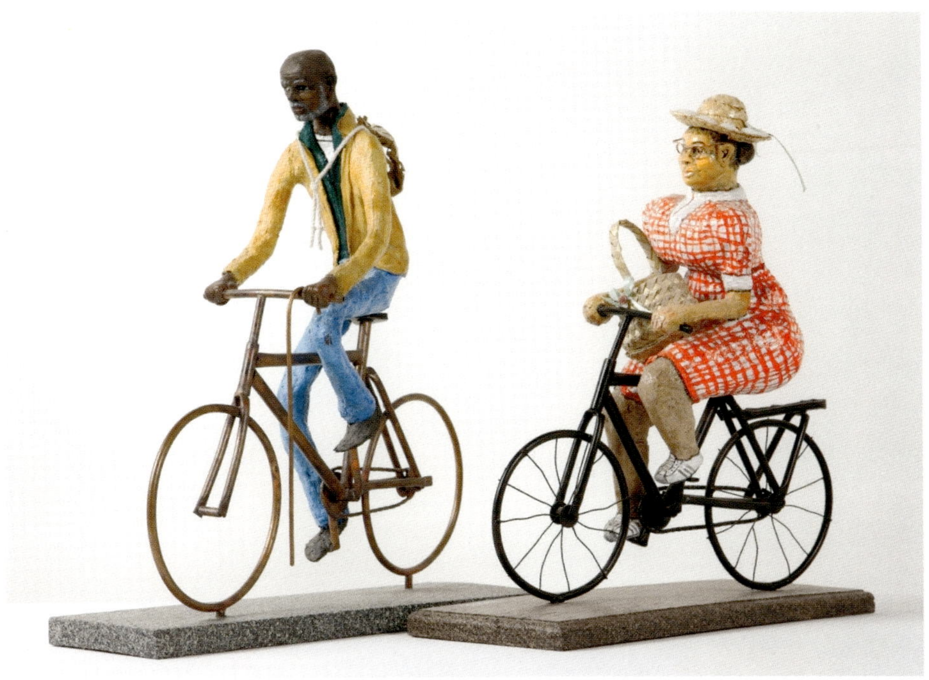

This work, which premiered at the 2005 Native Sons' *Fahive* exhibition at the National Gallery of the Cayman Islands, was created in response to the peace and reconciliation hearings in South Africa at the end of apartheid. The artist was moved by the stark truth that often the only people left to bear witness to the atrocities committed were the victims' wives, mothers, sisters: the women, with whom she identified. The work represents a proud people's struggle for honour in the face of dishonourable acts.

An accomplished artist, poet and performer, Suckoo-Chollette works primarily in a unique combination of acrylic with appliqué and traditional textile techniques. Her work is an introspective and social critique of the contemporary Caymanian experience, feminism and race.

This depiction of an elderly couple on their way to the market is typical of the artist's work. Frazer strives to capture the day-to-day activities of Cayman's residents, transforming mundane chores into the colourful and whimsical.

Frazer moved from the north of England to Grand Cayman in 1985, and since then he has taught high school–level art. He works in painting and sculpture and is inspired by the colours, people and culture of the Cayman Islands.

Randy Chollette (Caymanian, b. 1975)
Safe Harbour, **2008**
Acrylic on canvas; 30 x 22 inches
Gift of Truman Bodden
See also page 90, plate 40 and figure 14.

This tranquil scene, painted from a historical photograph found in the Cayman Islands National Archives, depicts fishermen returning home after a long day at sea. This is an early figurative work by the artist, who is better known for his large-format, semi-abstract paintings, and it is one of several created to celebrate his Caymanian heritage.

Chollette is an intuitive, self-taught artist whose work is often distinguishable by its signature black-outlined mosaic configuration. Chollette received public recognition very early in his career when he was awarded Best in Show (2002) from Kensington-Lott Fine Art Gallery and the People's Choice Award at The McCoy Prize (2003). A member of the Native Sons collective, he moves confidently between Realism and abstraction, and his Rastafarian beliefs are woven into the style and subject of his paintings.

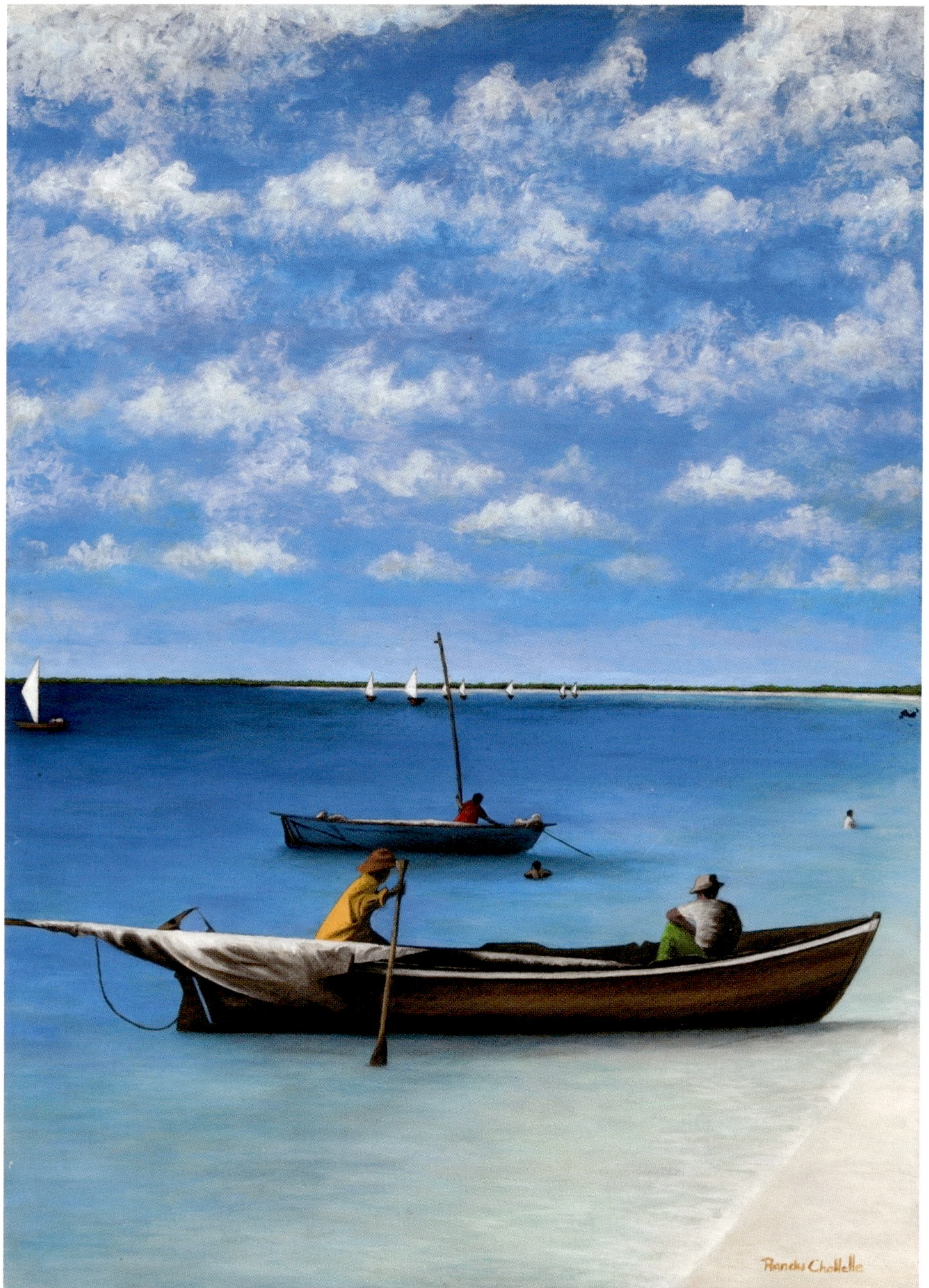

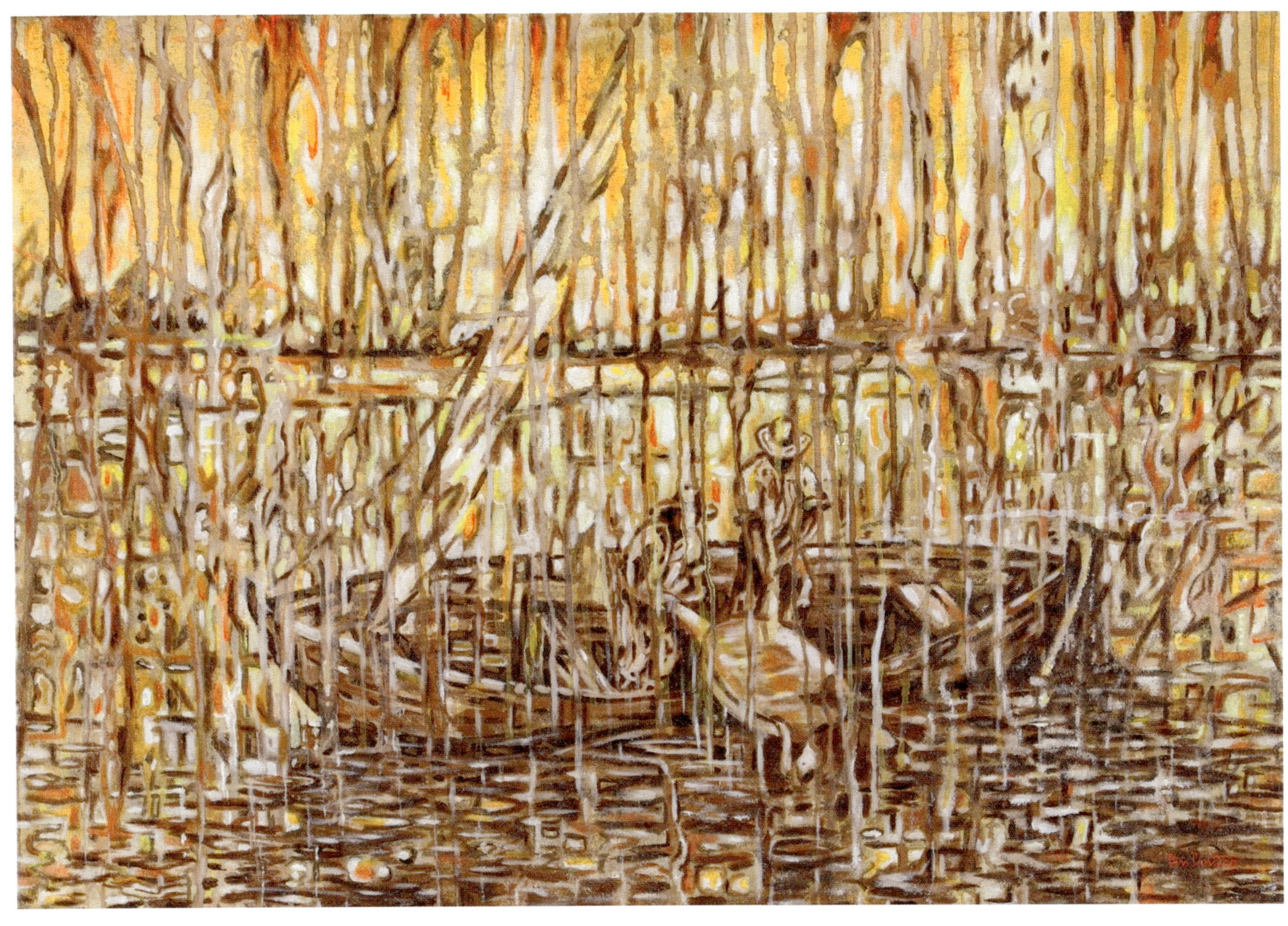

PLATE 34
Chris Christian (Caymanian, b. 1972)
Reflecting, 2007
Acrylic on canvas; 24 x 36 inches
Loaned by the artist
See also page 90.

Reflecting is a landscape fragmented by bold marks of paint that recalls the Divisionism technique used by the Neo-Impressionists. As the viewer's vision zooms in or out of the image, he can see either fishermen turtling or simply playful patches of colours.

Founder of Cayman Traditional Arts and a member of the Native Sons art collective, Christian has placed himself at the centre of the Cayman Islands' cultural scene, using his art to raise awareness about the islands' traditions.

Chris Mann (British-Caymanian, b. 1955)
Mangrove III, 2005
Oil, acrylic, mixed media on canvas; 56½ x 73 inches
See also page 92.

Mangroves are arguably the most vital natural
element in the Cayman Islands, and they have been
the inspiration behind much of the artist's work
over the past decade. This piece was created just
a few months after Hurricane Ivan had decimated
the mangroves surrounding Mann's home, and they
subsequently feature heavily in his art. The work
also references the arrival of Christopher Columbus
in the Cayman Islands, as evidenced by the sails
at the top centre of the image.

    Mann was born in England and trained at
Goldsmiths College before moving to the Cayman
Islands in 1987 to work as head of art at George Hicks
High School, a position he held for twenty-five years.
Working in oil, acrylic, mixed media and collage,
he creates pieces characterised by bold, sculptural
forms and the use of rich colour.

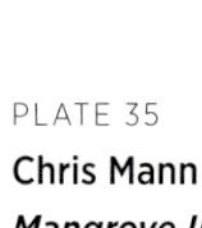

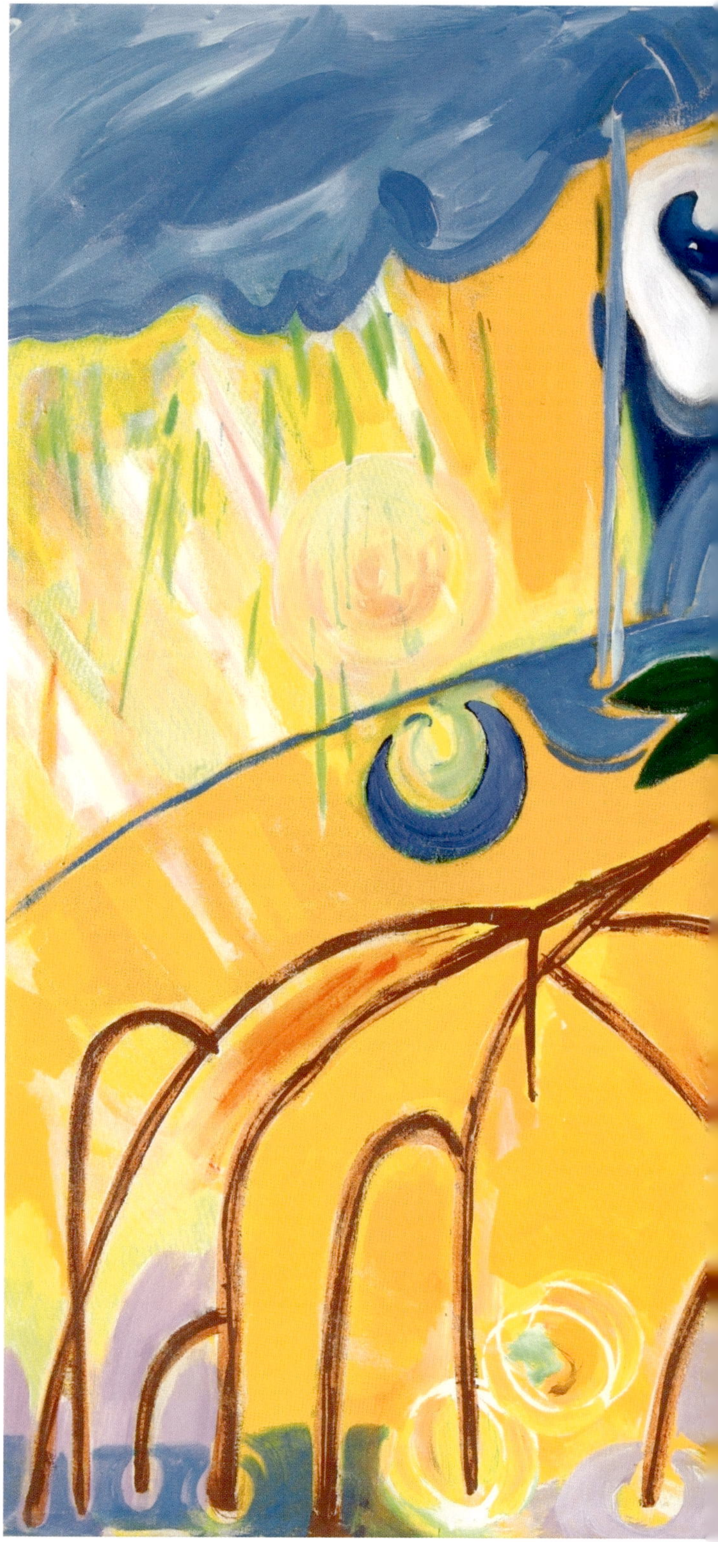

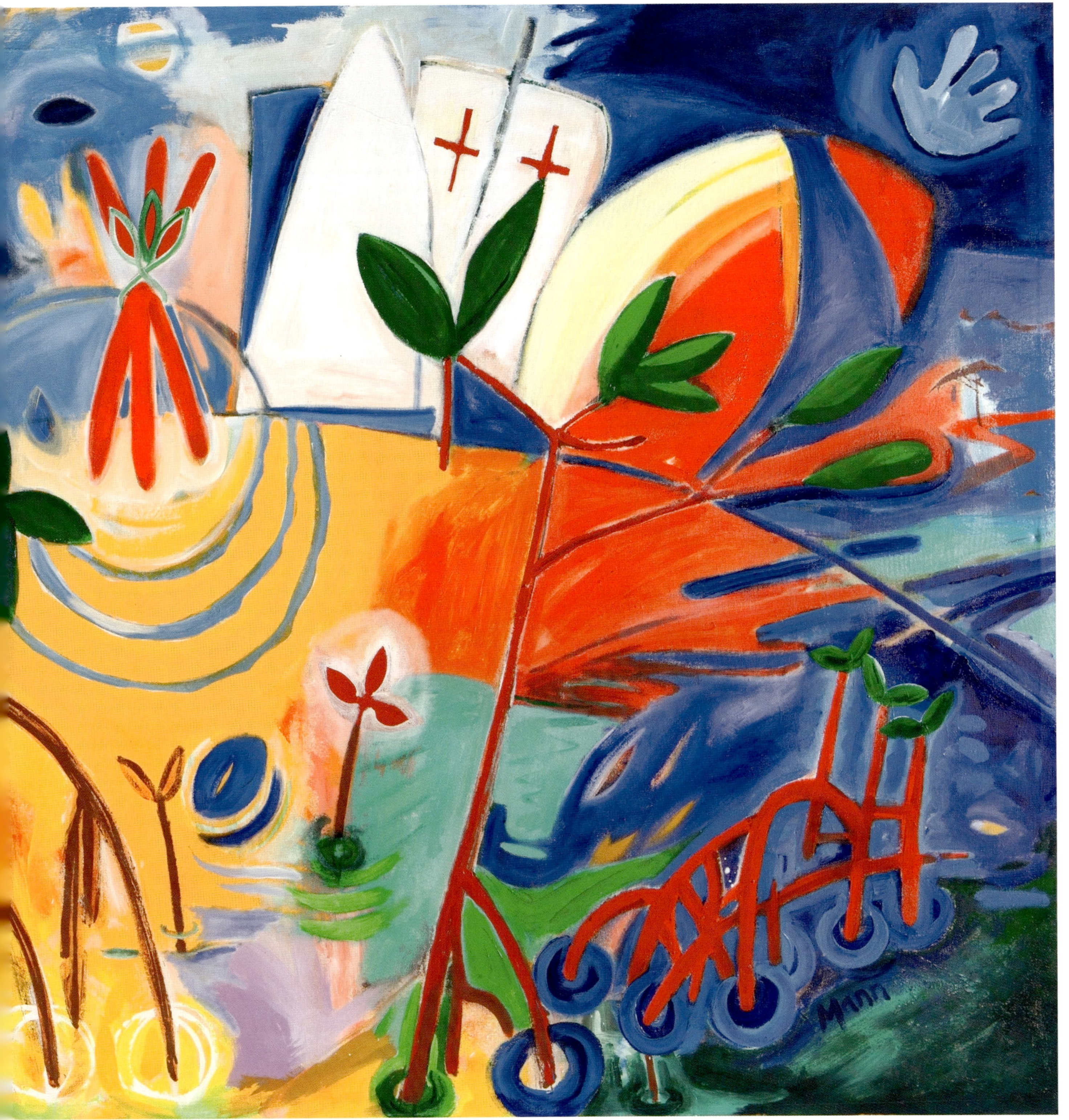

David Bridgeman (British-Caymanian, b. 1959)
Rain Gauge, 2007
Mixed media on canvas; 48 x 36 inches
See also page 89 and plate 40.

Explorations of cultural identity are central to Bridgeman's work, as are themes of nationality and transformation, which are evident in this painting. Here the artist has combined images drawn from his present reality and those from vivid childhood memories. He makes connections with various places he has lived, which have influenced his identity: the abandoned rain gauge and the barren landscape evoke Grand Cayman's 'iron shore,' and the bluebells represent England.

British-born artist Bridgeman arrived in the Cayman Islands from England in 1987. His work explores the duality between life in the Caribbean and his country of origin, predominantly through depictions of landscape. He works in a variety of media to convey this theme, often including underlying social commentaries about life in a small country.

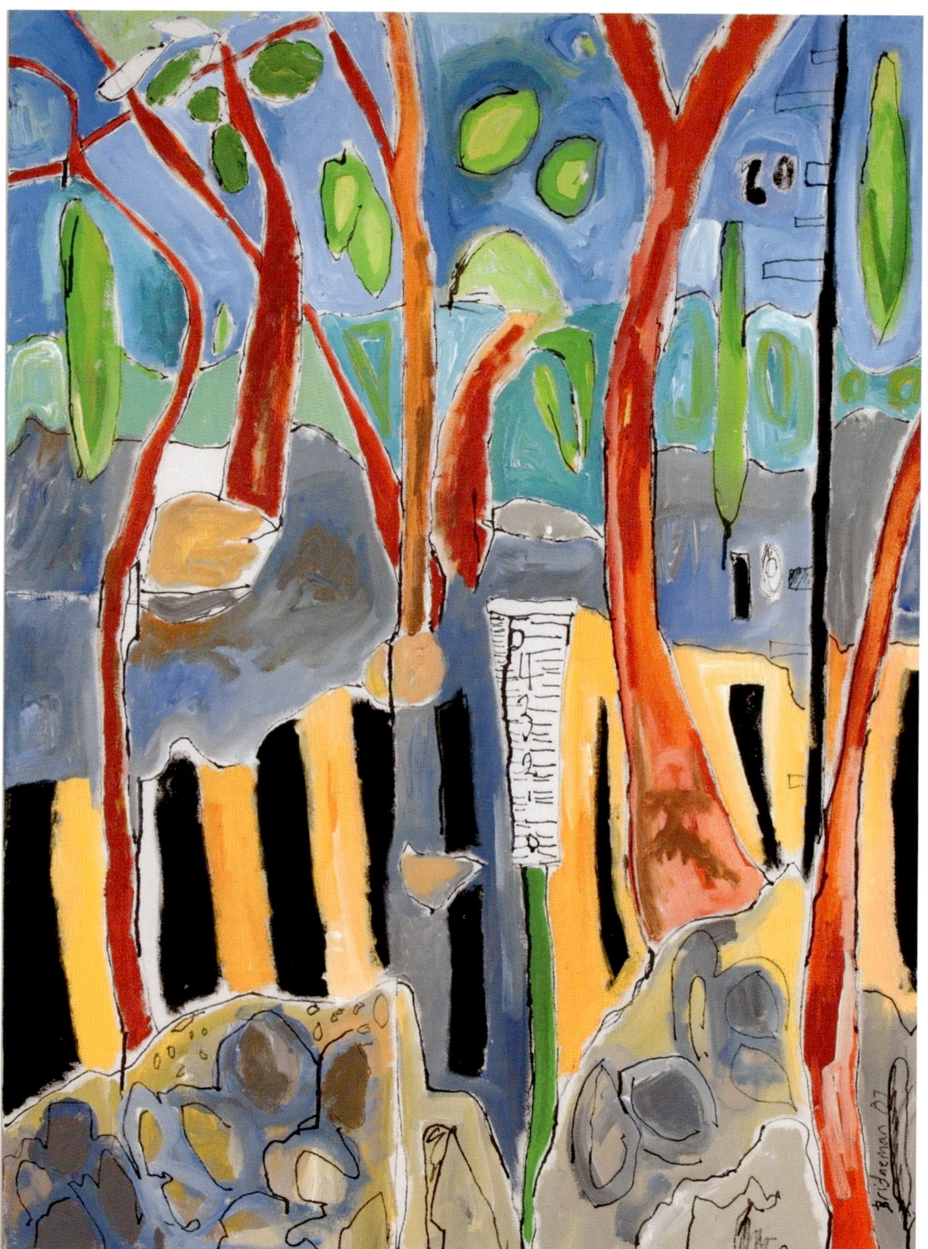

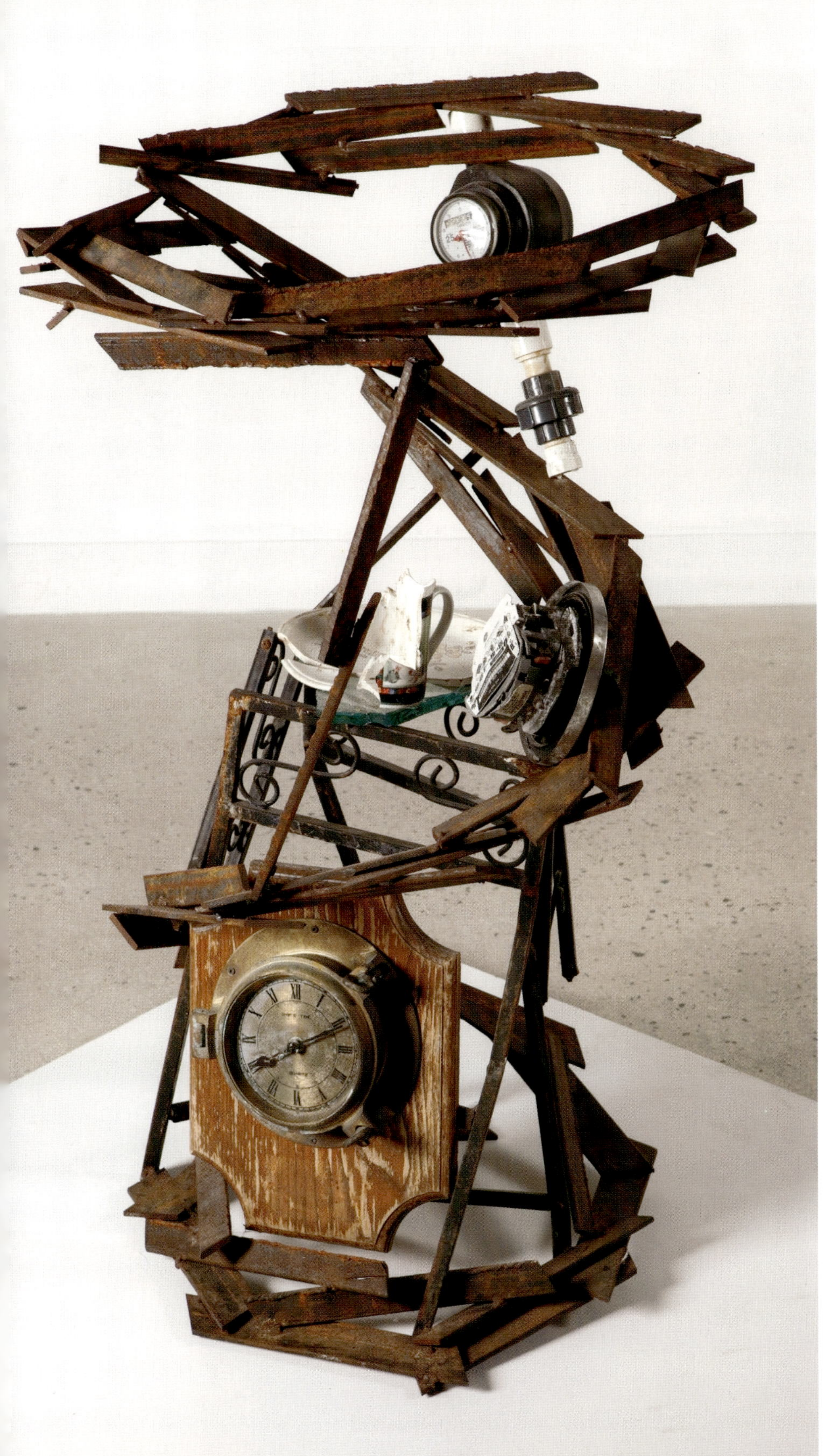

Karoly Szücs (Hungarian, b. 1965)
That Morning, 2004
Metal, found objects; 42 x 18 inches
See also page 93.

This sculpture was the opening piece in the National Gallery of the Cayman Islands' *Emergence* exhibition, held in 2005, in the wake of Hurricane Ivan. Standing almost four feet high, the swirling vortex of corroded iron rises up in a manner reminiscent of a hurricane. Embedded in the centre of the spiral are objects that the artist found when walking through the wreckage left behind by the storm—electricity and water meters, a broken mug and a clock that stopped at 8:10 a.m., when the storm was at its most violent—symbolising the complete upheaval of normality.

Hungarian-born metal fabricator and sculptor Szücs has lived in the Cayman Islands for several years. He has established himself as one of the islands' premier sculptors and has received commissions for several public works, including the memorial to the turtling industry in Heroes Square. Szücs was moved to create this piece after returning to his devastated Industrial Park studio to find his large supply of metal badly corroded by floodwater.

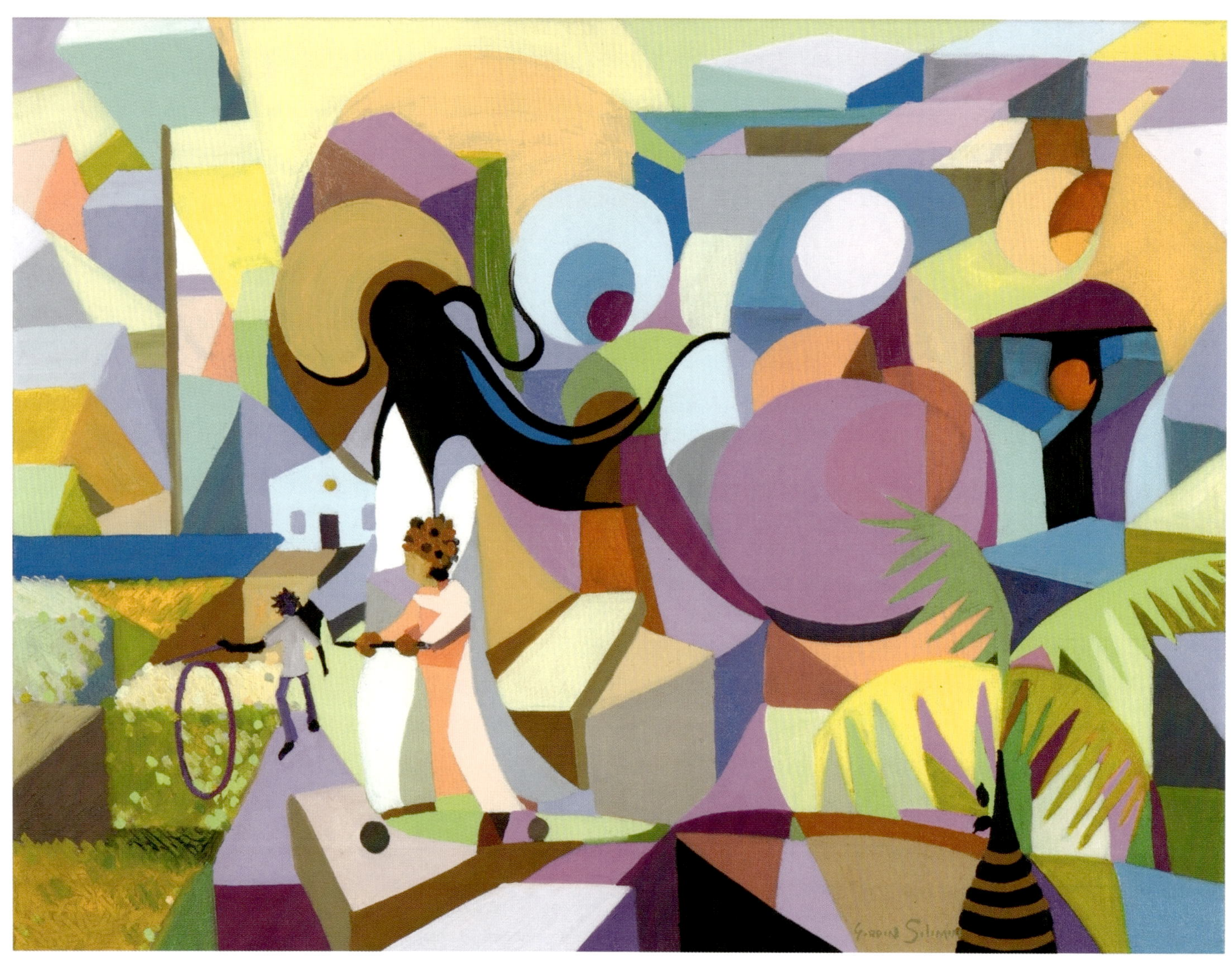

Gordon Solomon (Caymanian, b. 1977)
Harold's Picky Head Boy, **2010**
Acrylic on canvas; 16 x 20 inches
See also page 93.

The Cayman Islands did not escape the highly influential stylisation of Cubism, as Solomon demonstrates with this brightly coloured geometric composition. Its multiple vantage points result in a dizzying multitude of small facets engulfing two discernible figures. 'Picky head' is a patois term with negative racial connotations implying messy or unkempt hair. In this semi-autobiographical work, however, the derogatory nature of the phrase unfolds and collapses under the artist's positive and confident visual language.

Painter and musician Solomon is a member of the Native Sons art collective and was a recipient of the National Gallery's Artists Away programme, which sent him to further his studies in Cuba. His work is primarily concerned with Caymanian heritage, which he captures in a variety of genres from Cubism and Pointillism to Realism.

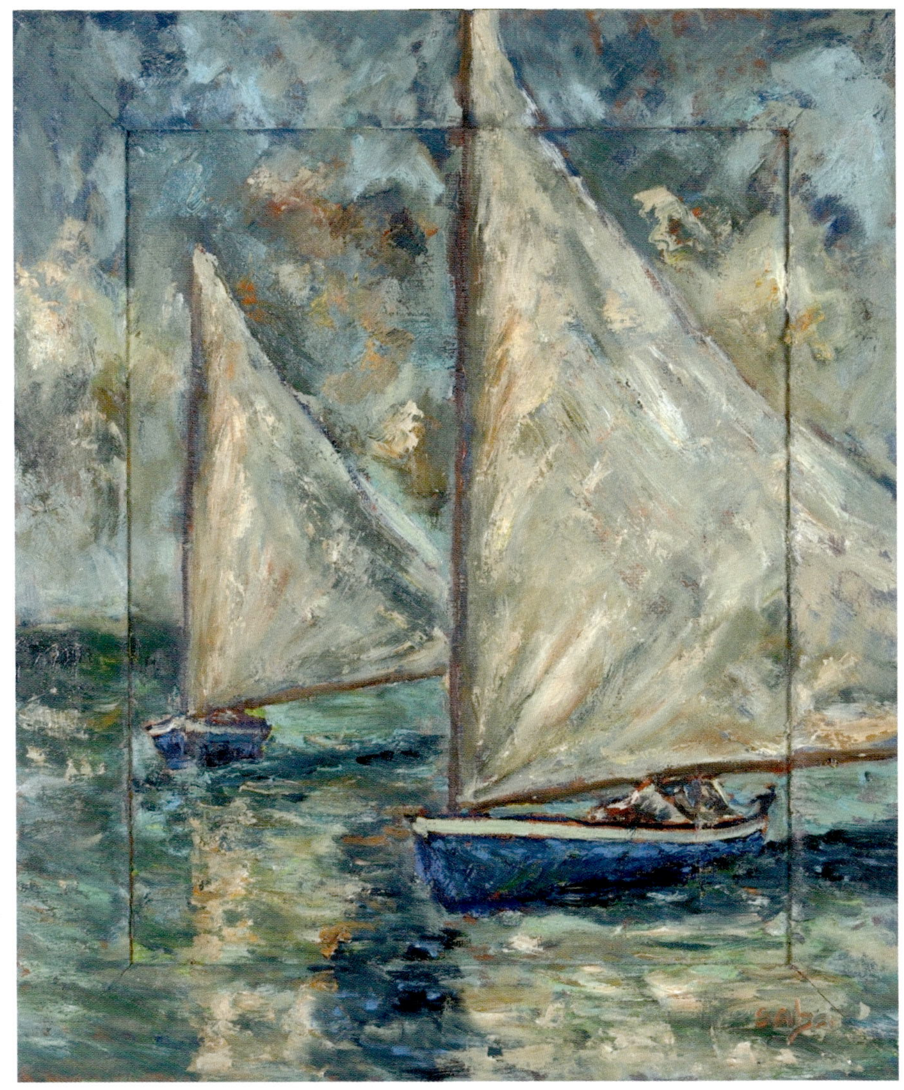

PLATE 39

Saba (Hungarian, b. 1965)
Spirits in the Rain, 2012
Acrylic on canvas; 27½ x 23½ inches
Gift of Robert and Satu Troyer
See also page 92.

The Cayman Islands' maritime heritage is a recurring theme in Saba's work, which usually depicts active scenes of vessels under sail or fishermen preparing to launch their boats. Here two traditional Caymanian catboats are chased by a pending storm, beautifully realised by the subdued palette and energised brushstrokes.

A self-taught artist, Saba (born Csaba Korsos) moved to the Cayman Islands in 1992 and was immediately inspired by Caymanian heritage, maritime scenes and local flora, which remain central themes in his work. He uses thickly textured strokes applied with a brush and palette knife and overpaints his frames, as he has done here, to add a three-dimensional, sculptural element.

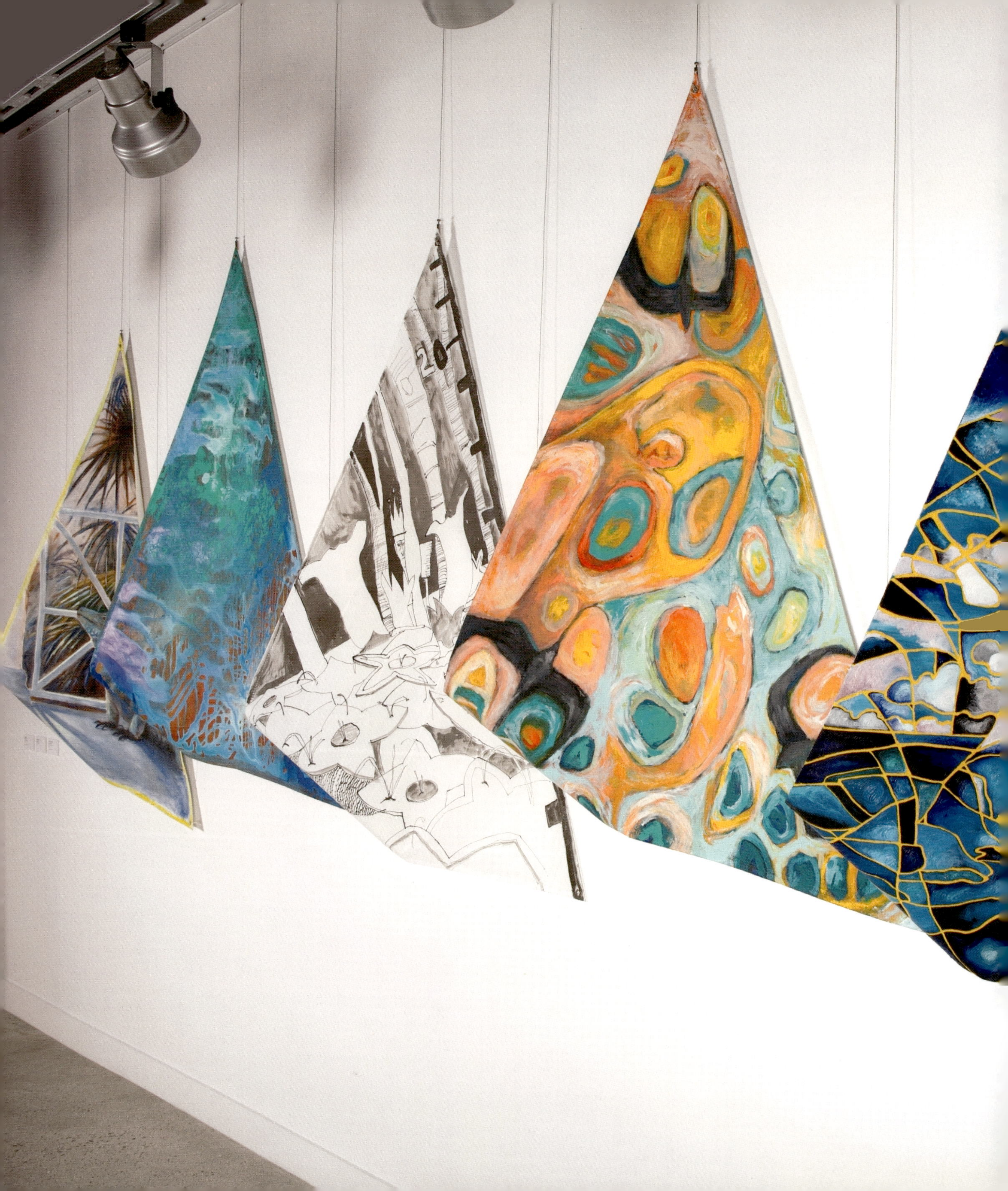

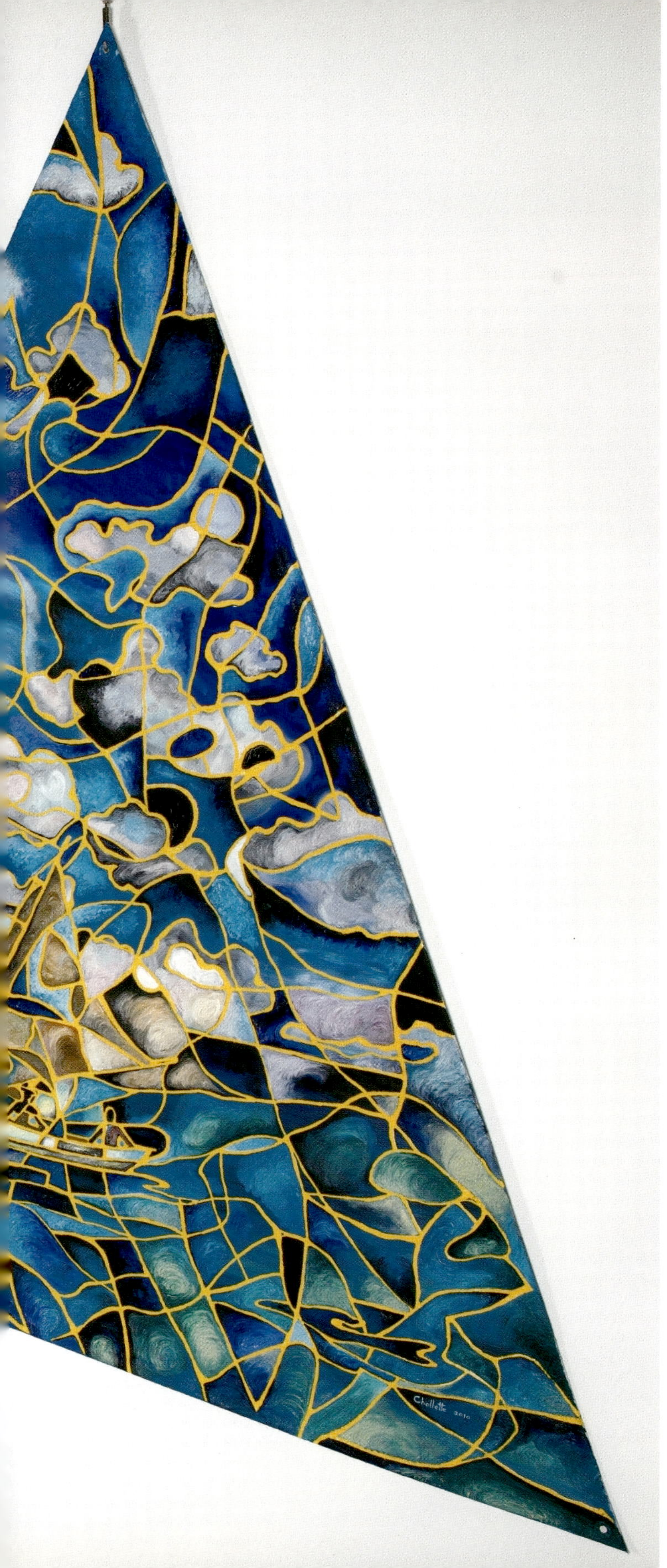

PLATE 40
Painted catboat sails (various), 2010
Acrylic on sail cloth; 68 x 52½ x 68 inches each

Left to right:

Miguel Powery (Caymanian, b. 1957)
Blue Iguana

Mikael Seffer (Caymanian, b. 1974)
Casting Nets

David Bridgeman (British-Caymanian, b. 1959)
Close to the Bark

Renate ('Ren') Seffer (Australian-Caymanian, b. 1971)
Warriors of Time

Randy Chollette (Caymanian, b. 1975)
Kings of Satwa

This series of artworks was commissioned as part of the National Gallery of the Cayman Islands' 2010 *21st Century Cayman* exhibition, which sought to reimagine aspects of traditional Caymanian heritage in the context of the islands' contemporary experience. Using the iconic catboat's sail canvas as a medium for contemporary art, the artists created a tangible connection between the past and the present.

61

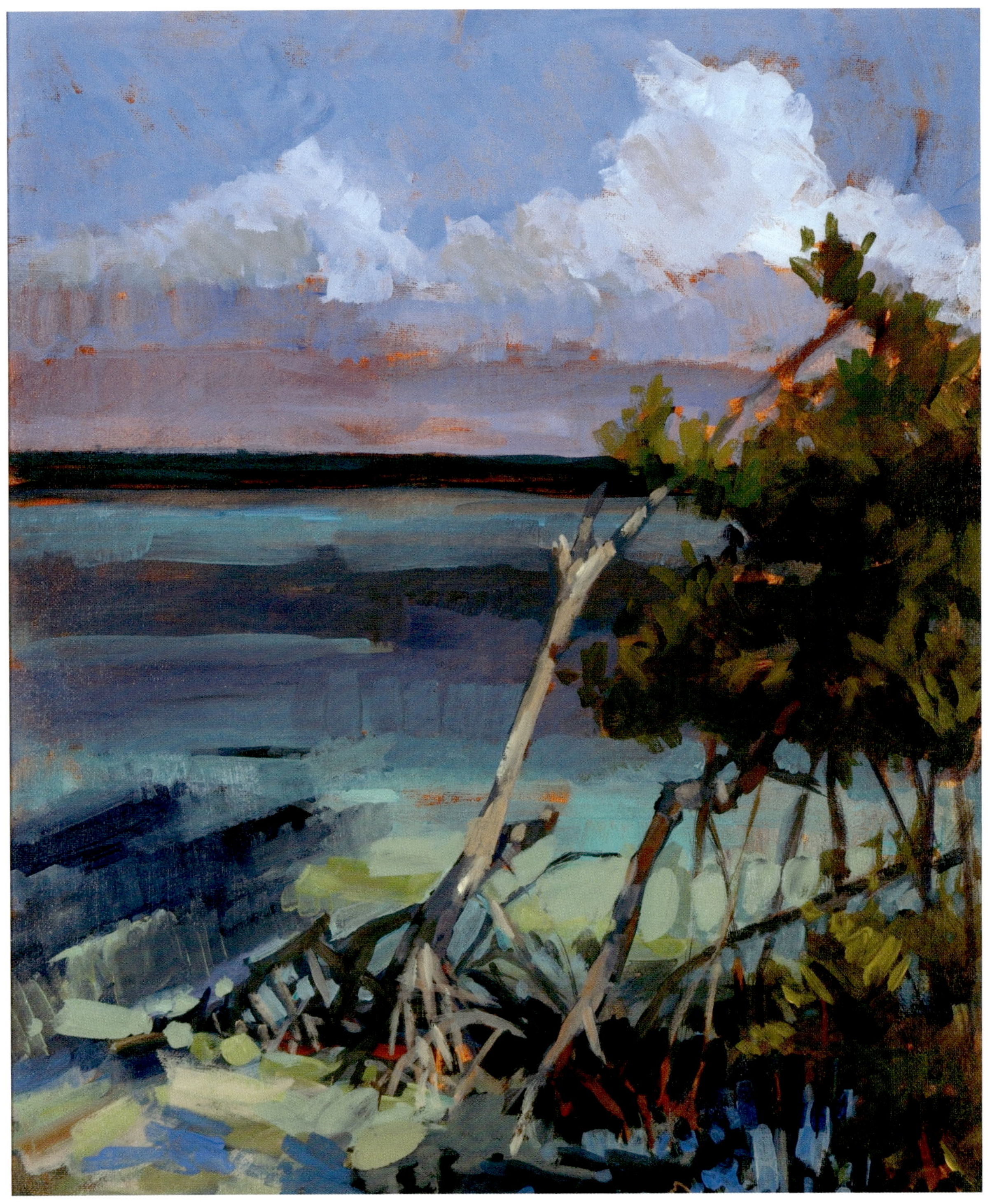

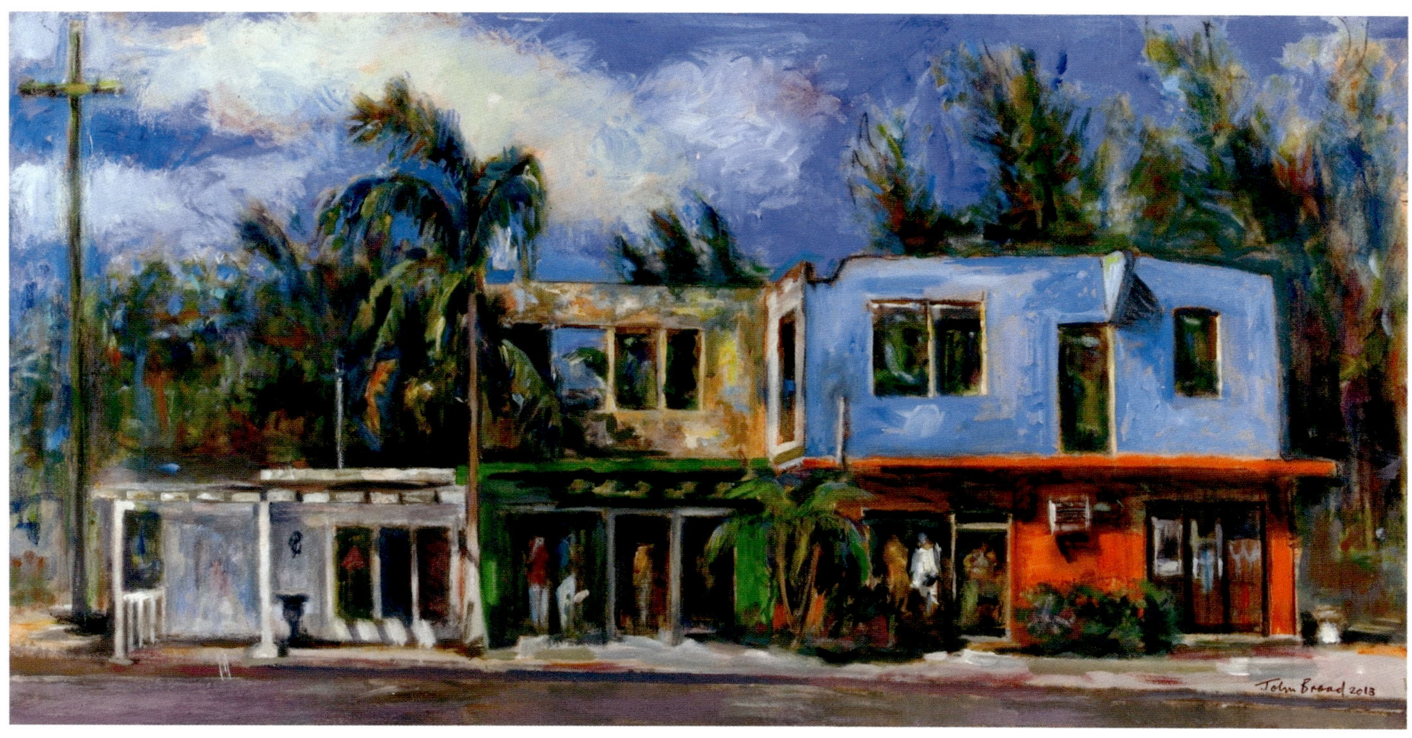

PLATE 41 (*opposite*)

Teresa Grimes (American-Caymanian, b. 1952)
East of Palmetto Point (*Barkers Plein Air* series), 2012
Acrylic on canvas; 24 x 18 inches
See also page 91.

Grimes's landscapes are created with acrylics or oils, and the smoothness and flow of her brushstrokes show how adept she has become with both media. She sketches *en plein air* studies before transforming them into formal paintings in her studio, where she creates compositions based on naturally abstract elements found in the landscape.

Grimes initially studied classical archaeology and classical art, and it was only after studying art restoration and life drawing in Ravenna, Italy, in 1975 that she began painting in earnest. She moved to the Cayman Islands in 1986 and became an active member of the burgeoning art scene.

PLATE 42 (*above*)

John Broad (British-Caymanian, b. 1947)
Fashion Shop, 2013
Acrylic on canvas; 24 x 48 inches
Gift of Susan A. Olde, OBE
See also page 89 and plate 1.

This view of a rundown building on Eastern Avenue offers a perspective of the islands rarely captured by artists and is a striking departure from John Broad's earlier work. The artist was struck by the store's vibrant character, which he depicts with seamless brushstrokes and a confident palette.

British artist Broad studied at the Edinburgh College of Art and taught art in Vanuatu, in the South Pacific, before settling in the Cayman Islands. His work is influenced by the islands' maritime culture and is recognisable by his loose brushwork and bold palette.

Nasaria Suckoo-Chollette
(Caymanian, b. 1968)
Five Hundren' Years in These Shoes?
(detail), 2007
Car tyres, silver thatch palm; 15 x 275 inches
See also page 93 and plate 31.

Suckoo-Chollette addresses themes of identity,
memory and survival in this installation, using
the traditional Caymanian footwear known
as 'whompas' to illustrate the idiom 'to walk a
mile in a man's shoes.' In this instance, she is
referring to time instead of distance—the five
hundred years of Cayman's recorded history.
'Walking' along the gallery wall, these footsteps
boldly question the viewer's ability to under-
stand the 'authentic' Caymanian experience
without a true connection to its historical past.

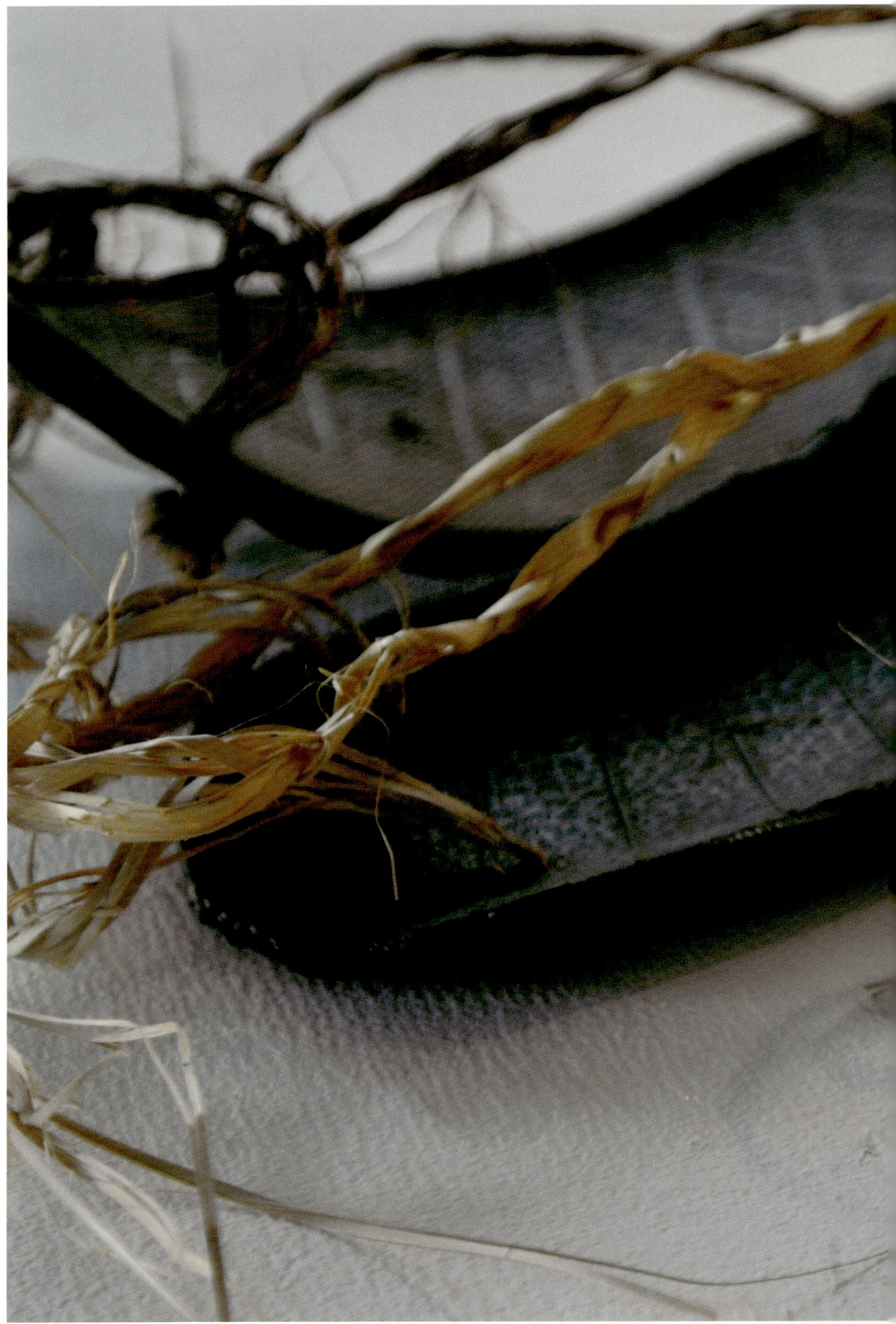

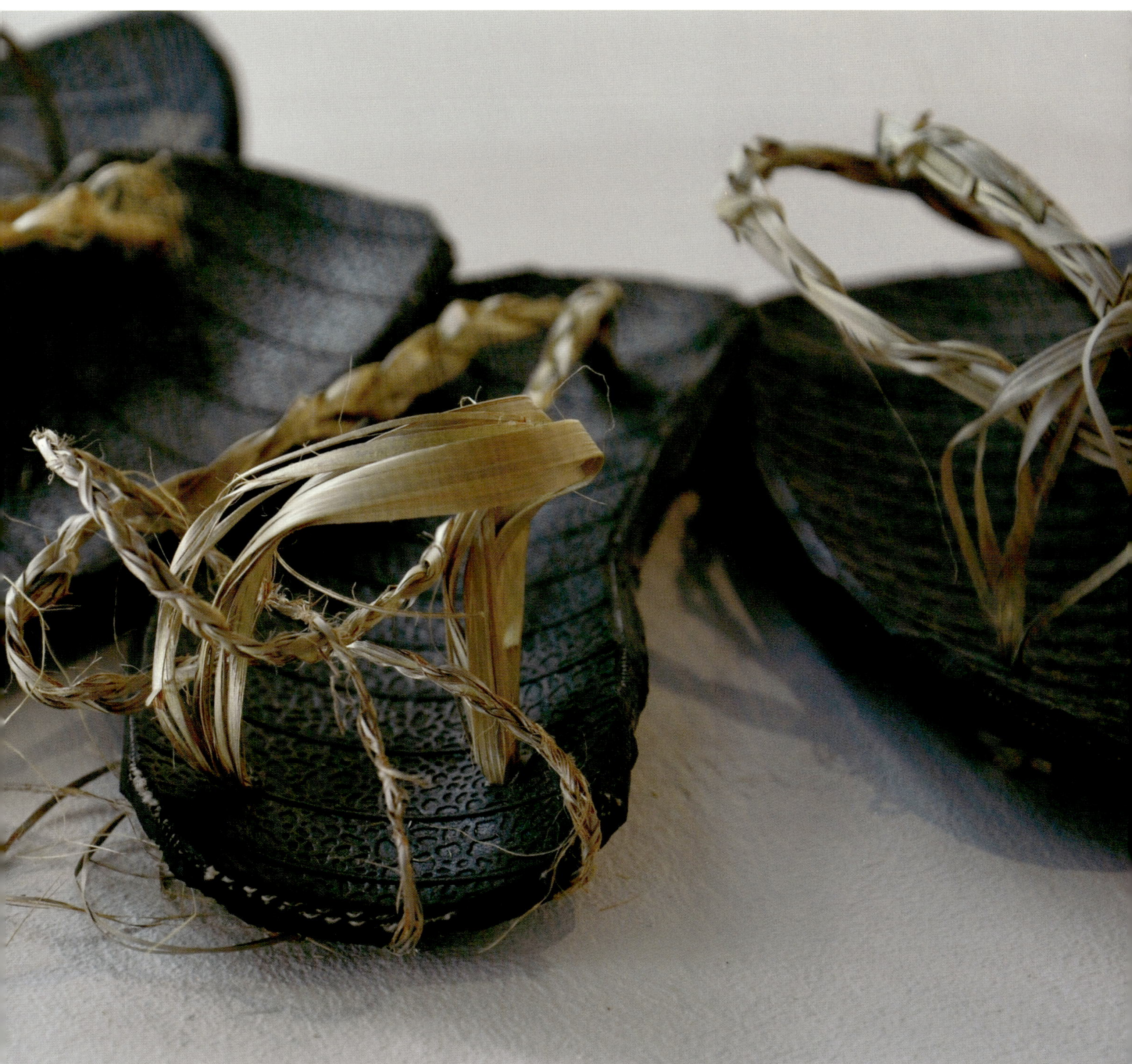

Davin Ebanks (Caymanian, b. 1975)
Blue Meridian: 80° W, Old Isaac's
(*Blue Meridian* series), 2009
Cast glass; 36 x 15 x 4 inches
See also page 91, plates 46 and 55 and figure 17.

The *Blue Meridian* series was inspired by the artist's
maritime heritage (he is the fifth generation of a
fishing family). *80° W, Old Isaac's* is one of several
studies of the ocean in which the artist created
rectangular glass castings with polished sides, glassy,
wind-blown surfaces, or granulated ridges. This
particular work renders the illusion that turquoise
water is miraculously suspended in the air, as if a
piece of ocean had been frozen in time.

Ebanks obtained a graphic design degree before
pursuing a master's degree in glass sculpture from
Kent State University, Ohio. To explore his personal
and cultural history, he utilises the difficult medium
of glass, which has won him university teaching
posts, artist-in-residence invitations, exhibitions and
prizes, including, in July 2014, the National Gallery
of the Cayman Islands' first sculptural commission
for the new site.

Bendel Hydes (Caymanian, b. 1952)
Belief, 2006
Oil on canvas; 36 x 36 inches
Gift of Atlantic Star Ltd
See also page 91, plate 14 and figures 13 and 18.

By the late 1990s, Hydes had moved away from
figurative work to a purely abstract visual language
that he refers to as 'luminescent abstraction.' *Belief*
is concerned primarily with the interaction of nature
and culture, reflecting on both the rational and the
ritualistic concerns of these perceived opposites.

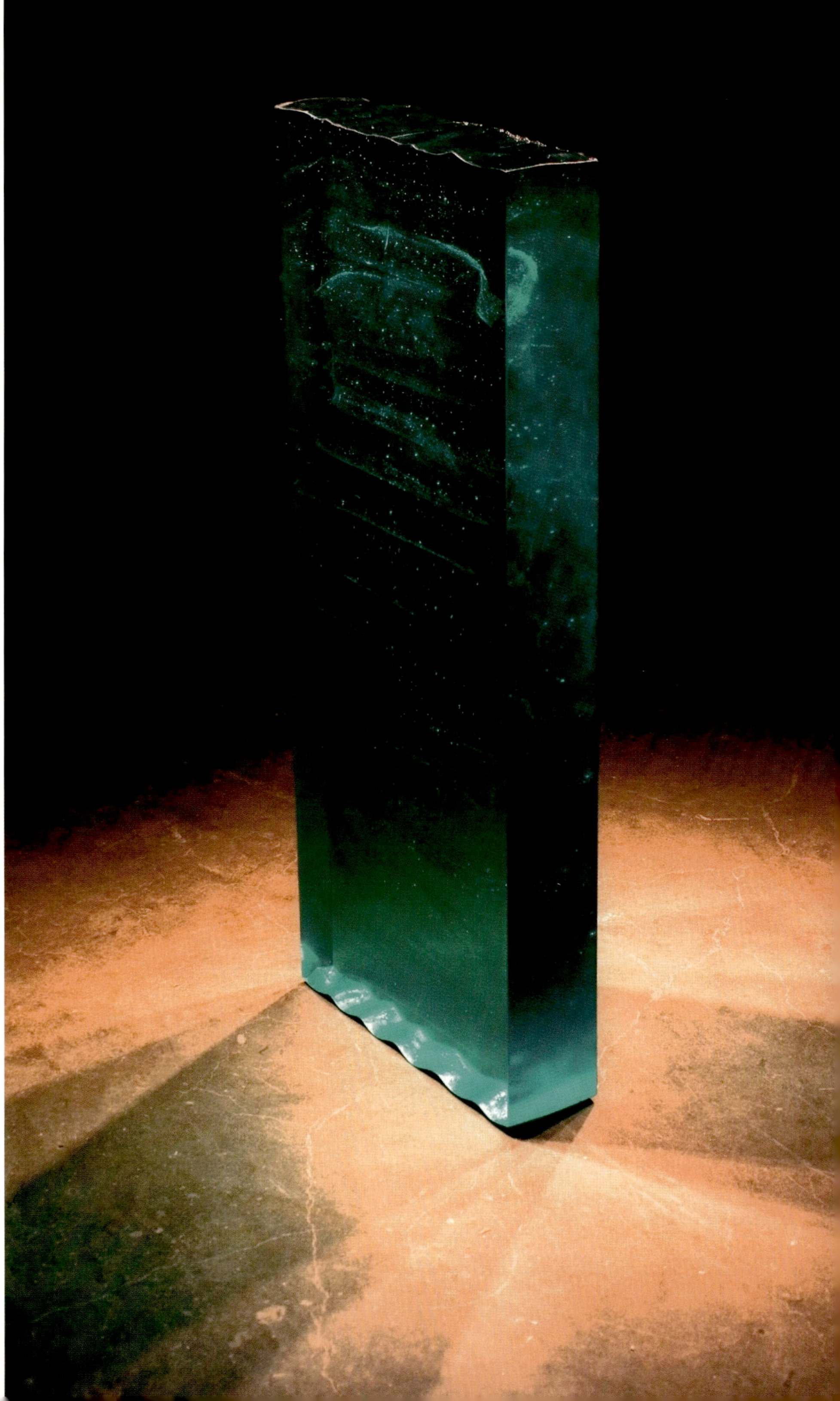

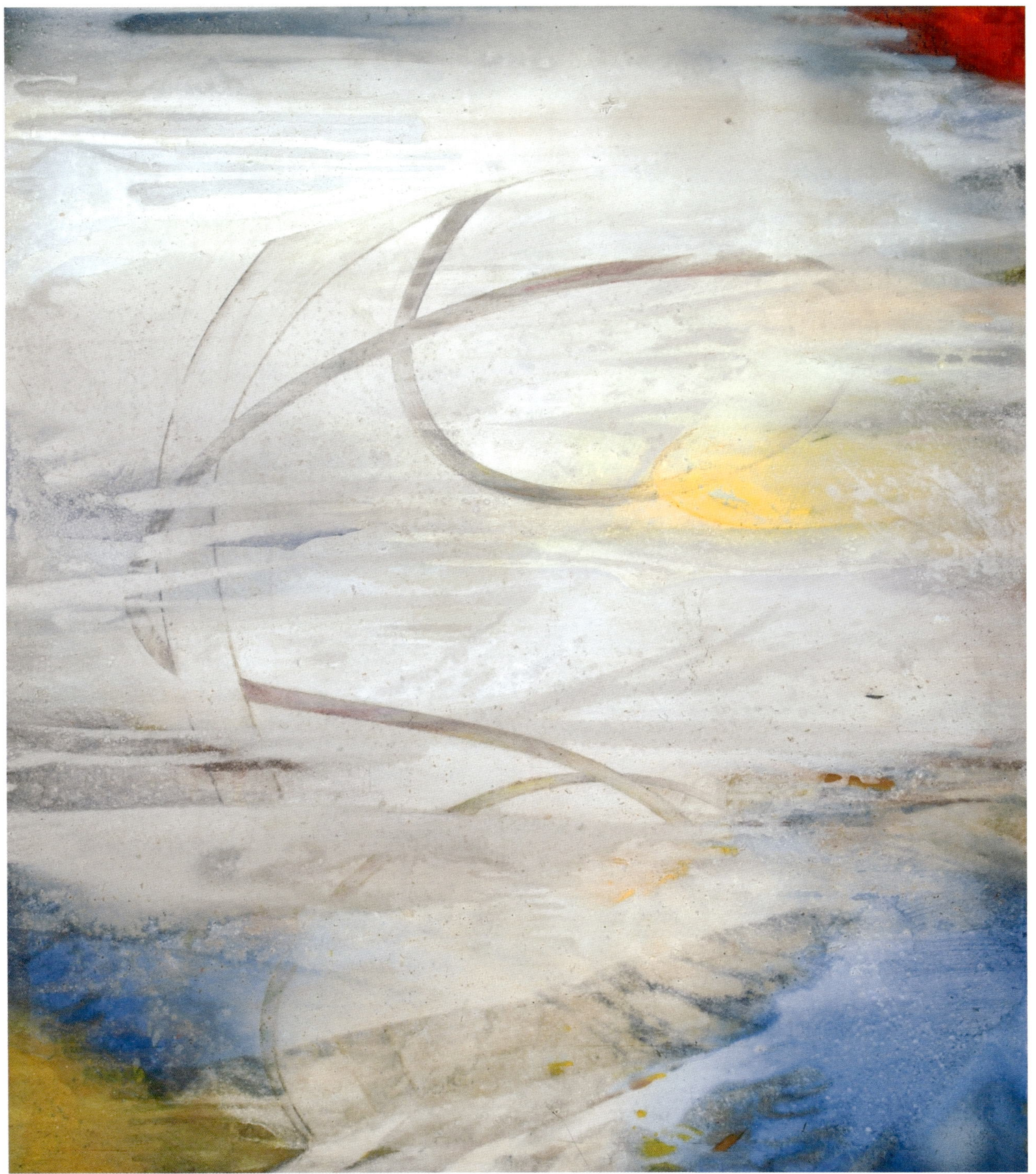

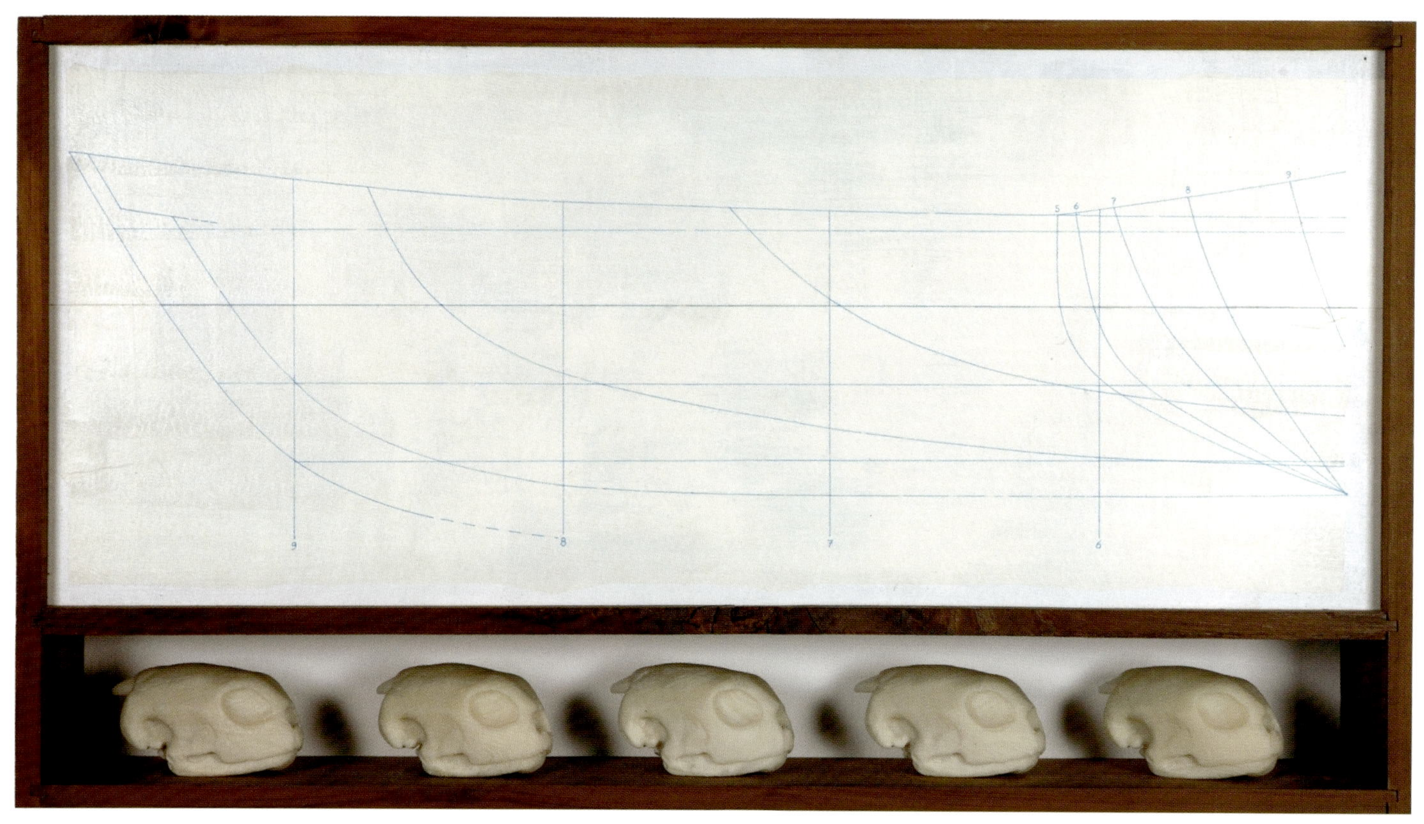

PLATE 46

Davin Ebanks (Caymanian, b. 1975)
***Death of the Ajax*, 2006**

Cast glass, wood, ink on paper; 26 x 96 x 7 inches
See also page 91, plates 44 and 55 and figure 17.

Death of the Ajax deals with a particular point in Caymanian history: the twilight years of the turtling industry in the 1940s and 1950s. Ebanks takes as his subject the *Ajax*, a traditional Cayman Brac catboat used to hunt turtles, which he illustrates through blueprints, its technical design and cast-glass turtle skulls. The amalgam of real, imagined and historical subjects evokes the continuous relationship between industry and nature, past and present, life and death. Whether it is seen as a lament on the disappearance of the historical vessel or the depletion of the marine resource, the work is permeated with a sense of bereavement and loss.

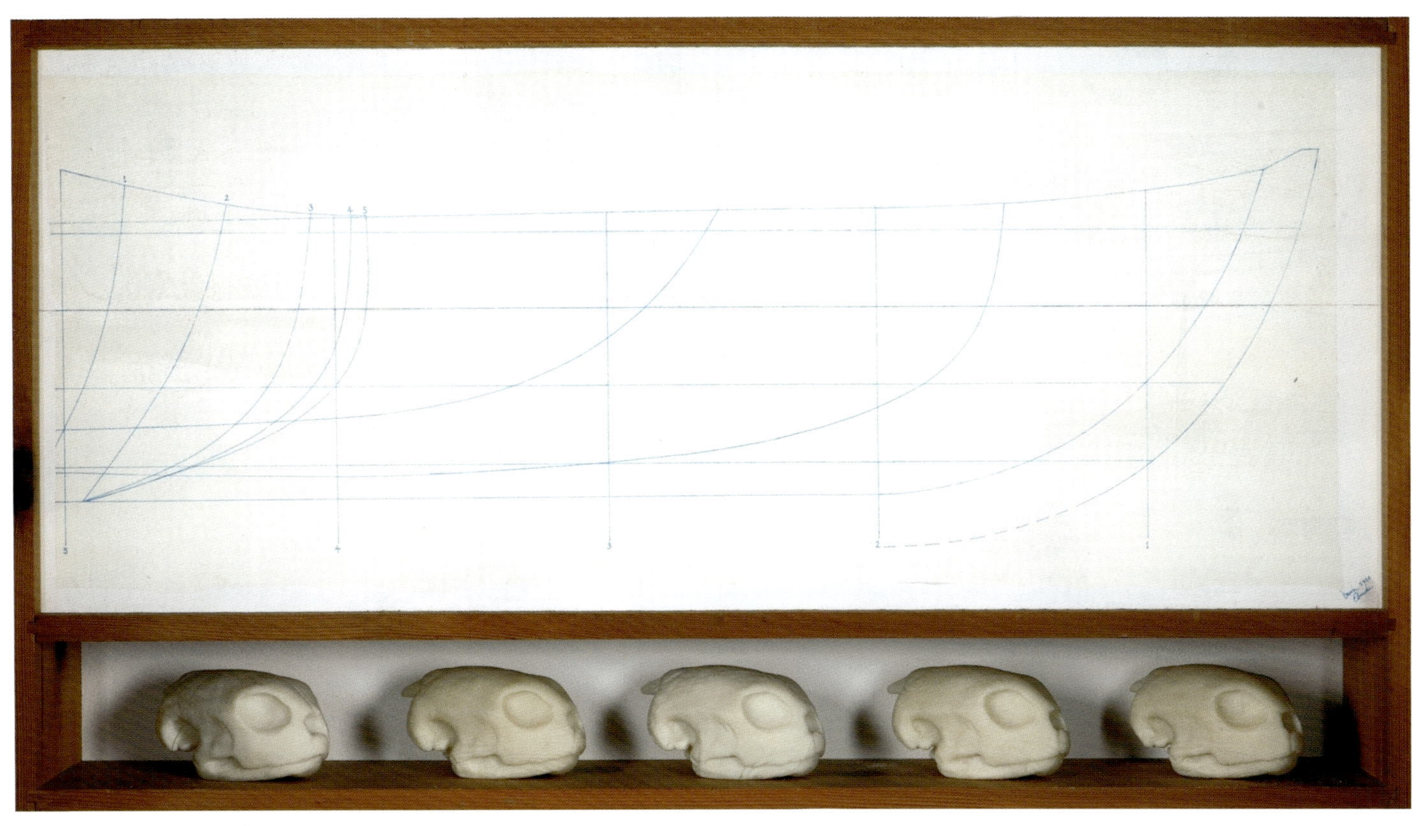

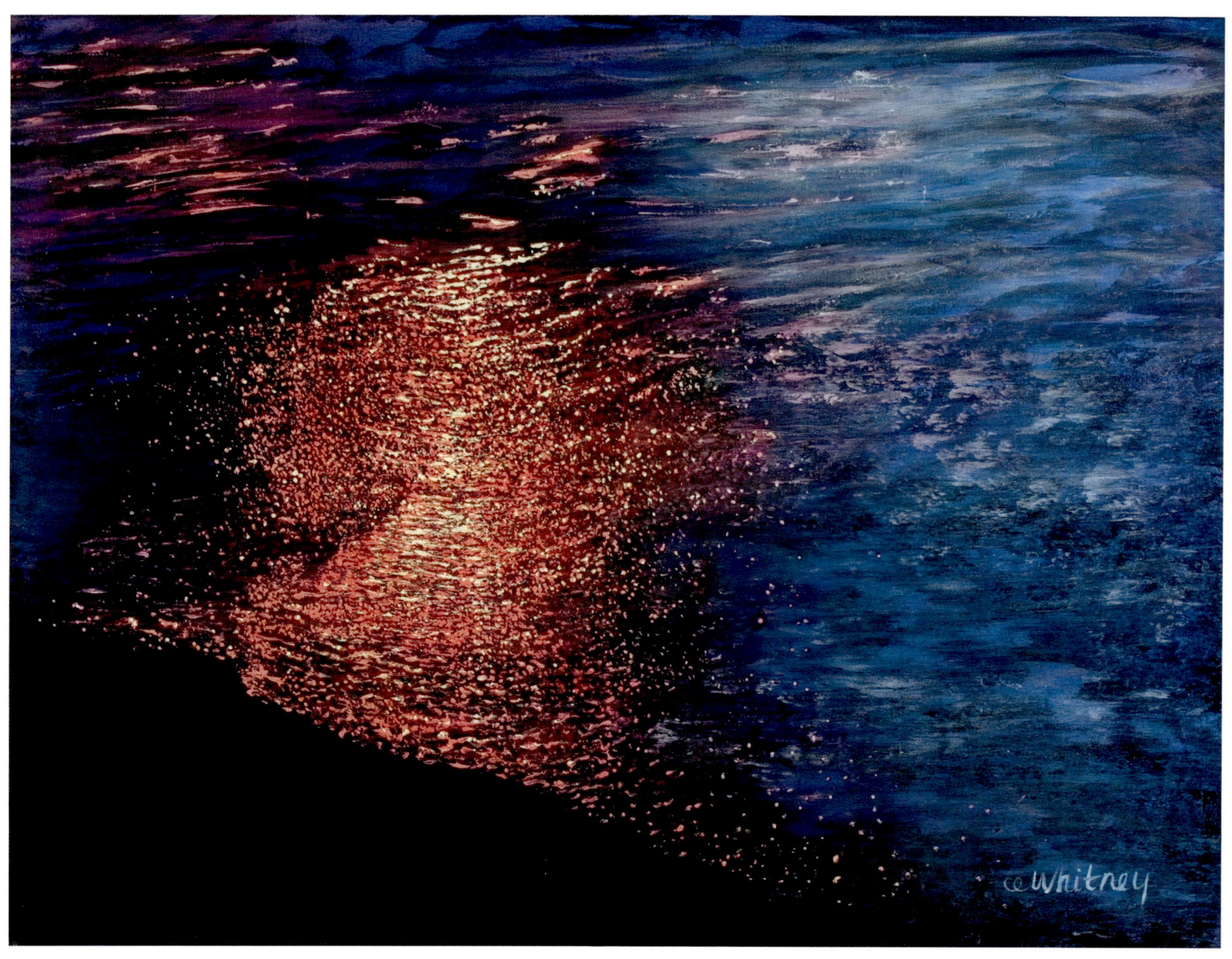

PLATE 47
C. E. Whitney (American-Caymanian, b. 1946)
Liquid Gold, **2011**
Oil on canvas; 30 x 40 inches
See also page 94.

This apparently abstract work in fact illustrates the play of sunlight on the ocean at sunset. Whitney has managed to so accurately capture the golden essence of the sun as it disappears that the painting seems to be illuminated from behind the canvas.

Whitney moved to the Cayman Islands in the 1970s and works primarily in Photorealism, a genre that began in the United States in the late 1960s, and she focuses on reproducing the effect of light. Her work has been shown in several international art fairs in Berlin, Miami and New York.

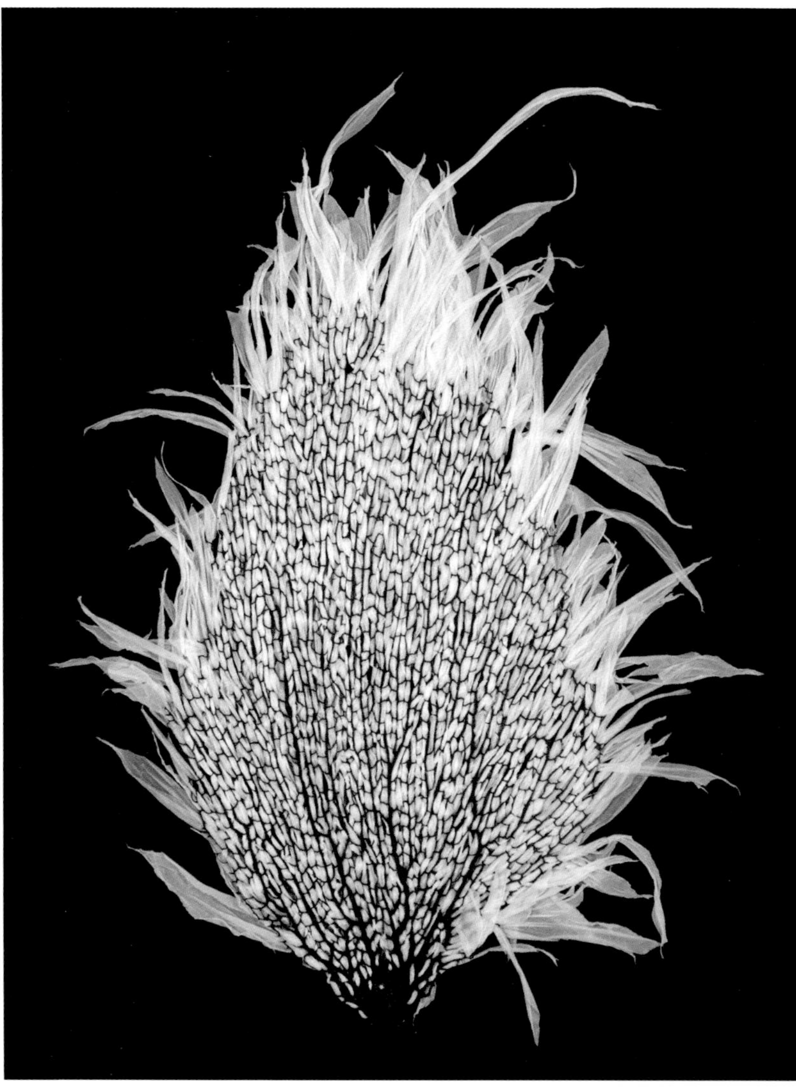

Kaitlyn Elphinstone (Canadian-Caymanian, b. 1985)
Woven Sea Fan, 2013
Found object assemblage; 22 x 18 inches
See also page 91 and plate 60.

Woven Sea Fan addresses Elphinstone's concerns about environmental sustainability and the polluting of the ocean. By carefully weaving plastic threads over and under the delicate lace pattern of the soft coral sea fan, she not only draws attention to the human need to control nature, but also creates an unexpected juxtaposition of the perfections and imperfections of the world.

Elphinstone is an interdisciplinary artist who works in digital media and assemblage, often with found objects. She is a member of the contemporary artists' collective C4.

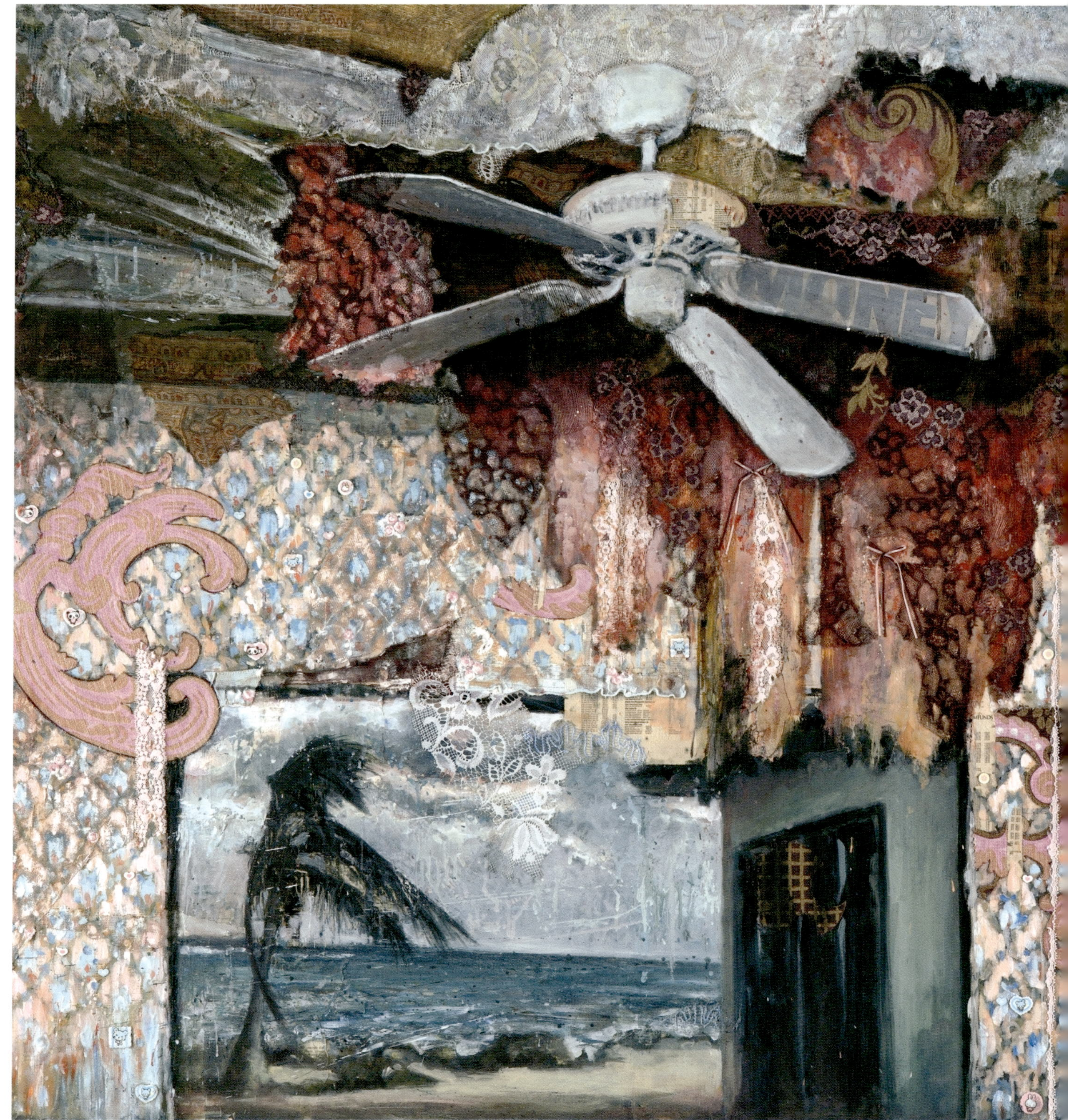

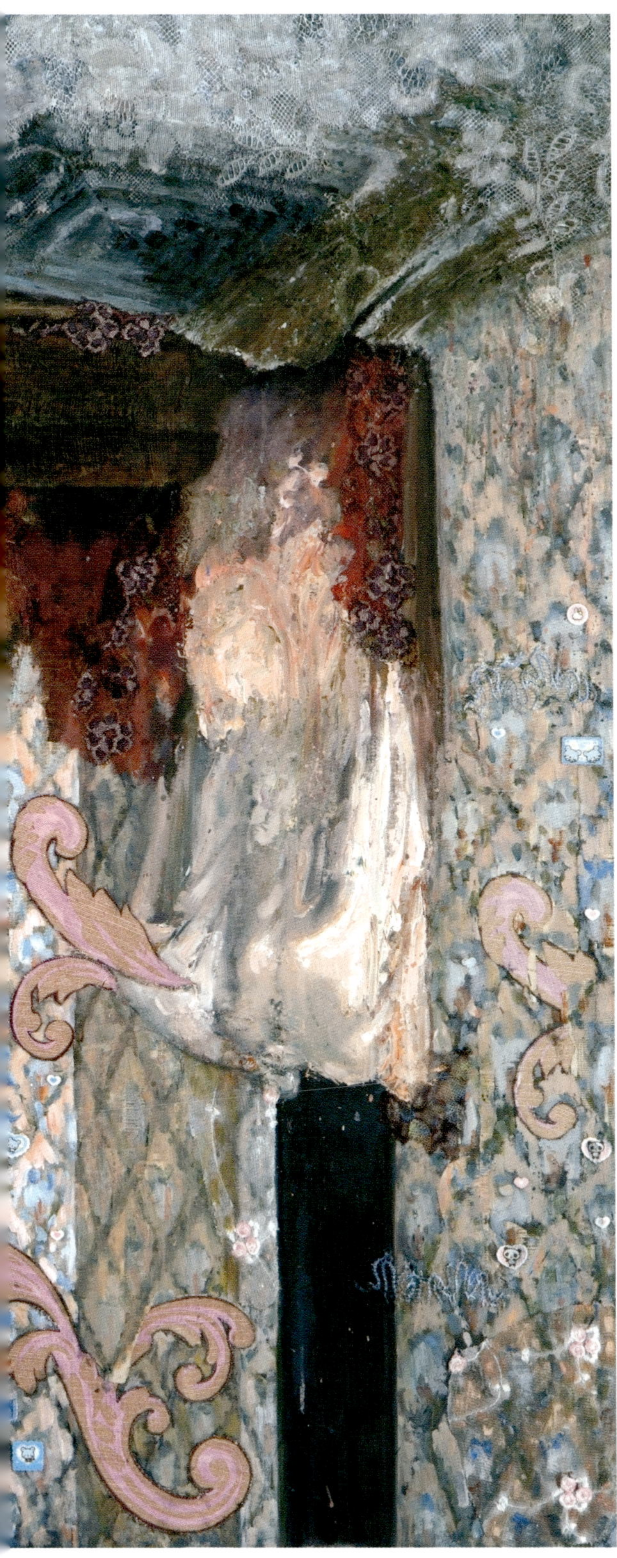

Pippa Ridley (British-Caymanian, b. 1980)
***'Ceci n'est pas un investissement,'* 2010**
Mixed media on canvas; 38½ x 47 inches
See also page 92.

Created in response to the damage wreaked by Hurricane Ivan in 2004, *'Ceci n'est pas un investissement'* ('This is not an investment') narrates the destruction of the artist's home and expresses post-Ivan economic concerns. The title plays on René Magritte's famous Surrealist painting *Ceci n'est pas une pipe* (1929) and questions our notions of certainty, authenticity and reality.

Ridley pursued her secondary education in the United Kingdom after winning an art scholarship. She graduated from the Slade School of Fine Art at University College London and the Prince's Drawing School, London. Her large-format mixed-media works initially appear to be tropical utopias. In fact, they explore darker narratives, such as social alienation and the aftereffects of colonialism.

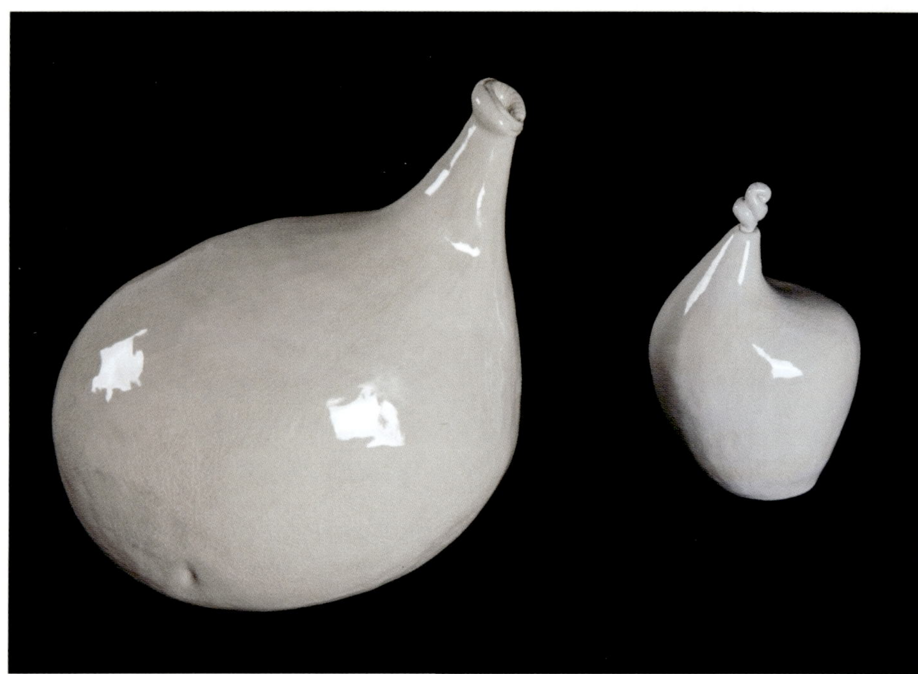

Virginia ('Auntie V') Foster (Belizean-Caymanian, b. 1950)
Arias in Mango Trees, ca. 2010
Ceramic, glaze, acrylic; 9 x 9 x 7 inches (*left*)
and 6½ x 4 x 3½ inches (*right*)
See also page 91.

Foster's clay sculptures are born out of a dialogue between minimalism and nature. Using the bird-like songs of the title as the inspiration for these works, the vessels are neither purely functional nor purely sculptural, but rather an inventive marriage of the two.

Originally from Belize, Foster is an educator, cultural administrator and professional storyteller who began practising ceramics as a hobby. Her work has been exhibited at key public institutions, and she is a recipient of the Cayman National Cultural Foundation's Gold Star for Creativity in the Arts.

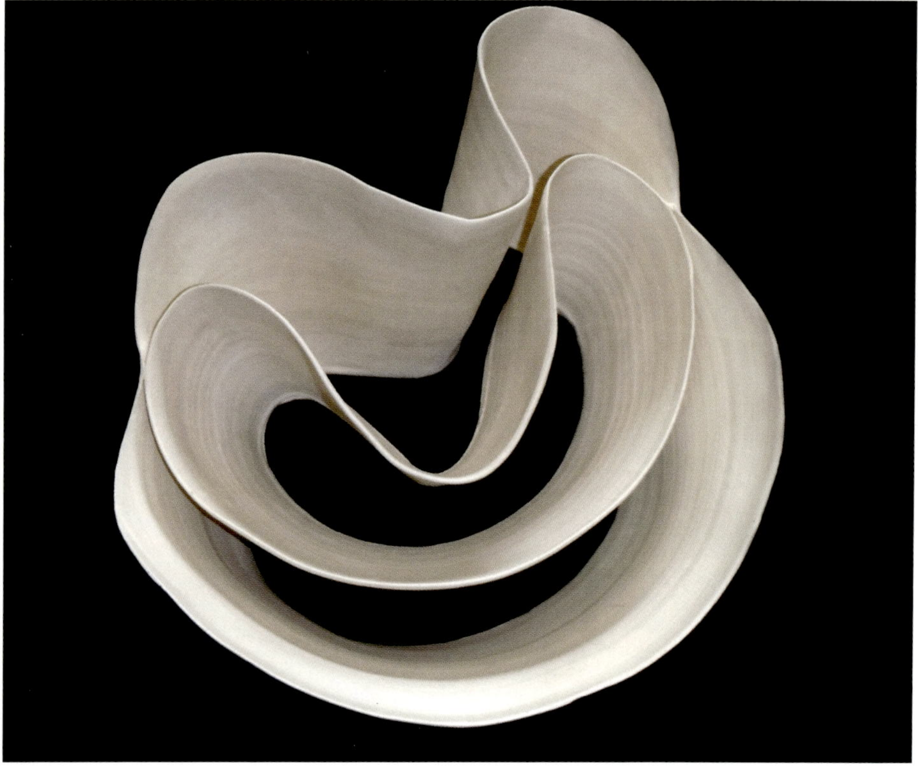

Cecilia Urdaneta (Venezuelan, b. 1967)
Wave, 2014
Ceramic, glaze, acrylic; 13 x 14½ x 5 inches
See also page 94 and plate 52.

Flattened and twisted into a ribbon-like form, this delicate sculpture defies the usual solidity of clay, creating a startlingly graceful effect. The sculpture is unassertive and yet evokes deep responses to its organic beauty.

Urdaneta studied ceramics at Stetson University in Florida and at the Akademia di Arte and Studio Giourette in Curaçao under the guidance of the artist Ellen Spijkstra. She moved to the Cayman Islands in 2002, and her highly collectible work has since been regularly featured in local exhibitions. Urdaneta was one of three artists to participate in the National Gallery of the Cayman Islands inaugural Art in Residency programme and exhibition in 2008.

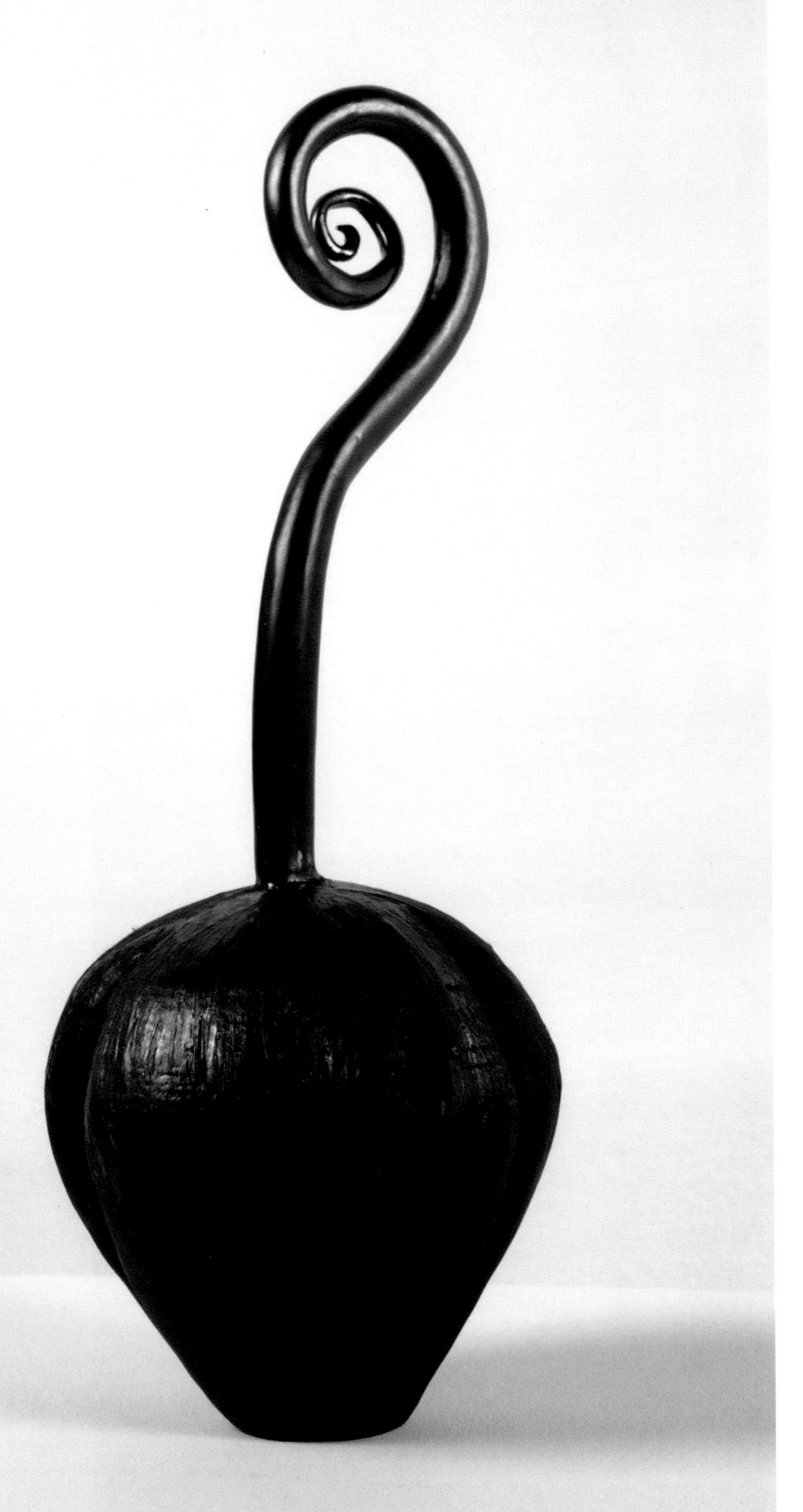

Cecilia Urdaneta (Venezuelan, b. 1967)
Calabaza, 2014
Ceramic, glaze, acrylic; 16½ x 6 x 6½ inches
See also page 94 and plate 51.

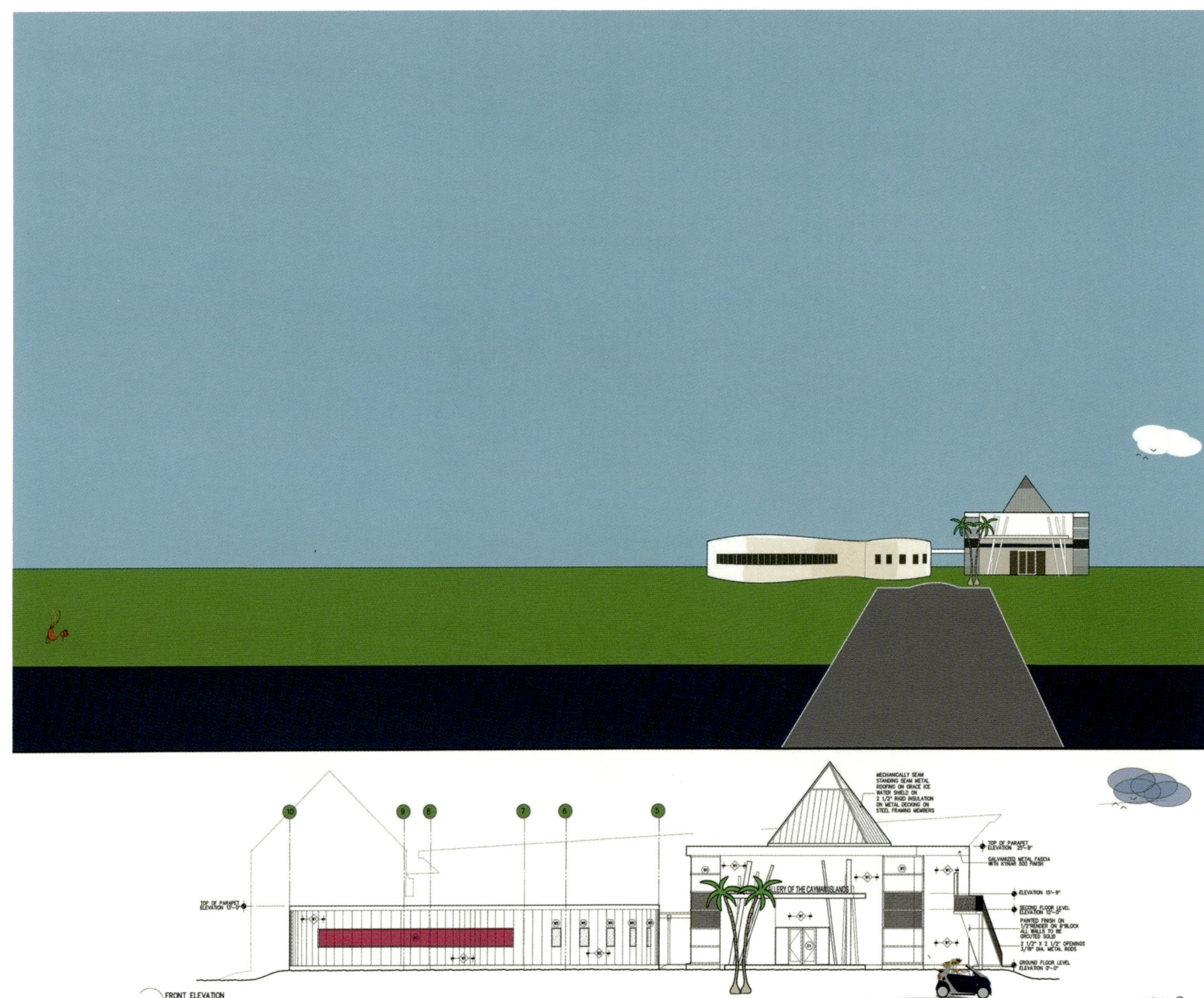

Shane ('Dready') Aquârt
(Jamaican-Caymanian, b. 1963)
The National Gallery, 2012
Digital art, ink on paper; 30½ x 36½ inches
See also page 88.

This image was created to celebrate the opening of the new NGCI facility in 2012 and formed part of a series by the artist of iconic architectural works from past and present Cayman. The extreme minimalist approach to, and use of, digital media underpins a complex design that successfully conveys the essential quality of the NGCI building.

Aquârt's graphic style is influenced by his Caribbean background and his itinerant life of English, Canadian and American education. The aesthetic criteria of flatness and bare compositions are instantly recognisable, and the artist's works often feature a whimsical stick figure, 'Dready,' his alter ego.

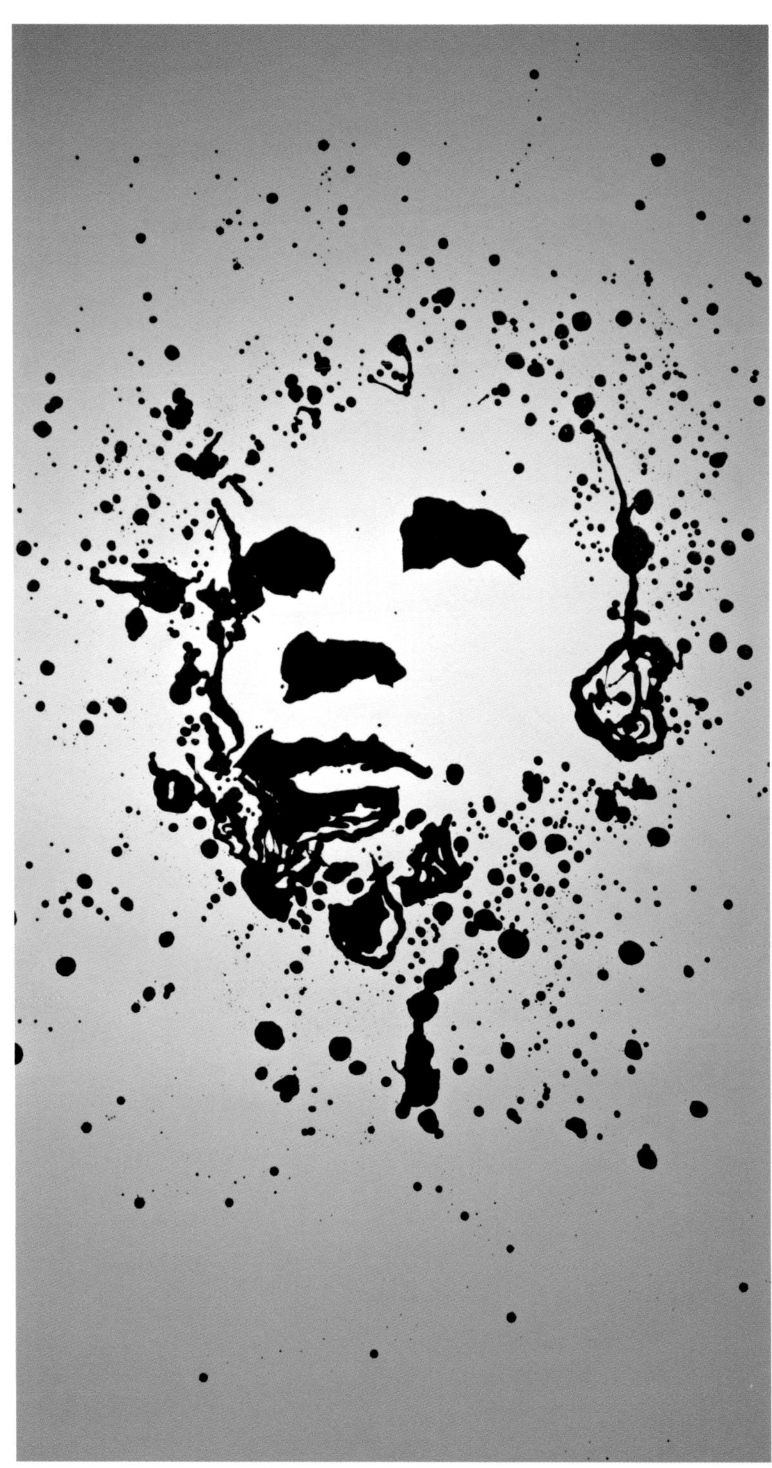

Greg Lipton (Canadian-Caymanian, b. 1975)
Passage, **2015**
Acrylic on canvas; 55 x 30 inches
See also page 92.

In this self-portrait, the artist places himself at the centre of what appears to be a burst of kinetic energy. In fact, it is a symbol of the rapid transformation—economic, social and cultural—that Lipton believes is presently occurring in the Cayman Islands. He draws attention to the chaos, noise and insecurity generated by the speed of this change and examines himself emerging from the past into a tumultuous present.

Lipton is a self-taught artist who works in many genres. His work is primarily concerned with identity and the social isolation driven by technology.

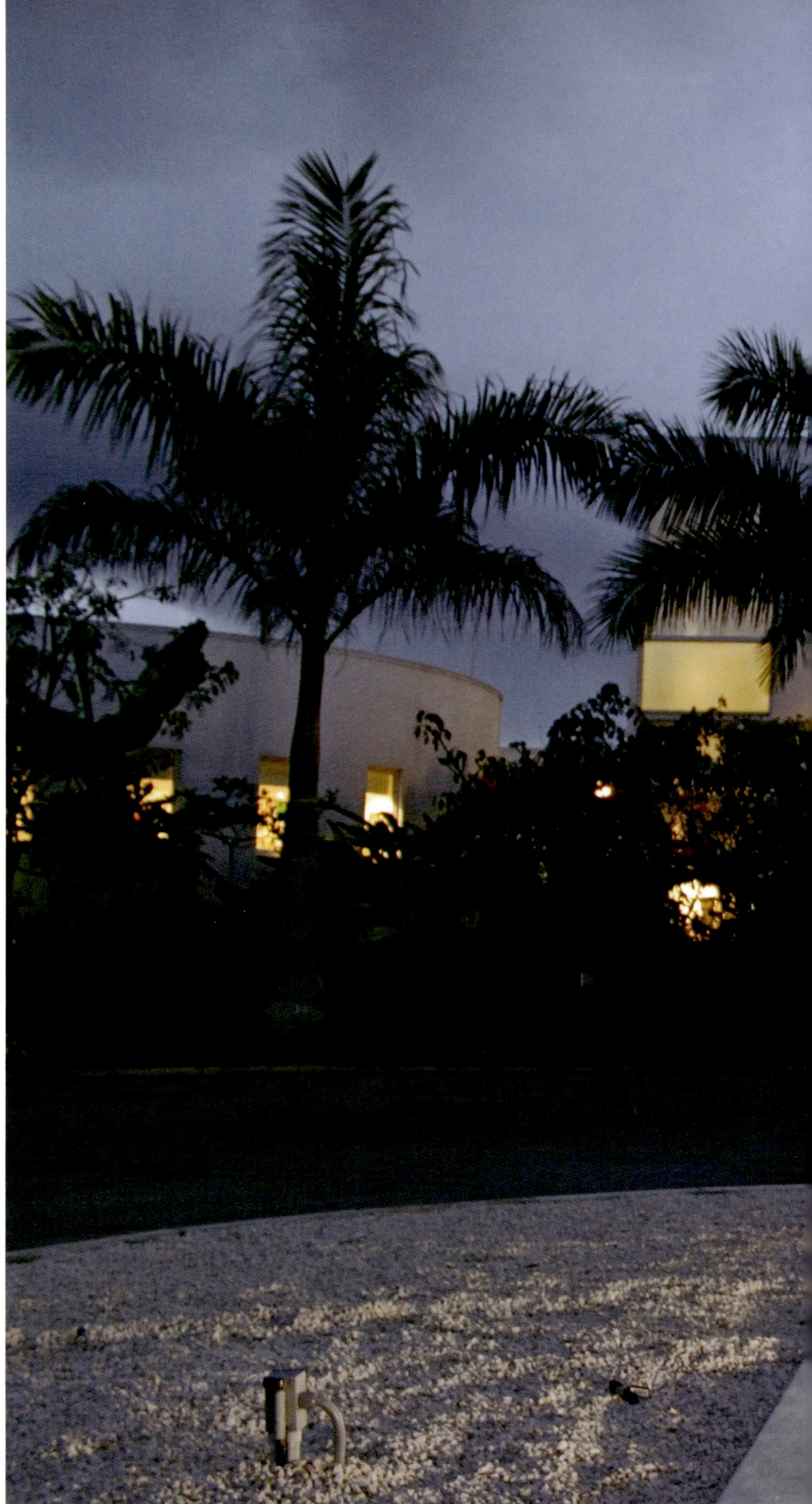

PLATE 55
Davin Ebanks (Caymanian, b. 1975)
Adjacent, 2014
Glass, cement; 132 x 48 x 72 inches
See also page 91, plates 44 and 46 and figure 17.

Adjacent, a public sculpture inspired by the iconic
Caymanian catboat, dynamically transforms the
National Gallery of the Cayman Islands' outdoor
space through its large scale and weight. The solemn
sculpture alludes to permanence and power, yet its
central glass makeup contradicts its external solidity.
Placed at the entrance of the museum, the two-part
structure marks a crossroads between individuality
and dialogue, permanence and timelessness.

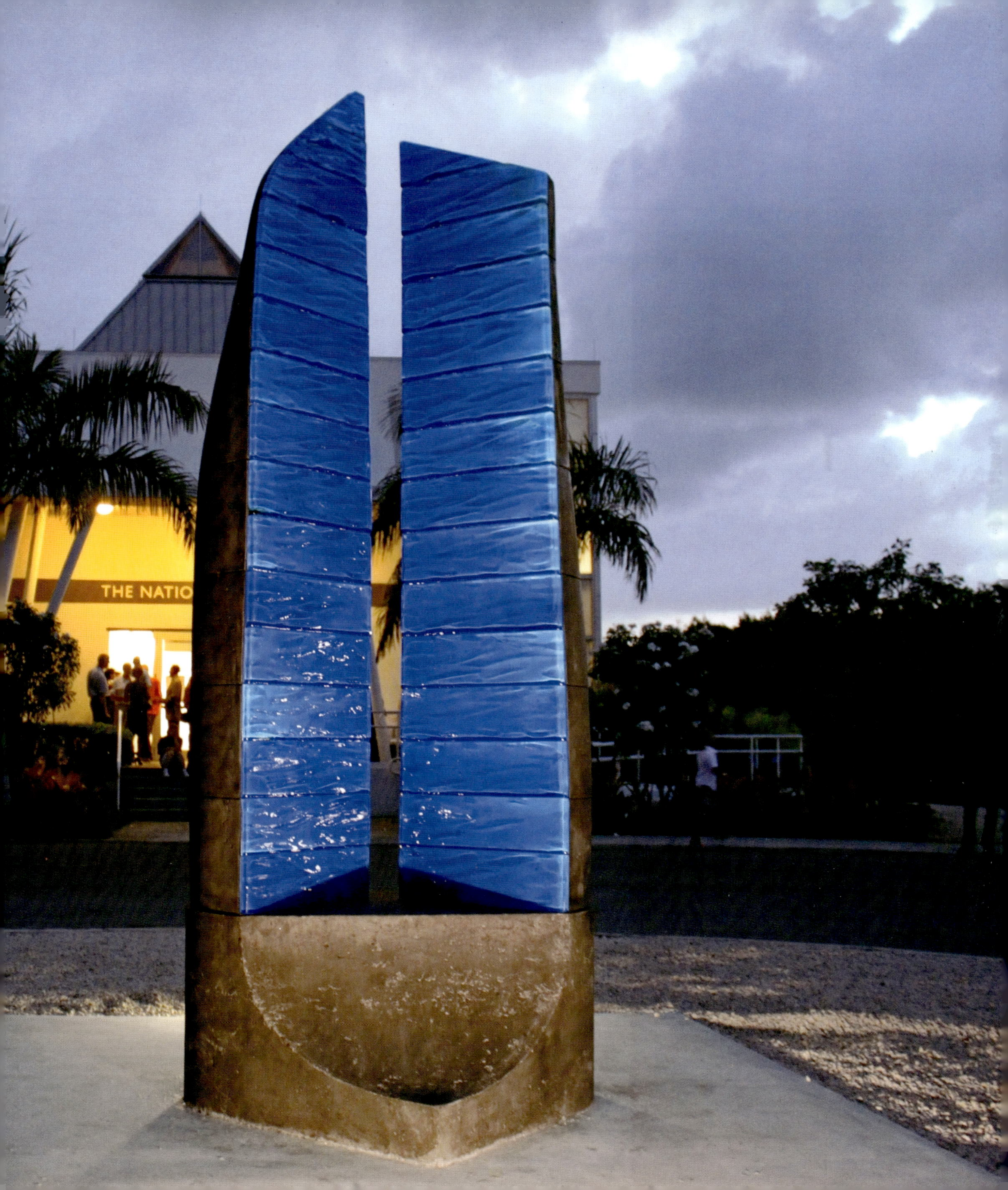
THE NATIO

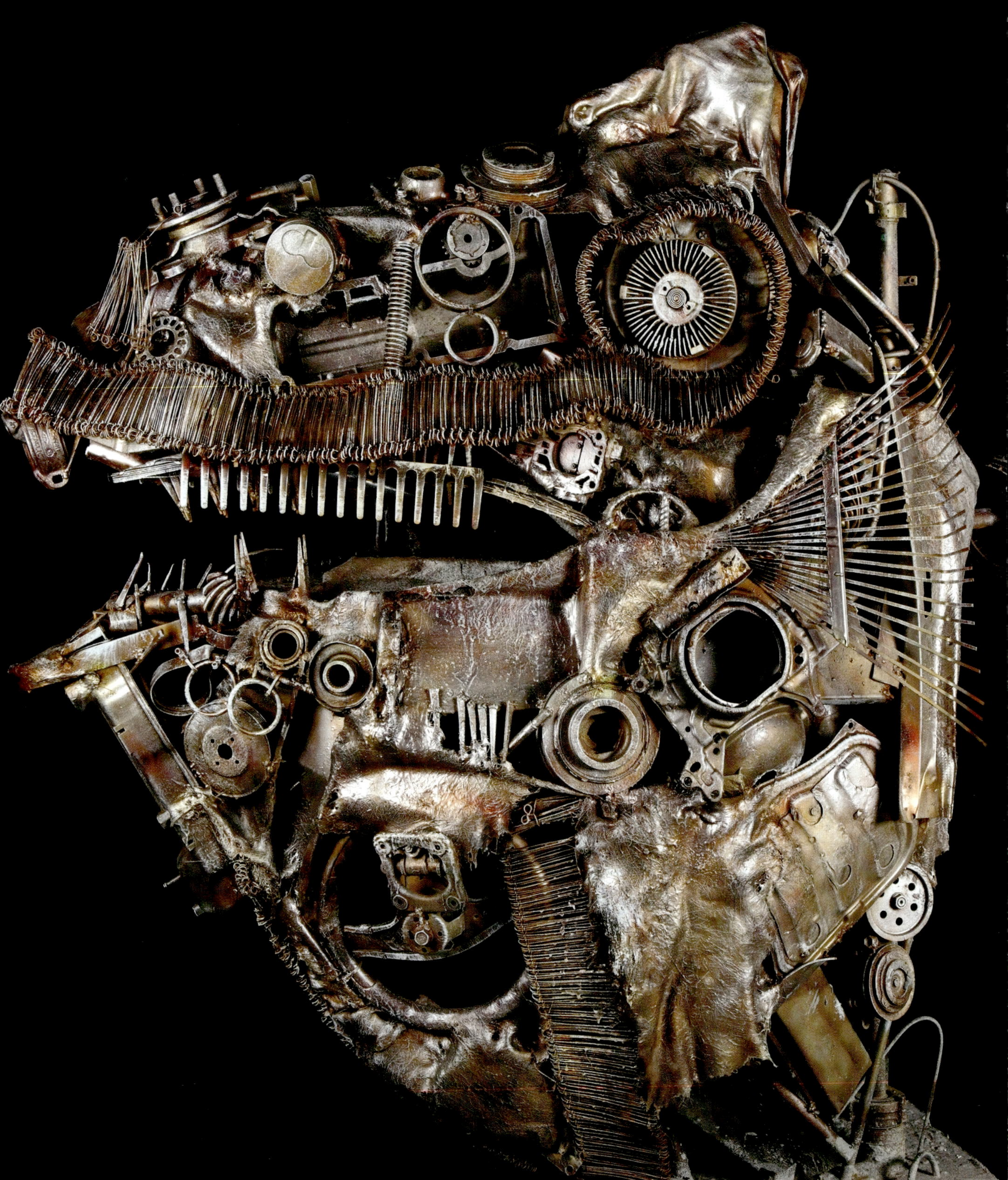

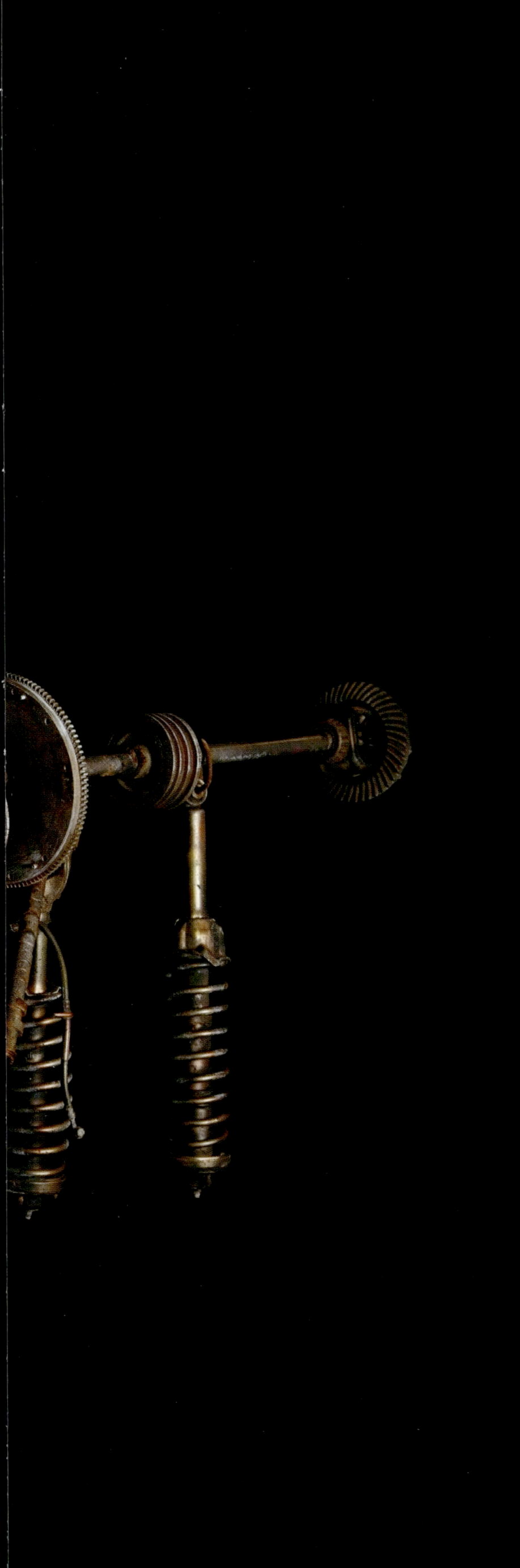

Rasitha Sanjeewa (Sri Lankan, b. 1972)
Fish Skeleton (detail), 2013
Mixed media; 108 x 72 x 45 inches
See also page 93 and figure 3.

Fish Skeleton, featured in the National Gallery of the Cayman Islands' 2013 exhibition *Art of Assemblage*, is a sculpture made from recycled domestic materials and car parts. Throughout the twentieth century, artists employed trash materials as part of the modernist revolt against the use of traditional materials in fine art. Here Sanjeewa draws attention to the islands' longstanding reliance on the ocean for sustenance and the increasing environmental pressures that threaten this relationship.

Sanjeewa arrived in the Cayman Islands after Hurricane Ivan and quickly began to transform pieces of the wreckage into works of art.

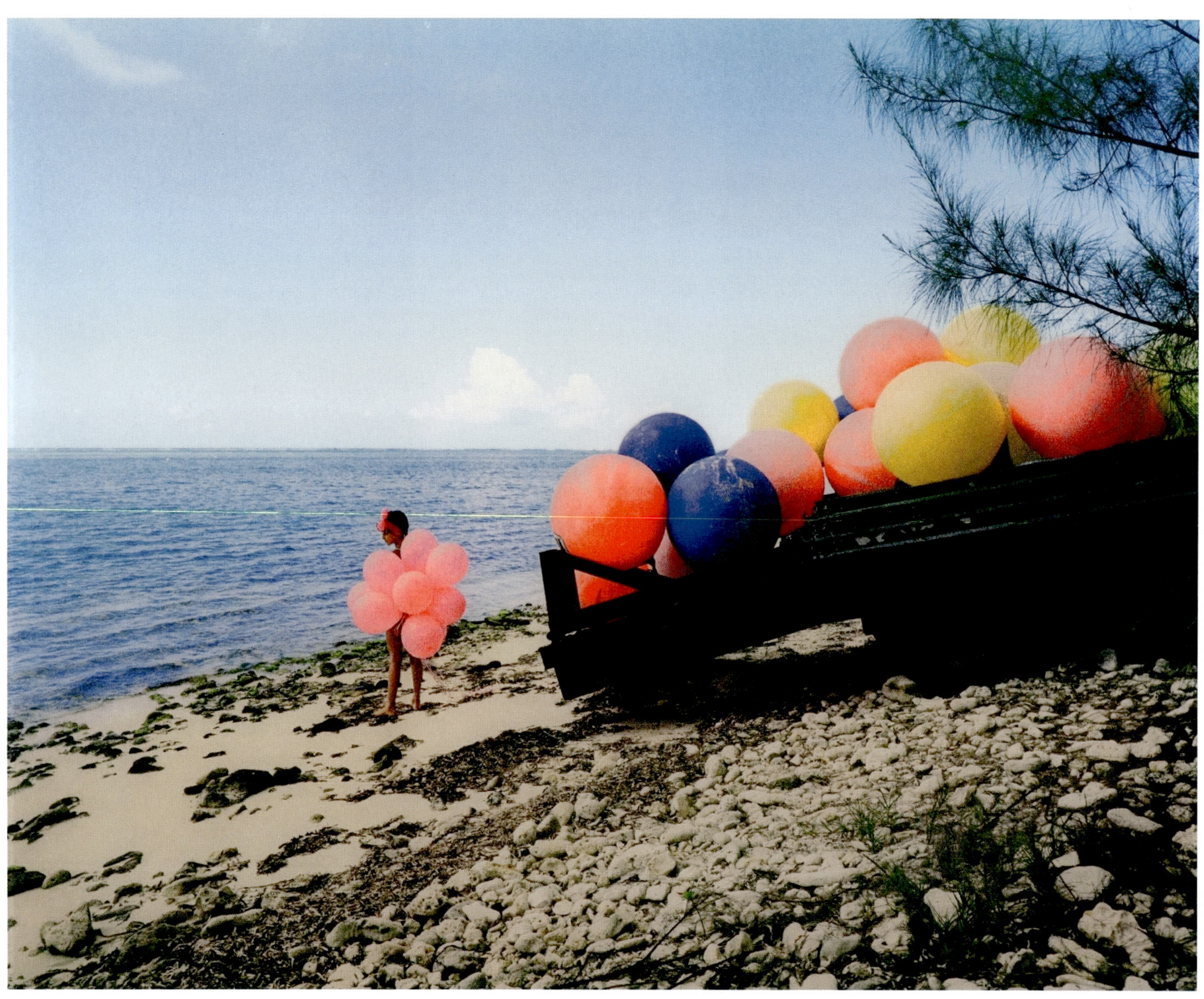

Heidi Bassett Blair (Canadian, b. 1969)
Forever Ten (*Plastic in Paradise* series), 2013
Medium-format film, archival giclée print in
Lucite frame; 36½ x 44½ inches
See also page 89.

This work is part of the larger series *Plastic in Paradise*, in which the artist explores the complex relationship between the natural and manmade environments. Her carefully staged compositions, which are influenced by nostalgic memory, art history and popular culture, are designed to resemble candid snapshots—truth and fiction are woven together to create a narrative of both a real and an imagined world, where helium balloons compete with coconut palms and nature intersects with the factory-made.

Now a Cayman Islands resident, Bassett Blair studied photography at university before moving to France to work with video-digital artist Peter Campus at Parsons Paris. Her work has been exhibited in galleries across the United States and Canada, and she has won several prestigious awards, including the Jack Goodman Award for Art and Technology and *American Photo*'s Portraits and People contest.

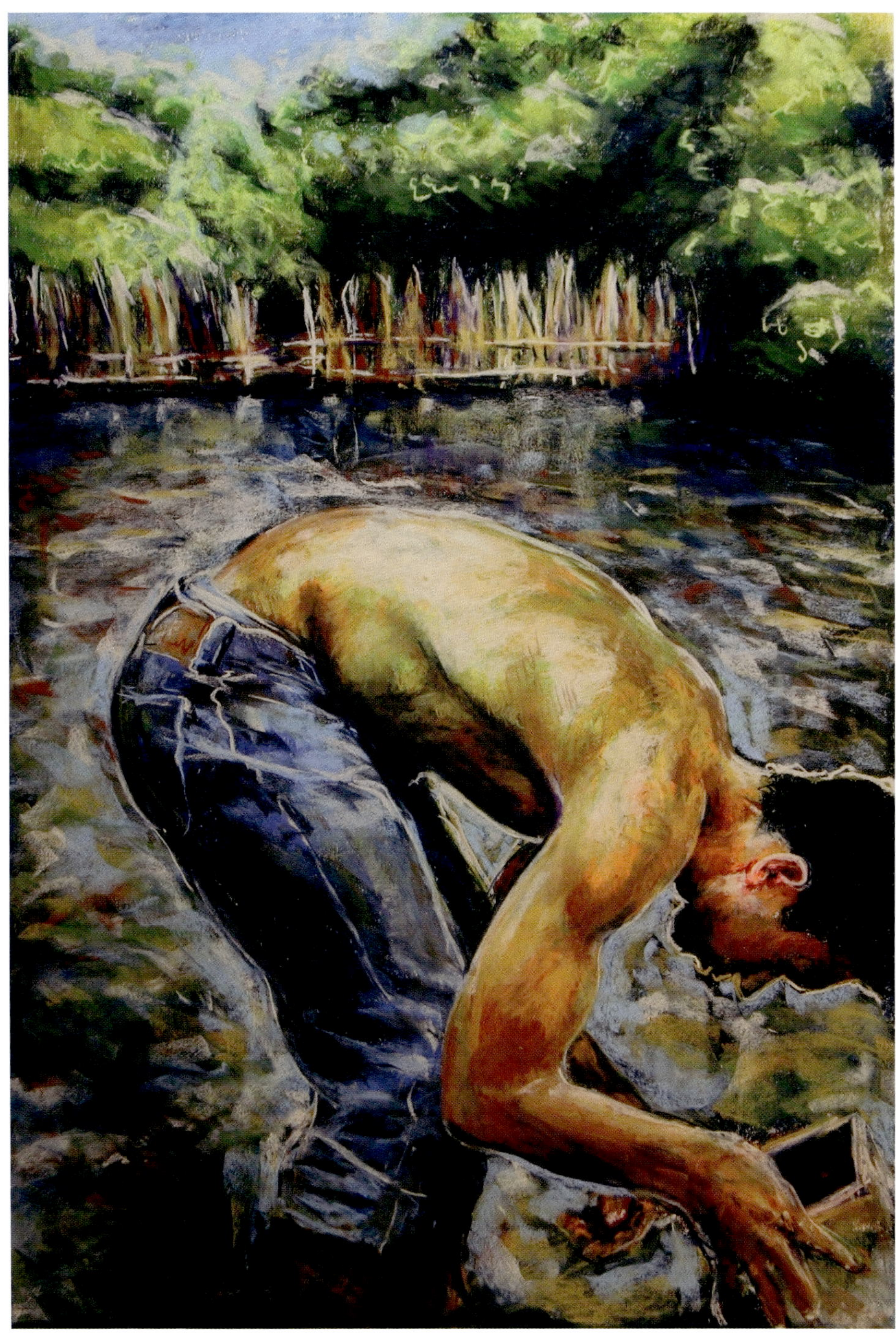

Simon Tatum (Caymanian, b. 1995)
Looking Glass, 2014
Ink and pastel on paper; 28 x 20 inches
See also page 93.

The 'looking glass' of the title is used in both a literal sense—it is the traditional tool used by turtle fishermen to see under the water—and as a symbol for the seeking of self-knowledge. The artist has depicted himself as a traditional turtle fisherman in an effort to connect to the customs and history of his forefathers. The work speaks to the challenging role of a young Caymanian trying to hold on to his heritage in a rapidly changing environment.

Tatum is currently pursuing his BA at the University of Missouri, Columbia, for which he received the Cayman Islands Government Overseas Scholarship and the Deutsche Bank National Gallery Visual Arts Scholarship. His recent body of work, which explores Caymanian heritage, was featured in a three-artist exhibition, *Evoke* (Imago Gallery and Cultural Center, Columbia, 2015), and in *tIDal Shift: Explorations of Identity in Contemporary Caymanian Art* (NGCI, 2015).

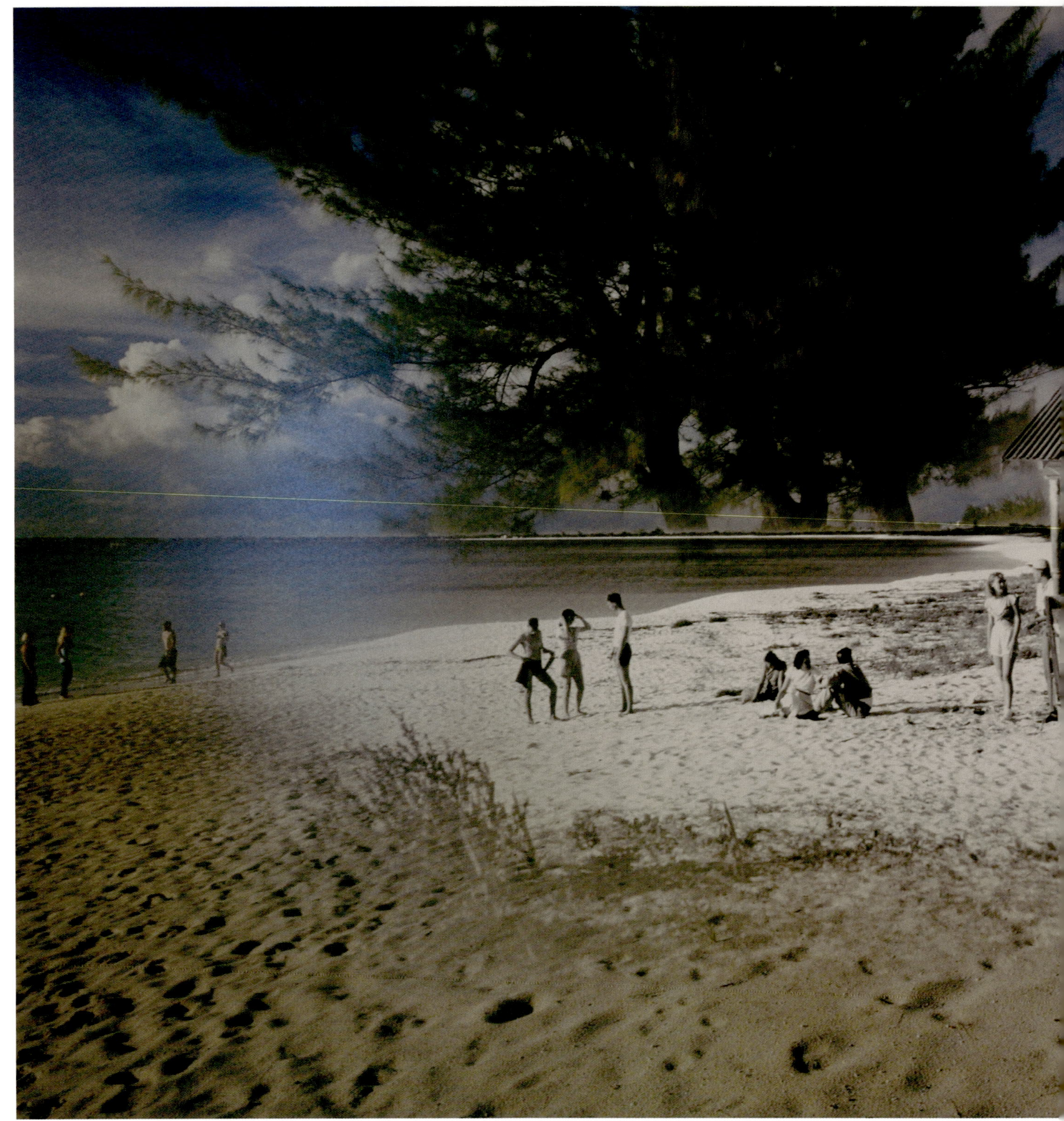

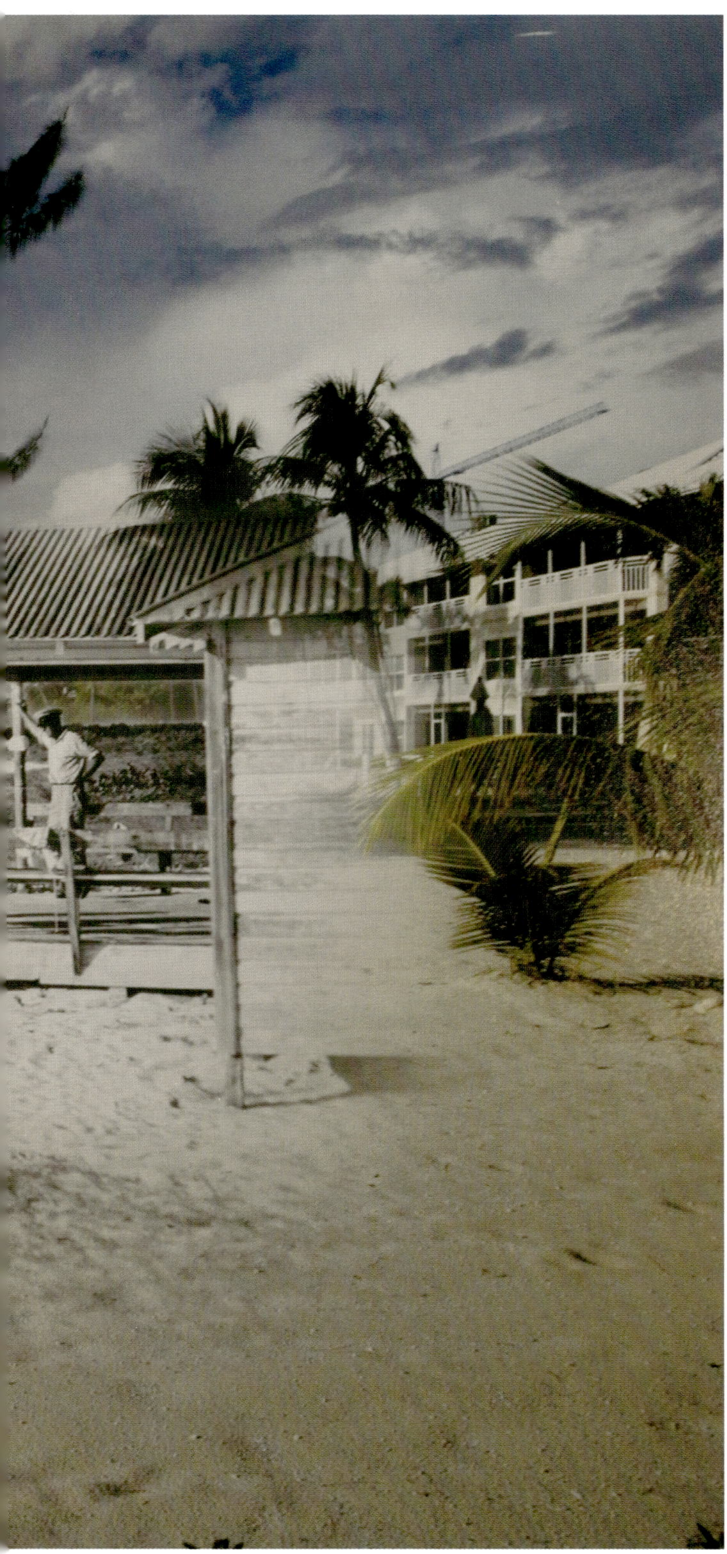

Courtney Platt (American-Caymanian, b. 1957)
***Seven Mile Beach (Now and Then* series), 2012**
Digital print; 32 x 48 inches
Original image by Joseph Steinmetz, 1950
Courtesy of the Steinmetz Collection
See also page 92.

This is one of a series of twenty-four images created
for the National Gallery of the Cayman Islands'
2012 *Now and Then* exhibition, which sought to
encourage dialogue around the islands' rapid
development and disappearing landscape and the
importance of preserving the past. As a result of
Platt's clever manipulation of the original photo, past
and present landscapes, buildings and generations
of people blend together into a surreal and at times
haunting mix of images.

Platt is a prolific photographer who moved to
the Cayman Islands in 1983. He developed this series
in collaboration with the author, Natalie Urquhart,
a Caymanian curator whose practise focuses on
explorations of identity and memory.

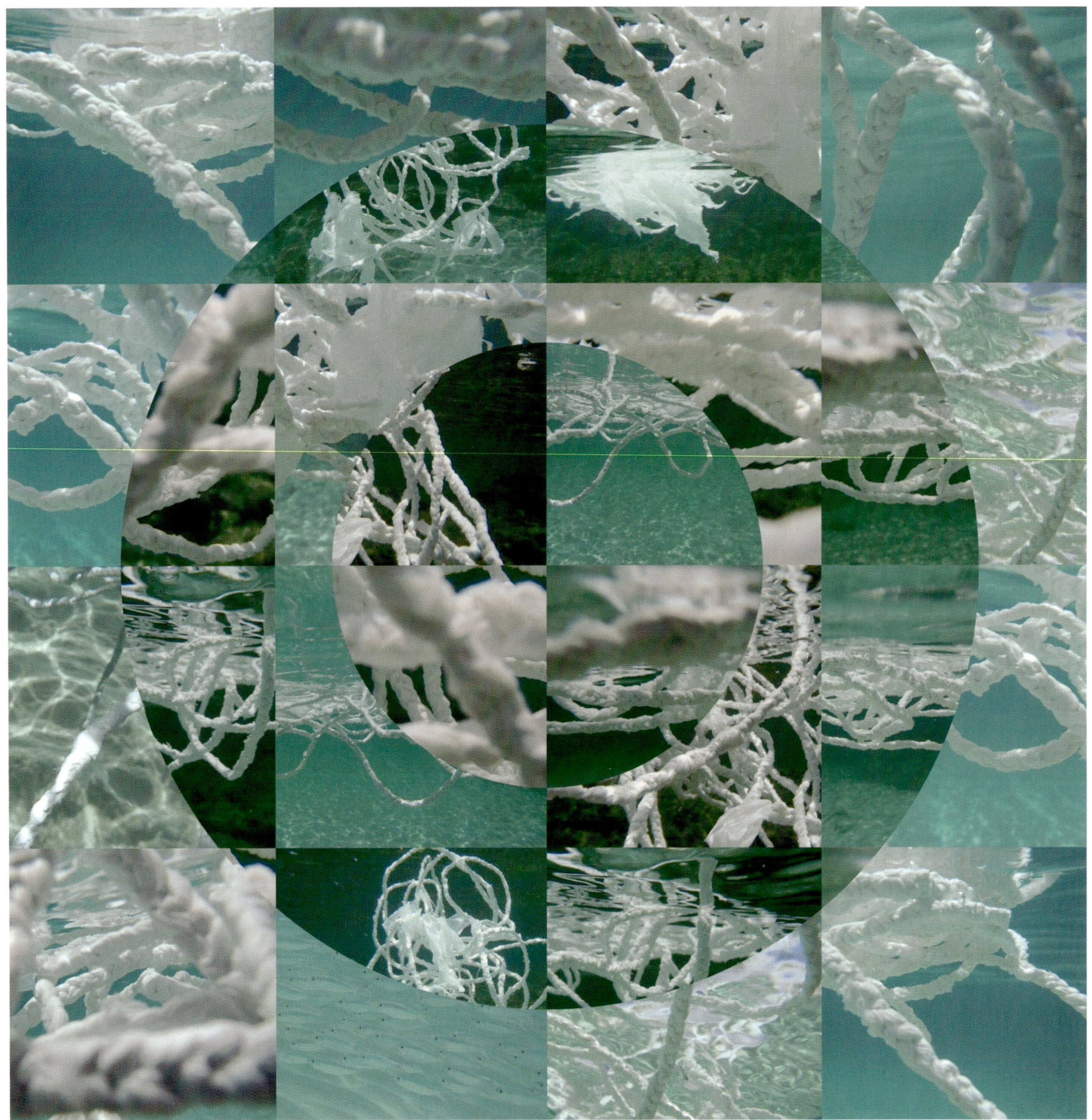

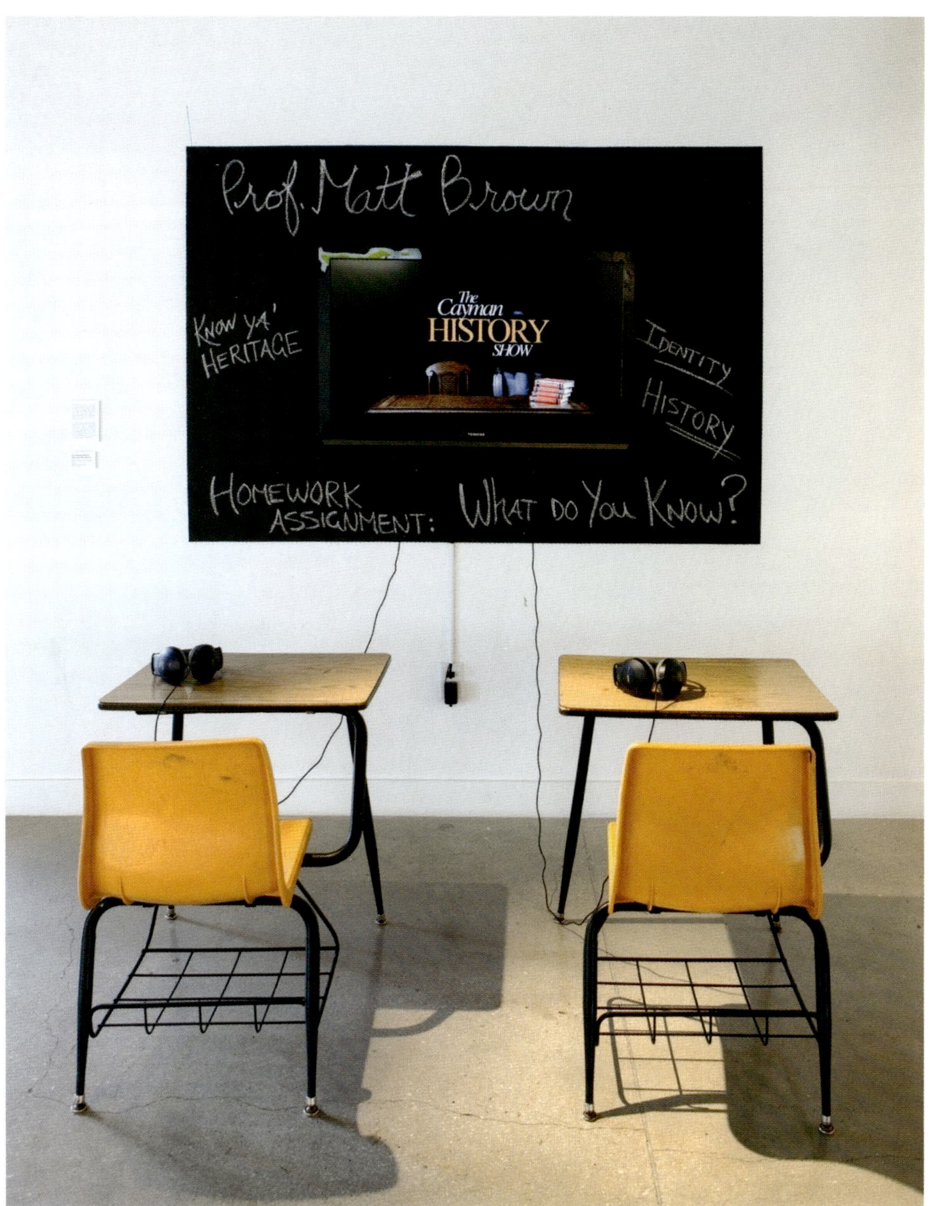

PLATE 60 (*opposite*)

PLATE 60 (*opposite*)

Kaitlyn Elphinstone (Canadian-Caymanian, b. 1985)
White Plaits, Blue Braids **(detail), 2015**
Metallic photographic prints, installation;
44 x 44 inches
See also page 91 and plate 48.

Braids have been made for thousands of years and for a variety of uses. In contrast, plastic bags are new but can take hundreds of years to decompose. In this ethereal image, Elphinstone combines the two to narrate many commentaries, from the local practises of fishing and thatching to broader themes of time, functionality and conservation.

PLATE 61 (*this page*)

Ben Hudson (Belizean, b. 1976) and
Matt Brown (Caymanian, b. 1985)
The Cayman History Show, **2014**
Digital video, acrylic, plastic, metal, wood, chalk;
71½ x 64 x 72 inches
See also pages 89 and 91 and figure 19.

This video installation is styled as a game show in which the professor (played by Matt Brown) challenges the audience with multiple-choice questions on the Cayman Islands' history and cultural heritage. Topics range from commonplace trivia to significant historical events, figures and institutions in the islands' history. The artists' humorous approach belies their more serious concern about the increasing disconnection between contemporary society and its past.

Hudson is a filmmaker who has received several awards for his socially conscious documentaries. Brown is a Caymanian actor and radio personality. Together they have created several popular music and video projects on the islands.

Moira Abbott (British-Caymanian, b. 1945). Abbott studied textile design at Manchester College of Art, United Kingdom, and worked as a conservation officer at the Victoria and Albert Museum, London, before moving to Jamaica in the 1970s and then to the Cayman Islands in 1983 to teach art. She became an active member of VAS and was a prolific artist from the 1980s until the early 1990s. *See plate 16.*

Marlena Anglin (Caymanian, b. 1933). Born in West Bay, Grand Cayman, Anglin learned thatching from her mother and soon became a highly skilled rope maker and weaver of baskets, hats and other items. She is an active member of the Cayman Islands Traditional Arts Council, creating work for festivals and heritage days as well as teaching crafts to local schoolchildren. She participated in the *21st Century Cayman* exhibition (NGCI, 2010), and her work is included in public and private collections. *See plate 5.*

Shane ('Dready') Aquârt (Jamaican-Caymanian, b. 1963). Jamaican-born Aquârt, who signs his art 'Dready,' has a whimsical graphic style influenced by his rich mixture of cultural experiences: a Caribbean childhood and education at an English boarding school, a Canadian high school and a U.S. college. Aquârt has illustrated several publications, and his solo exhibition *Cayman Panorama: Things That Exist Only in My Fading Memory* was featured at NGCI in 2013. In addition to fine art, Aquârt has created work extensively used in merchandising, commercial graphics and interiors. His work also can be found in the permanent collection of NGCI. *See plate 53.*

Wray Banker (Caymanian, b. 1968). Born in West Bay, Grand Cayman, Banker studied graphic design in Houston and is a founding member of the Native Sons art collective. Career highlights include designing pins for the Cayman Islands 1996 Olympic Committee and the 2003 Pan Am Games (both voted Best of Countries). Notable exhibitions include *Serious bout Makin' Fun* (NGCI, 2001); Art Basel Miami (2003); the Santo Domingo Biennale (2003); the Griffin Gallery, Chicago (2006); and Carifesta X, Guyana (2008). Banker has received numerous awards, including the Lifetime Achievement in Arts award from the Cayman Islands government (2003); The McCoy Prize's Second Commendation in Photography (2005) and People's Choice for Fine Art (2006); CNCF's Artistic Achievement Award (2007); and an Emerging Pioneer recognition at Cayman Islands' National Heroes Day (2014). His work is in private and public collections, including those of NGCI and CINM. *See plate 30 and figure 20.*

Edrid Banks Jr. (Caymanian, 1923–91). Banks, a prolific intuitive artist, was struck with polio and left deaf at the age of seven. Despite (or because of) this early setback, the artist developed a love of music and singing that later evolved toward the visual arts, particularly photography and painting. Banks's artwork is in private collections and the public collections of NGCI and CINM. *See figure 12.*

Jan Barwick (New Zealander–British, b. 1953). Born in New Zealand, Barwick spent her childhood in the Solomon Islands, Kiribati and Malawi before becoming a resident of the Cayman Islands. She studied at Hornsey College of Art, London, and at the Fine Arts Faculty of Florida State University. She has enjoyed a prolific and highly successful artistic career in the Caribbean, and many of her paintings have been used in the production and merchandising of decorative household objects. She is a daughter of Margaret Barwick (below). *See plates 10 and 13.*

Margaret Barwick (British-Caymanian, b. 1931). New Zealand-born Barwick arrived in the Cayman Islands in 1977 via the Solomon Islands, Kiribati and Malawi. She quickly became involved in the establishment of VAS, the islands' first formal art collective. Subsequently, she headed the first Cayman Islands contingent to Carifesta in 1981, designed national stamps and Tortola's J. R. O'Neal Botanic Gardens, played a leading role in the design of the Cayman Islands' Queen Elizabeth II Botanic Park and wrote the authoritative *Tropical and Subtropical Trees: A Worldwide Encyclopaedic Guide* (2004). Barwick's work has been exhibited in London, New Zealand, Malawi, Barbados, France and the Cayman Islands, where NGCI held a retrospective of her work in 2007. *See figure 11.*

Maureen Andersen Berry (British-Caymanian, b. 1927). Born in Derby, United Kingdom, Andersen Berry studied fine art at the Slade School of Fine Art, London, and gained an art teacher's diploma from the Institute of Education, London. While in the United Kingdom, Andersen Berry taught art and exhibited at the Royal Academy of Arts in Burlington House, Whitechapel Gallery and the Paddington Art Society. She moved to the Cayman Islands in 1976 and taught art in Grand Cayman and Cayman Brac until her retirement in 1991, painting profusely in oil and watercolour throughout this time. *See plate 15.*

Heidi Bassett Blair (Canadian, b. 1969). Born in Toronto, Bassett Blair has a BA from McGill University and an MA from New York University; she also studied at Parsons Paris, where she worked as assistant to video-digital artist Peter Campus. Her work has won several prestigious awards, including the Jack Goodman Award for Art and Technology and *American Photo*'s Portraits and People award. Her work appears in many private, corporate and museum collections and is represented by the Benrubi Gallery, New York. In 2015, NGCI held *Plastic in Paradise: Scenes of Real Life Fictions*, a solo exhibition of her series of the same name. *See plate 57.*

Luelan Bodden (Caymanian, b. 1968). Born in Grand Cayman and self-taught, Bodden was quickly recognised as an intuitive artist of merit by CNCF, which awarded him its Cultural Award for Artistic Endeavour in 2001. Highlights of his artistic career include the *Blue Dragon* public art project (2004; figure 15), co-led by NGCI and the National Trust; the Bienal del Caribe, Dominican Republic (2004); and the Golden Star Award for Creativity from CNCF (2010). One of his works was selected as a 2007 Golden Jubilee gift from the Cayman Islands to Jamaica. *See page 13.*

Lois Brezinski (American, b. 1952). Brezinski received her formal art education at the Rhode Island School of Design and studied graduate print-making at Montclair State College before starting her own textile design firm in New Jersey. She resided in the Cayman Islands in the 1990s, where she helped to reinvigorate the outdoor, or *en plein air,* tradition of painting. Her work is included in the permanent collections of NGCI, CINM and The Ritz-Carlton—Grand Cayman. *See plate 22.*

David Bridgeman (British-Caymanian, b. 1959). Born in Oxford, Bridgeman acquired a BEd (Hons) at Worcester College of Higher Education and moved to the Cayman Islands in 1987 to teach. As a professional artist, he has received important commissions from the Cayman Islands government and from CNCF, and his work is in private collections and the public collections of CNCF, CINM, NGCI and the Governor's Residence. His significant exhibitions include *Anchored in Landscapes* (NGCI, 2005) and *Arreckly: Towards a Cultural Identity* (NGCI, 2007), in addition to a solo exhibition, entitled *The Road Not Taken*, at NGCI in 2014. He is a founding member of the Cayman art collective C4. *See plates 36 and 40.*

John Broad (British-Caymanian, b. 1947). Born in Essex, Broad studied at Southend School of Art and Edinburgh College of Art before moving to the Cayman Islands in 1989 to teach art. Career high-lights include the public art project *Wall of History*, a mural commissioned in 2003 by the Quincentennial Celebrations Committee to commemorate five hundred years of Cayman Islands history; CNCF's Artistic Achievement Award (2004); and exhibiting in the *Art Below* initiative in the London Underground (2008) and in *Art Below Pillar of Art* in Berlin (2009) as one of sixteen artists selected from around the globe. His work is in both private and public collections, including the permanent collections of NGCI and CINM. *See plates 1 and 42.*

Patrick Broderick (Caymanian, b. 1960). Born in Jamaica, Broderick is a self-taught photographer who developed his skills via specialised training from the New York Institute of Photography, Winona International School of Photography, a Santa Fe workshop with U.S. artist Joyce Tenneson and

collaborations with Cuban artist Roberto Sala, among others. His work has been featured in numerous publications, including the *New Yorker*, *Travel and Leisure*, *Bon Appétit* and *Modern Bride*. Key exhibitions include Carifesta IV (Barbados, 1981); *People Time Forgot* (NGCI, 2002); *Dos Visiones* (NGCI, 2002), which travelled to Fototeca, Havana, and the Commonwealth Institute, London; Carifesta VII, Suriname (2003); and Carifesta X, Guyana (2008). Broderick has been awarded CNCF's Artistic Achievement Award (2000) and the Jamaica Festival of Arts Kodak Award. He serves on CNCF's board of directors and is a mentor for the U.S. magazine *Popular Photography*.

Matt Brown (Caymanian, b. 1985). A filmmaker, Brown holds a degree in professional recording arts and has worked in media production with DMS Broadcasting in the Cayman Islands. His broadcasting career brought him to present at large national festivals in the Cayman Islands, such as Pirates Week and the Homecoming Music Festival, and to host on radio the Kiss FM Morning Show. His video work *The Cayman History Show*, coproduced with Ben Hudson, was featured in *tIDal Shift: Explorations of Identity in Contemporary Caymanian Art* (NGCI, 2015). *See plate 61 and figure 19.*

Gladwyn K. ('Miss Lassie') Bush (Caymanian, 1914–2003). A fourth-generation Caymanian, Miss Lassie was a self-taught artist who began painting at the age of sixty-two following a visionary experience. Her work, which she referred to as her 'markings,' was featured in the 1994 *Carib Art* exhibition and is profiled in several books on intuitive art worldwide, including *Raw Creation* (Phaidon Press, 1996), *Caribbean Art* (Thames & Hudson, 1998), *Fantasy*

Worlds (Benedikt Taschen Verlag, 1999) and *My Markings: The Art of Gladwyn K. Bush* (CNCF, 1994). Her work is in private and public collections, most notably that of the American Visionary Art Museum in Baltimore, Maryland. In her lifetime, the artist was honoured as a Member of the British Empire (MBE) in 1997 and received a CNCF Heritage Award in 1993 and the Excellence Award in 1999. Her home, in Grand Cayman, was added to the World Heritage Watch List in 2012. *See plates 11 and 12a–d.*

Cayman Quilters (est. 1993). This collective of local quilters is dedicated to continuing the long tradition of craft in the Cayman Islands and raising funds for charitable organisations. The group was created at the suggestion of Monica Gore, wife of former Cayman Islands Governor Michael Gore, and includes Debbie Calder, Maureen Collins, Carmen Connolly, Lucinda Cruikshank, Geraldine Duckworth, Doreen Gray, Glenys James, Sandra Joseph, Julia Kandiah, Pam de Lisser, Judy Massie, Meg Paterson, Suzanne Smith, Jilly Stone, Val Strang, Sybil Watler and Jill Wood. Their work is in the collections of CINM and NGCI. A special commission, *Creation*, which won The McCoy Prize in 2004, hangs in the Baptist Church in Little Cayman. *See plate 2.*

Randy Chollette (Caymanian, b. 1975). George Town–born Chollette is an intuitive, self-taught artist who earned recognition early in his career by winning Best in Show in *Blue*, an exhibition at Kensington-Lott Fine Art Gallery (2002), and The McCoy Prize People's Choice Award (2003). He is a member of Native Sons and has exhibited extensively, both with the group and independently, in the Cayman Islands and abroad, notably in *Arreckly: Towards a Cultural Identity* (NGCI, 2007), *The Persistence of Memory* (NGCI, 2011) and *Founded upon the Seas* (NGCI, 2012). His work forms part of many private collections and the public collections of NGCI, CNCF and CINM. *See plates 33 and 40 and figure 14.*

Chris Christian (Caymanian, b. 1972). Grand Cayman–born Christian is a self-taught artist who began painting in the early 2000s, joining the Native Sons art collective soon thereafter. He has exhibited widely with the group and has been a regular demonstrator of Caymanian traditional arts at the Art@Governors, Looky Ya and Red Sky at Night community art festivals. Notable exhibitions include *See Me Ya* (2007) and Native Sons' *Grass Piece* (2008), both at The Morgan Gallery, and *Emerging* (2015) at The Gallery at The Ritz-Carlton—Grand Cayman. He is the founder of Cayman Traditional Arts, a company that teaches heritage crafts to students across the Cayman Islands. He also curates the exhibition schedule of The Gallery at The Ritz-Carlton—Grand Cayman. In 2003, Christian received a CNCF lifetime achievement award recognising his accomplishments in fine art. His work can be found in the public collections of NGCI and CINM. *See plate 34.*

Carmen Connolly (Caymanian, b. 1936). Born in East End, Grand Cayman, Connolly began basket making as a child, learning thatching techniques from her aunt. By the early 1970s, her skills became more advanced, and she has subsequently become one of the most respected of all of Cayman's craftspersons. Her unique thatch designs are a regular feature at national festivals, and she has been recognised with a Heritage Award (CNCF, 2000), a Heritage Cross Gold (CNCF, 2011) and a National Heroes Day Award. Her work can be found in many private and public collections, including the permanent collections of NGCI and CINM. *See plate 4.*

John Doak (British-Caymanian, b. 1954). Born in Scotland, Doak graduated from the Mackintosh School of Architecture, Glasgow, in 1979 and arrived in the Cayman Islands the same year. His extensive architectural portfolio includes the F. J. Harquail Theatre and the Cayman Islands National Museum renovation. Doak is also a skilled artist and was an early member of VAS. Key fine art awards include first prize in the 1994 CINM art competition *Wreck of the Ten Sails*; a commendation in *Facelift*, the 1979 *Sunday Times* competition of ideas; Top Award in the 1978 national contest *Measured Drawings* (United Kingdom); and first prize in the 1977 international competition *Art into Landscape* (United Kingdom). His fine art is in the permanent collection of NGCI and CINM.

Al Ebanks (Caymanian, b. 1963). Born in George Town, Grand Cayman, sculptor and painter Ebanks was awarded a scholarship from CNCF in 1995 to study sculpture with renowned Barbadian artist Karl Broodhagen and later learned bronze casting in Tuscany through NGCI's Artists Away grant programme (2004). Ebanks cofounded the Native Sons art collective in 1996 and was awarded CNCF's Artistic Achievement Award in 2001. He has exhibited locally and abroad, including a solo show at the Jackie Gleason Theatre, Miami. His paintings were used onscreen for the feature film *Haven* (written and directed by Frank E. Flowers; 2004). Ebanks's work is included in the permanent collections of CINM, NGCI and the Griffin Gallery, Chicago. *See plate 28.*

Annalee Ebanks (Caymanian, b. 1933). Born in Cayman Brac, Ebanks learned to master complex thatching techniques from her father and became an active teacher and demonstrator of her craft. Her work can be found in the collections of NGCI, CINM and the Cayman Brac Museum. Ebanks was recognised with a Heritage Award from CNCF in 2002. *See plate 6.*

Annie Joy ('Mrs Annie') Ebanks (Caymanian, b. 1950). Born in Cayman Brac, Mrs Annie began straw work at the age of five and made her first basket at the age of six under the teaching of her mother. She has a reputation for creative artistic interpretations of original thatch designs and is considered an innovator in the field of basketry. She is a member of the Cayman Islands Traditional Arts Council and has contributed to numerous community events and heritage days, where she continues to share her skills. Mrs Annie was the recipient of a CNCF Silver Heritage Cross (2012), and her work is in public collections, including the permanent collections of NGCI and CINM. *See plate 7.*

Aston Ebanks (Caymanian, b. 1974). A self-taught conceptual artist, Jamaica-born Ebanks now resides permanently in Grand Cayman, after stints in Switzerland and Western Samoa. He was awarded The McCoy Prize (2005) and has since become well known for using recycled materials in remarkable site installations such as *The Maze* (constructed out of three thousand shipping pallets in 2007) and the on-going permanent project *The Faley*. Notable exhibitions at NGCI include *Arreckly: Towards a Cultural Identity* (2007), *21st Century Cayman* (2010) and *The Persistence of Memory* (2011). He is a founding member of the C4 collective. Ebanks's work is included in the permanent collections of NGCI and CINM.

Davin Ebanks (Caymanian, b. 1975). Born in Grand Cayman, Ebanks acquired a BA in graphic design at Anderson University, Indiana, and an MFA in glass sculpture at Kent State University, Ohio. He has been artist-in-residence at Jacksonville University and Anderson University and has taught at New York's Urban Glass (the first and largest glass studio in the United States), at Kent State University and at Salisbury University. His work has been displayed at the Glass Art Society's Annual Conference; the National Biennial Exhibition: Fine Contemporary Craft; and NGCI exhibitions including *Blue Meridian* (solo show, 2010–11), *The Persistence of Memory* (2011) and *tIDal Shift: Explorations of Identity in Contemporary Caymanian Art* (2015). He won The McCoy Prize for Fine Craft (2003) and NGCI's 2012 Public Sculpture competition. His work is included in the permanent collections of NGCI and CINM. *See plates 44, 46 and 55 and figure 17.*

Harvey Ebanks (Caymanian, 1921–2012). Seaman and World War II veteran Ebanks began painting at the age of seventy-five, having been moved after his retirement 'to draw old-time things.' A self-taught artist, he painted predominantly from memory, capturing scenes of Cayman's dwindling turtling industry and maritime heritage. His work was exhibited at Carifesta XII (Haiti, 2015) and can be found in the permanent collections of NGCI and CINM.

Rose May Ebanks (Caymanian, b. 1951). Born in West Bay, Grand Cayman, Ebanks was taught thatching techniques by her mother, who in turn had been taught by her own mother. A prolific weaver who creates mainly traditional functional items, she regularly demonstrates the craft at local arts festivals such as Art@Governors and CNCF's Red Sky at Night cultural festival. Her work was featured in NGCI's exhibitions *Merging Cultures* (2003) and *21st Century Cayman* (2010) and is included in the permanent collections of NGCI and CINM. *See plate 1.*

Kaitlyn Elphinstone (Canadian-Caymanian, b. 1985). Elphinstone is an interdisciplinary artist who works in digital media and assemblage. She studied visual art and art history at the University of Toronto and has a master's degree in arts policy and management from the University of London (Birkbeck). She has coordinated several local arts festivals and works in cultural communications and administration. Select

exhibitions include *A Day in the Life II* (NGCI, 2009), *The Persistence of Memory* (NGCI, 2011) and *tIDal Shift: Explorations of Identity in Contemporary Caymanian Art* (NGCI, 2015). She was recognised with a CNCF Silver Star for Creativity (2016) and is a founding member of the contemporary artist collective C4. Her work is included in the permanent collection of NGCI. *See plates 48 and 60.*

Horacio Esteban (Caymanian, b. 1963). Born in Cuba, Esteban was raised in Cayman Brac and is primarily a sculptor and jeweller known for his use of the local semi-precious stone Caymanite. Esteban is a member of the Native Sons art collective. Notable exhibitions include NGCI's *Emergence* (2005) and *Fahive* (2005). In 2015, Esteban was selected for residency in the Inter-Island Artist Lock-In project in Jersey, United Kingdom, produced by the Jersey Arts Trust in partnership with Jersey Heritage and Wild Works Theatre Company.

Virginia ('Auntie V') Foster (Belizean-Caymanian, b. 1950). Born in Belize, Foster arrived in the Cayman Islands in 1977. Here she became an educator, a youth librarian in the Public Library Service and a board member of CNCF. Auntie V is a performer and storyteller at Gimistory (CNCF's storytelling festival) and on Radio Cayman and is also an accomplished ceramicist, designer and poet. Foster won the 2014 Emerging Pioneer Certificate at the National Heroes Day Award ceremony and the 2012 Gold Star for Creativity in the Arts from CNCF. Her ceramic work was featured in the exhibition *Ceramic Art* (NGCI, 2014) and is included in the permanent collections of NGCI, CINM and the Cayman Islands Turtle Farm. *See plate 50.*

Mark Frazer (British-Caymanian, b. 1960). Born in the United Kingdom, Frazer received a degree in arts education from Middlesex Polytechnic, United Kingdom, and arrived in Grand Cayman in 1985 to teach art. A painter and sculptor, Frazer is best known for his wire-and-plaster figures on bicycles, which have been exhibited in *Our Story of Art* (NGCI, 2013) and the Art@Governors festivals and are included in the permanent collection of NGCI. *See plate 32.*

Teresa Grimes (American-Caymanian, b. 1952). Born in Baltimore, Maryland, Grimes received a BA in classical archaeology and classical art from the University of Maryland. She later studied art restoration and life drawing in Ravenna, Italy. Her work was selected to represent the Cayman Islands in the *Carib Art* travelling exhibition (1993), the Bienal del Caribe, Dominican Republic (1994), and Carifesta X, Guyana (2008). She was awarded First Prize at the 2010 Ogier Art Award, and her work is included in the permanent collections of the Governor's Residence, NGCI, CNCF and CINM. *See plate 41.*

Ben Hudson (Belizean, b. 1976). Born in Belize, filmmaker Hudson studied commercial art at PTEC, Florida. In 2008, he teamed with Matt Brown to create several music and video projects in Grand Cayman as well as *The Cayman History Show*, which was featured in *tIDal Shift: Explorations of Identity in Contemporary Caymanian Art* (NGCI, 2015). In 2013, the Ministry of Education awarded him the Socially Conscious Filmmakers Award for *Boy's Voice: A Documentary,* coproduced with his wife, the filmmaker Mari Abe Hudson. *See plate 61 and figure 19.*

Bendel Hydes (Caymanian, b. 1952). Born in West Bay, Grand Cayman, Hydes has lived and worked in New York City since 1982. He received a BA in fine art at Canterbury College of Art, United Kingdom, and pursued his studies in philosophy and international relations at Clark University, Massachusetts. He has been featured in exhibitions at the Commonwealth Institute, London (1986); the 23rd International Bienal de São Paulo, Brazil (1996); the 30th Festival International de la Peinture, Cagnes-sur-Mer, France (1998); *Caribbean Visions: Contemporary Painting and Sculpture,* a North American travelling exhibition (1995–98); and numerous exhibitions at NGCI, notably a solo exhibition for the museum's grand opening in 2012. Hydes has been the subject of two solo exhibitions at NGCI: *Soundings* (2003) and *Circumnavigating the Globe* (2012). His work is also featured in several publications, including *Caribbean Art* (Thames & Hudson, 1998) and *He Hath Founded It upon the Seas* (Ian Randle Publishers Inc., 2003). Works by Hydes are held in the permanent collections of NGCI, CINM, CNCF, the Cayman Islands Health Services Authority, the Cayman Islands National Archive (CINA), UBS (Cayman Islands) and the private collection of HRH Prince Philip, Duke of Edinburgh. *See plates 14 and 45 and figures 13 and 18.*

Csaba Korsos (Saba) (Hungarian, b. 1965). Saba came to the Cayman Islands in 1992 to teach. Initially he began painting as a hobby, until he received second prize in CINM's competition *Wreck of the Ten Sails* (1994). Career highlights include first prize in VAS's competition *Dramatic Light in Artwork* (1998) and an Artist of the Year nomination by *What's Hot* magazine (2002). Key exhibitions include Art Miami, with the Kensington-Lott Fine Art Gallery (2003); the travelling exhibition *Carib Art: Contemporary Art of the Caribbean* (1995); and *All Access* (NGCI, 2015). Saba is represented by Kennedy Gallery in Grand Cayman, and his work is in the permanent collections of NGCI and CINM. *See plate 39.*

Greg Lipton (Canadian-Caymanian, b. 1975). A self-taught artist, Lipton first received critical acclaim when he was selected for the exhibition *Persistence of Memory* (NGCI, 2011). His work is distributed primarily by Acme Archives, the official licensee for Lucasfilm, Disney, Marvel, DreamWorks and Fox. His prints for Lucasfilm are available in galleries across North America and Europe. *See plate 54.*

Charles Long (British-Caymanian, b. 1948). Born in West Africa, Long grew up in Swaziland and England, where he attended Farnham School of Art. He settled in the Cayman Islands in the late 1960s and became a founding member and first secretary of VAS. Long has been dubbed a chronicler of our times, a phrase that became the title of a 2002 retrospective of his work at NGCI. Other key exhibitions include the Santo Domingo Biennale (2003) and Carifesta X, Guyana (2008). Long's highly collectible work forms part of the permanent collections of NGCI and CINM. *See plates 8–9 and figures 1 and 8.*

Chris Mann (British-Caymanian, b. 1955). Born in England, Mann studied fine art and ceramics at Goldsmiths College, London, before moving to the Cayman Islands in the late 1980s to teach art. Key exhibitions include the second Biennial of Painting in the Caribbean & Central America at the Museo de Arte Moderno, Santo Domingo, Dominican Republic (1994); Carifesta X, Guyana (2008); the

Commonwealth Games Art Exhibition, New Zealand (2002); and NGCI's exhibitions *Watermarks* (2005), *Anchored in Landscapes* (2005), *Emergence* (2005) and *Arreckly: Towards a Cultural Identity* (2007). He is a founding member of the C4 collective. Mann's work is included in the permanent collections of NGCI, CINA, CINM, CNCF and the Royal College of Music, London. *See plate 35.*

Nickola McCoy-Snell (Caymanian, b. 1974). Born in Savannah, Grand Cayman, McCoy-Snell studied art at University College of the Cayman Islands. She rose to prominence in 2002, when she won the first McCoy Prize for Excellence in Caymanian Art. She also won CNCF's Artistic Achievement Award in 2002 and the Honours and People's Choice awards in The McCoy Prize in 2007. Select exhibitions include *Portrait of an Artist* (NGCI, 2003), *Emergence* (2005), Native Sons' *Fahive* (NGCI, 2005), *See Me Ya* (Morgan Gallery, 2007) and Native Sons' *Grass Piece* (Morgan Gallery, 2008). Her work was selected for the cover of the Cayman Islands Poetry Society's first annual edition (2005) and is included in the permanent collections of NGCI, CINA and many private collections. *See plate 29.*

Ed ('Mr Ed') Oliver (American-Caymanian, ca. 1918–2005). Oliver worked in advertising and industrial design in the United States before he moved to the Cayman Islands in 1969. A talented artist himself, he dedicated much of his time to encouraging and nurturing emerging artistic talents such as Bendel Hydes through regular painting classes at a time when art was not taught in Caymanian schools. His work can be found in the permanent collections of NGCI, CINA and CINM.

Carol Owen, MBE (British, b. 1948). Owen founded NGCI in 1997, for which she was awarded an MBE in 2000. She came to the Cayman Islands in 1995 as the wife of former Governor John Wynne Owen, CBE. She acquired a BA (Honours) from Portsmouth College of Art and studied art teaching at Manchester University. In addition to landscapes, Owen has painted many portraits, and her sitters have included Anne, HRH The Princess Royal, whose portrait is permanently displayed at the Guildhall Art Gallery in the City of London. Owen's work is held in the permanent collection of NGCI. *See plate 25.*

Courtney Platt (American-Caymanian, b. 1957). A self-taught photographer, Platt moved to the Cayman Islands in 1983. He is primarily a documentary photographer, and his work has been featured in numerous publications, including *National Geographic.* Platt has been involved in several fine art projects, the most celebrated being his *Now and Then* series, developed in collaboration with NGCI curator Natalie Urquhart and exhibited at NGCI in 2012 and 2015. *See plate 59.*

Elizabeth ('Lizzie') Powell (Caymanian, b. 1937). Born in West Bay, Grand Cayman, Powell learned the skill of thatching from her mother, who made baskets for use on the family farm. In the early 1970s, she learned advanced techniques from a visiting teacher and became a professional basket maker. Powell, a central member of the Cayman Islands Traditional Arts Council, has work in both NGCI's and CINM's permanent collections. *See plate 3.*

Miguel Powery (Caymanian, b. 1957). Born in Grand Cayman, Powery is a self-taught painter and sculptor who carves black coral and semi-precious stones. A founding member of the Native Sons art collective, he was recognised with a lifetime achievement award from CNCF in 2003 and as a Cultural Heritage Pioneer at the 2014 National Heroes Day ceremony. Key exhibitions include a solo exhibition at NGCI (1999) and the NGCI exhibitions *Fahive* (with Native Sons; 2005), *21st Century Cayman* (2010) and *Founded upon the Seas* (2012). His work can be found in the permanent collections of NGCI, CINM and the Cayman Islands government. *See plates 26 and 40 and figure 2.*

Pippa Ridley (British-Caymanian, b. 1980). Born in the Cayman Islands, London-based Ridley won a scholarship to study art at the Slade School of Fine Art at University College London and the Prince's Drawing School, London. In addition, Ridley has completed several artist residency programmes in the United Kingdom and Italy. Key exhibitions have included *Noise*, a solo show (Barbican ArtWorks Project Space, London, 2010); *tIDal Shift: Explorations of Identity in Contemporary Caymanian Art* (NGCI, 2015); *Ivan Remembered* (NGCI, 2014); and regular shows at Thomas Williams Fine Art, London. Ridley's work has been in several publications, and she has won several prizes, most notably a prize from the Barbican Arts Group Trust Open Exhibition (2010). Her work is included in NGCI's permanent collection. *See plate 49.*

Saba. *See* Csaba Korsos.

Rasitha Sanjeewa (Sri Lankan, b. 1972). Sanjeewa, from Ambalangoda, Sri Lanka, began his professional career as a culinary artist. He has been a regular participant in various presentations by the George Keyt Foundation in Sri Lanka, where he received the Young Artist of the Year award in 2001. Sanjeewa moved to the Cayman Islands in the late 2000s and came to prominence by winning First Prize in the 2012 Ogier Art Award. Key exhibitions include *Art of Assemblage* (NGCI, 2013) and *All Access* (NGCI, 2015). His work is in the permanent collection of NGCI. *See plate 56 and figure 3.*

Mikael Seffer (Caymanian, b. 1974). Born in the United States, Seffer moved to the Cayman Islands as a child, an experience that left an indelible mark on his artwork. A self-taught artist, he began painting in earnest in the early 2000s, quickly developing a unique technique that combines paint, powdered pigments and resin, which are manipulated by pouring and tilting the canvas. Seffer is a regular exhibitor at Art@Governors, VAS exhibitions and The Gallery at The Ritz-Carlton—Grand Cayman. Key exhibitions include *21st Century Cayman* (NGCI, 2010). He is represented by the Kennedy Gallery and the White Dog Gallery. *See plate 40.*

Renate ('Ren') Seffer (Australian-Caymanian, b. 1971). Born in Australia, Seffer travelled extensively before settling in Grand Cayman in 1995, when she began painting full time. Her work has been featured in group shows in Spain, Canada and the United States. Key exhibitions include *Arreckly: Towards a Cultural Identity* (NGCI, 2007), *21st Century Cayman* (NGCI, 2010), *A Day in the Life III* (NGCI, 2010), *Raw Arts Exhibit* (Carrozini Von Buhler Gallery, 2006) and *Changes* (Arteccentrix Gallery, 2011). Her work is represented by the White Dog Gallery and the Kennedy Gallery and features in the permanent collections of NGCI and CINM. *See plate 40.*

Jeremy Sibley (Jamaican-Caymanian, b. 1929). Born in Jamaica, Sibley studied architecture in Canada and practised in Jamaica before moving to the Cayman Islands in 1980. His work has been exhibited several times at VAS and NGCI and in Salt Spring, British Columbia. He is represented by the Kennedy Gallery and Pure Art in the Cayman Islands, and his work is included in the permanent collection of NGCI. *See plate 21.*

Joanne Sibley (Canadian-Caymanian, b. 1930). Sibley studied interior design at the University of Manitoba before moving to Jamaica in 1954, where she designed the interiors of Jamaica House, the prime minister's residence. Sibley also had a successful painting career, with important commissions including portraits of Jamaica's national heroes and of George William Gordon for Headquarters House. In 1980, she moved to the Cayman Islands, where she exhibited widely with VAS. She was awarded the 1995 Creativity Prize by CNCF. Key exhibitions include the solo show *Faces and Figures* (NGCI, 2007), *Our Story of Art* (NGCI, 2013) and *Metamorphoses* (NGCI, 2014). Sibley is represented by the Kennedy Gallery and Pure Art in Grand Cayman and by Gallery Diamante in Carmel, California. The artist received a honourable mention from *American International Artist* magazine, and her works are in the permanent collections of NGCI and CINM. *See plates 17–20.*

Gordon Solomon (Caymanian, b. 1977). Born in George Town, Grand Cayman, Solomon studied fine art at the University of Superior Art, Cuba, and is a member of the art collective Native Sons. He is the recipient of CNCF's Artistic Endeavour Award (2002), CNCF's Silver Star Medal for Creativity in the Arts (2009) and Second Prize in the 2012 Ogier Art Award. Key exhibitions include *Cayfest* (1999); Natives Sons' *Fahive* (NGCI, 2005), *Metamorphoses* (NGCI, 2014) and *tIDal Shift: Explorations of Identity in Contemporary Caymanian Art* (NGCI, 2015). Solomon has been commissioned for several public murals in the Cayman Islands and is represented by several galleries, including Pure Art and The Gallery at The Ritz-Carlton—Grand Cayman. His work is included in the permanent collection of NGCI, CINM and CINA. *See plate 38.*

Josie Solomon (Caymanian, b. 1932). Born in Bodden Town, Grand Cayman, Solomon learned thatch, embroidery and sisal techniques from her aunt and other district elders. She is best known for her embroidery and crochet work, which she demonstrates at national arts festivals and heritage days. Her work is on permanent display at the Heritage Senior Centre of Bodden Town and at NGCI and CINM. She was awarded CNCF's Gold Heritage Cross in 2012. *See figure 10.*

Nasaria Suckoo-Chollette (Caymanian, b. 1968). Born in George Town, Grand Cayman, Suckoo-Chollette received a BA in theatre and a MA in educational theatre from New York University. She is a member of the artists' collective Native Sons and has exhibited widely both with the group and as a solo artist. Key exhibitions include Native Sons' *Fahive* (NGCI, 2005), *Arreckly: Towards a Cultural Identity* (NGCI, 2007), *The Persistence of Memory* (NGCI, 2011) and *tIDal Shift: Explorations of Identity in Contemporary Caymanian Art* (NGCI, 2015). Her work is in the permanent collections of NGCI and CINM. *See plates 31 and 43.*

Karoly Szücs (Hungarian, b. 1965). In the early 2000s, Szücs moved to the Cayman Islands, where he established his company, Artisan Metal Works, specialising in ornamental custom metalwork. The award-winning artist has received several important public commissions, including projects for Heroes Square, the Cayman National roundabout and the Dart Family Park in George Town. Szücs has exhibited widely, and his sculptural work *That Morning* (2004) was selected as the centrepiece of NGCI's exhibition *Emergence* (2005) and is now included in the permanent collection of NGCI. *See plate 37.*

Simon Tatum (Caymanian, b. 1995). Born in Grand Cayman, Tatum received two scholarships to study for his BA at the University of Missouri, Columbia. Exhibitions to date include *Evoke* (Imago Gallery and Cultural Center, Columbia, 2015) and *tIDal Shift: Explorations of Identity in Contemporary Caymanian Art* (NGCI, 2015). Tatum was selected to represent the University of Missouri in the SEC Academic Symposium's Undergraduate and Graduate Fine Art Showcase (2015). His work is part of the permanent collection of NGCI. *See plate 58.*

Cecilia Urdaneta (Venezuelan, b. 1967). Born in Caracas, Venezuela, Urdaneta studied ceramics at Stetson University, Florida, and at the Akademia di Arte, Curaçao, as well as with several ceramicists in their studios. She moved to the Cayman Islands in 2002, where she taught ceramics at NGCI and VAS and showed work in several exhibitions, notably Cayfest (CNCF, 2006 and 2009), *A Day in the Life* (NGCI, 2008) and *Ceramic Art* (NGCI, 2014). Other key exhibitions include those at the Duncan Gallery (Stetson University, 1996), Arawak Clay Products (Curaçao, 1998) and Studio Giourette (Curaçao, 2002). Her work is included in the permanent collection of NGCI. *See plates 51–52.*

Debbie Chase van der Bol (American-Caymanian, b. 1956). Chase Van der Bol acquired a BA from Edinboro University, Pennsylvania, with majors in painting and printmaking and minors in drawing and communication graphics. In the early 1980s, she moved to the Cayman Islands, where she opened the store and gallery Pure Art. She is a board member of VAS and has exhibited widely, notably at the NGCI exhibitions *Emergence* (2005), *Watermarks* (2005) and *Metamorphoses* (2014). In 1999, Chase van der Bol won the Radley Gourzong Award from CNCF. Her work is included in the permanent collections of NGCI and CINM. *See plate 27.*

Janet Walker (Canadian-Caymanian, b. 1938). Walker trained at the Ontario College of Art before moving in 1963 to Grand Cayman, where she traded oil paints for watercolours and began to paint outdoors. She was prolific in the 1980s and 1990s, exhibiting frequently with VAS. She was the recipient of CNCF's 1995 Creativity Award and was the subject of a retrospective exhibition at NGCI in 2009. Her work is included in the permanent collections of NGCI and CINM and in several corporate art collections. *See plates 23–24.*

C. E. Whitney (American-Caymanian, b. 1946). Born in Toronto, Canada, Whitney moved to the Cayman Islands in the 1970s. She is a graduate of City Lit Art and Design, London, where she developed her Photorealist technique. Key exhibitions include Bridge Art Fair in Berlin, the Affordable Art Fair in New York (2009) and *All Access* (NGCI, 2015). She is represented by Sandon Feat Gallery in Grand Cayman, and her work is included in the permanent collection of NGCI. *See plate 47.*

Sue Widmer (British-Caymanian, ca. 1955–2012). Born in England, Widmer trained in education and art before moving to the Cayman Islands in 1982 to teach art. She was an avid painter and costume maker who exhibited widely and was a regular demonstrator at Art@Governors and with VAS, and her work is found in the collection of CINM. *See figure 9.*

NOTES

The chapter 'A Brief History of Cayman Islands Art' has been adapted from the author's curatorial essay 'A Survey of Cayman Islands' Art History,' which accompanied NGCI's *Our Story of Art* exhibition (November 2013–March 2014) and was published in the *Journal of the University College of the Cayman Islands* (2016). It is intended as a starting point for future in-depth scholarship and discourse rather than a complete history of the art of the Cayman Islands, the story of which is still being explored.

1   For the purposes of this essay, the definition of *art* encompasses works of fine art (painting, sculpture, drawing, printmaking, photography, video and filmmaking) that are created to be appreciated primarily or solely for their imaginative, aesthetic or intellectual content rather than as functional items. In the remainder of this essay, the terms *fine art* and *art* are used interchangeably.

2   For an in-depth discussion of the contributions of both European and African cultures to the formation of early Caymanian identity, and the resulting creolization process, see Christopher A. Williams, *Defining Caymanian Identity: The Effects of Globalization, Economics, and Xenophobia on Caymanian Culture* (Lanham, MD: Lexington Books, 2016), ch. 1, 3–30.

3   Art historian Anne Walmsley has noted that the religion, and subsequently the cultural norms, of the initial colonising country has significant effects on the rate at which fine art has developed in the region. For example, many early fine art commissions in the region were for religious paintings in churches and public buildings, predominantly in the Catholic, French and Spanish colonies. On islands colonised by the British and Dutch, whose Protestant faith focused more on text than on religious iconography, there was less incentive for the local production of fine art in the colonial period. Religion also informed the African traditions brought to the region during the Middle Passage, as evidenced in the dance, music, stories and practises relating to Eshu and to Obeah found across the region, which subsequently had a great influence on artistic practise. See Anne Walmsley and Stanley Greaves, *Art in the Caribbean: An Introduction* (London: New Beacon Books, 2010).

4   Given its geographical size and limited natural resources, Cayman never boasted large-scale plantocracies like those found in the neighbouring islands of Jamaica and Cuba. However, chattel slavery played an inherent role in the development of Caymanian society throughout the eighteenth and early nineteenth centuries, when the ratio of freemen to slaves averaged 1:1. See Williams, *Defining Caymanian Identity*, 20–21, for further discussion.

5   As late as the 1950s, Caymanian government annual reports listed 'seamen' as the main 'export' of the islands (www.gov.ky). While traditional Caymanian cultural identity is now viewed almost entirely through the lens of its maritime heritage, it is important to acknowledge that agriculture, primarily logging and cotton, initially played a substantial role in the early economic development of the islands from 1734 (when permanent settlement began) until the late 1830s, following the abolition of slavery.

6   One exception to this rule was Jervis Jackson, who is recognised as the first Caymanian artist. Born in 1881, Jackson was a commercial house painter who created artworks as a hobby (CINA interview with Deborah Barnes-Tabora, collections manager, CINM, 10 November 1998, CINA Oral History Programme). Artworks and drawings that others may have created during this early period have either succumbed to the tough climatic conditions or did not make their way into public collections.

7   NGCI has only a small collection of traditional crafts, as the mandate to collect heritage arts falls to the Cayman Islands National Museum (CINM). NGCI's samples of such works are also generally more experimental in their execution than earlier works would have been. We express our gratitude to CINM for loaning traditional items for display in the NGCI Collection Gallery, which help visitors to put the islands' formal visual art history into context.

8   The Southwell Years, which extended from the late 1940s to the mid-1980s, were a time when Caymanian seamen worked on supertankers, sending their money home and helping to lay the foundations of the modern Caymanian economy. Merill G. Southwell was the National Bulk Carrier (NBC) recruiting officer who hired hundreds of Caymanians to work on the company's ships. See Consuelo Ebanks, *The Southwell Years: Recollections of Caymanian Seamen and Those Who Served at Home* (George Town: Cayman National Cultural Foundation, 2003). It should be noted that Caymanian men also travelled during this period as seasonal agricultural labourers in addition to turtling and seafaring.

9   Author emails with Bendel Hydes, 28 September 2013.

10   The first official VAS meeting was called in 1977, and the first committee, elected on 20 September of the following year, consisted of Betty Wise, Meg Paterson, Jane Porter

(president), Nina Tiessen (secretary), Lady Frances Jenkinson (treasurer), Dr Joe Jackman and Tony Virtue (vice-president).

11   The growth of the tourism industry, and with it the increased opportunity to sell artwork to tourists, influenced the subject and style of artwork created in this period. Artists inevitably produced work that catered to visitors' expectations of the 'exotic island paradise,' which was also promoted in tourism literature and marketing. For a wider discussion of this subject, see Natalie Coleman, '"A Distinctly Caymanian Experience"—Cultural Tourism and Identity Politics in the Cayman Islands,' MA thesis, University of London, Birkbeck College, 2006.

12   The influence that Pirates Week and later Batabano (Carnival), as vehicles for creative expression, had on the development of fine art and vice versa warrants further discussion, but it is outside the remit of the current publication.

13   See www.artscayman.org/mind-s-eye.

14   The museum formally opened in 1990, but the organisation's beginnings can be traced to the 1930s, when local resident Ira Thompson began collecting Caymanian artefacts as a hobby. In 1979, the government purchased Thompson's collection, which now makes up a major portion of the museum's collection (www.museum.ky).

15   Caymanian artists had also participated in the earlier Carib Art Selection Competition (*Caribe Art: Cayman Selection Exhibition*, CNCF, 1992).

16   Original members included Wray Banker, Al Ebanks, Miguel Powery and Anthony Ramoon, but the group soon grew to include Pearl Parker, Nasaria Suckoo-Chollette, Randy Chollette, Chris Christian, Nickola McCoy-Snell, Gordon Solomon and Horacio Esteban.

17   This number was over one hundred by 2005.

18   Curated by Nancy Barnard, former director of NGCI, and by the author, respectively.

19   Curated by NGCI founding director Leslie Bigelman.

20   The Artists Away (AA) programme was developed to provide training opportunities for local artists that are not readily available in the islands. Many of the Cayman Islands' best-known artists have been recipients of the AA grant. To name only a few, Wray Banker, Miguel Powery and Gordon Solomon studied printmaking at the Taller Experimental de Gráfica in Havana; Patrick Broderick studied photography in New Mexico with Joyce Tenneson; and Al Ebanks and Horacio Esteban studied bronze casting in Florence.

21   The first full-time formal curator's position at NGCI was created in 2004.

22   Curated by artist David Bridgeman and by the author, respectively.

23   The UK Government Department for Culture, Media and Sport (DCMS) describes the creative industries as 'those industries which have their origin in individual creativity, skill and talent and which have a potential for wealth and job creation through the generation and exploitation of intellectual property' (DCMS 2001, 4).

REFERENCES

Bodden, J. A. Roy. 2007. *The Cayman Islands in Transition: The Politics, History and Sociology of a Changing Society.* Kingston, Jamaica, and Miami, FL: Ian Randle.

Coleman, Natalie. 2003. *Twenty Five Years On—The History of the Visual Arts Society.* Quincentennial Celebrations Exhibition Catalogue. Cayman Islands: Quincentennial Celebrations Committee.

———. 2006. '"A Distinctly Caymanian Experience"—Cultural Tourism and Identity Politics in the Cayman Islands.' MA thesis, University of London, Birkbeck College.

Craton, Michael. 2003. *Founded upon the Seas: A History of the Cayman Islands and Their People.* Kingston, Jamaica, and Miami, FL: Ian Randle.

DCMS. 2001. *Creative Industries Mapping Document.* 2nd ed. London: Department for Culture, Media and Sport.

Ebanks, Consuelo. 2003. *The Southwell Years: Recollections of Caymanian Seamen and Those Who Served at Home.* George Town, Cayman Islands: Cayman National Cultural Foundation.

Eckmeyer, Ruby, and Frank Elstak. 1993. *Carib Art: Contemporary Art of the Caribbean.* Curaçao: National Commission for UNESCO of the Netherlands Antilles.

Eden, William T., and E. Noel McLaughlin. 1891. *The Island of Grand Cayman at the Jamaica Exhibition: Historical Sketch and Descriptive Catalogue.* Jamaica: DeCordova & Co.

Muttoo, Henry, with Karl ('Jerry') Craig. 2003. *My Markings: The Art of Gladwyn K. Bush, Caymanian Visionary Intuitive.* Edited by David Martins. George Town, Cayman Islands: Cayman National Cultural Foundation.

Urquhart, Natalie. 2016. 'A Survey of Cayman Islands' Art History.' *Journal of the University College of the Cayman Islands* (Spring).

Walmsley, Anne, and Stanley Greaves. 2010. *Art in the Caribbean: An Introduction.* London: New Beacon Books.

Williams, Christopher A. 2016. *Defining Caymanian Identity: The Effects of Globalization, Economics, and Xenophobia on Caymanian Culture.* Lanham, MD: Lexington Books.

WEB LINKS

Cayman Islands Government: www.gov.ky

Cayman Islands National Museum: www.museum.ky

Cayman National Cultural Foundation: www.artscayman.org

National Gallery of the Cayman Islands: www.nationalgallery.org.ky

Pirates Week Office: www.piratesweekfestival.com

INDEX OF ILLUSTRATIONS

COLLECTIONS SUPPORT AND ART FUND DONATIONS

Call for Collections Support

The majority of artworks featured in this publication were acquired for the NGCI Collection via donation. These successes were made possible with help from people who share our belief in the importance of securing and commissioning great artworks of national significance and in keeping them publicly accessible. We need your help to ensure that the collection continues to grow and to inspire visitors long into the future. There are several ways to get involved.

Donations to the NGCI Art Fund

In 2015, NGCI established the National Gallery Art Fund, with the support of Susan A. Olde, OBE, to fund major acquisitions of works by artists from the Cayman Islands. To date, several key works have been secured, including *Kitchen Window I–IV*, a series of rare painted window panels, circa 1980, by Gladwyn K. ('Miss Lassie') Bush (plates 12a–d), and *White Plaits, Blue Braids*, 2015, by Kaitlyn Elphinstone (front cover and plate 60). Artworks for consideration are identified by the NGCI Collections Committee based on their historical significance, strength of execution and authorship. Anyone can donate to the fund, with amounts based on personal circumstances. In addition to helping us secure artwork, funds contribute to our collections-based public education programmes, artwork conservation and related research projects.

Donations and Bequests of Artwork

As illustrated in these pages, donations of paintings have greatly enhanced our national collection over the years. Furthermore, bequests to NGCI, of whatever size, help to strengthen and conserve the collection long-term. These gifts stand as a lasting tribute to the generosity and vision of NGCI's benefactors.

For further information on donations and support, contact the NGCI Collections Committee:

Tel: +1 (345) 945 8111
Email: director@nationalgallery.org.ky

Alternatively, mail enquiries to:

NGCI Collections Committee
c/o The Director
PO Box 10197
KY1-1002
Cayman Islands

Thank you.

ACKNOWLEDGMENTS

Discussions for this publication first grew out of NGCI's seminal survey exhibition *Our Story of Art* (2013), which was the first comprehensive overview of Cayman Islands art history. During the research phase of the exhibition, it had become clear that there was a lack of published material on the subject and, further, that much of this 'history' had yet to be formally recorded. Subsequently, this book was developed with the dual purpose of sharing highlights from NGCI's collection and as an introduction to our history of art. It does not seek to tell the full story; indeed, many artists practising in our islands are not represented owing to the fact that they are not formally part of our collection, but it is hoped that this will be a starting point for further scholarship and discourse around this important subject.

Our story has been drawn from primary resources (interviews and letters) and supplemented by NGCI and CNCF exhibition catalogues, local media articles and historical archives. As such, we wish to express our sincere thanks to the many artists and private collectors who agreed to be interviewed during the research phase of this project; to NGCI interns and volunteers who helped to gather materials, especially Karina Harford, Joe Roberts, Simon Tatum and Paige Jordison; to CINM collections manager Debra Barnes-Tabora for information relating to Caymanian traditional art; and particularly to the team at CINA, headed by director Josette Kimlon Lawrence.

Importantly, this publication marks the twentieth year of our organisation's history and the development of our collection as an invaluable national cultural resource. So many people have contributed to this journey that while we are not able to acknowledge each of them individually, we do wish to extend a sincere, heartfelt thank you to all the members, donors, artists, volunteers, past and present board members, and staff who have made it a success.

In terms of collections development, NGCI is indebted to the following organisations and individuals who have each made a significant and sustained contribution to this area: the Cayman Islands Government via the Ministry of Health and Culture; founding NGCI Chairperson Carol Owen, MBE; Helen Harquail, OBE; Susan A. Olde, OBE, NGCI Chairperson; Michael and Monica Gore; former NGCI directors Leslie Bigelman, OBE, and Nancy Barnard; Richard and Elaine Christiansen; Andreas and Natalie Ugland; Henry Harford; Truman Bodden; Anita Ebanks; Jennifer Woodford; Anne Goulden; King and Lisa Flowers; Ernest Jacob Olde VI; the Dart Foundation; Deutsche Bank (Cayman) Ltd; Butterfield Bank (Cayman) Ltd; Atlantic Star Ltd; Coutts (Cayman) Ltd; and IAMCO, in addition to the artists and all those persons who have been involved in numerous fundraising efforts that have helped to secure important works of art. Thanks are also on-going to our fellow cultural agencies—CNCF, CINM and CINA—which continue to generously loan artworks to supplement current gaps in NGCI's collection.

I would like to extend a personal thank you to the exceptional project team, whose dedication and commitment have helped to guarantee its success: Emérentienne Paschalides for her editorial contribution to the plate descriptions and biographical profiles; assistant curator Kerri-Anne Chisholm for her invaluable logistical support; educational consultant Robert Bailey; Carol Drake and Lise Hurlstone for proofreading; legal advisor Andrea Williams; photographer Justin Uzzell; graphic designer Andrea Hemmann; and editor Laura Harger.

I would also like to recognise the on-going work of my colleagues in NGCI's curatorial, education and communications departments, who help to make our collection accessible to schools and the general public on a daily basis.

Finally, a very special thank you must be reserved for NGCI Chairperson, board member and patron Susan A. Olde, OBE, whose vision and support have made this landmark publication, and the accompanying schools guide, a reality.

NATALIE URQUHART

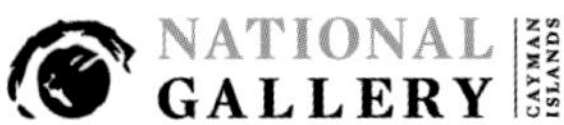

First published in 2016 by Scala Arts Publishers Inc.
141 Wooster Street, Suite 4D
New York, NY 10012
www.scalapublishers.com

In association with the National Gallery
of the Cayman Islands
www.nationalgallery.org.ky

Distributed in the book trade by
ACC Distribution
6 West 18th Street, 4th Floor
New York, NY 10011

ISBN 978-1-78551-058-8
Designed by Andrea Hemmann
Project manager: Laura Harger
Printed in China
10 9 8 7 6 5 4 3 2 1

Photograph and Artwork Credits

Front cover: Kaitlyn Elphinstone, *White Plaits,
Blue Braids* (detail), 2015 (see plate 60).

Back cover: Janet Walker, *Mending Nets* (detail), 1987
(see plate 24).

All other photographs, including artwork
photographs, are by Justin Uzzell, excluding the
following: figure 4: David Wolfe; figure 5:
Veronica Platt; figures 6–7: Kaitlyn Elphinstone;
figures 10 and 16: Courtney Platt; figure 14: courtesy
of Randy Chollette; figure 17: courtesy of
Davin Ebanks; figure 20: courtesy of Wray Banker.